2/97

D1442174

The European
Royal Families

© **Norden Publishing House Ltd. St. Gallen, Switzerland 1993**

Authors: Bobby Andström (Sweden), François Billaut (Remaining), Bodil Cath (Denmark), Philippe Delorme (Belgium), Ismael Fuente (Spain), Vincent Meylan (Remaining), Annemor Møst (Norway), Mirjam J. Spiering (Netherlands) and Judy Wade (Britain).

Photo: *Belgium:* Crochet, Darryl, Dhont, Geeraerts, Lebrun, Yves Smets, Versele *Bureaus:* Archives Point de Vue (PDV), Nordfoto, Photonews/Gamma. *Britain:* Alan Band, Jayne Fincher. *Bureaus:* Bandphoto, Berlingske Tidene, Nordfoto, Photographers International Ltd. *Denmark:* Palle Hedemann, Jørgen Jessen, Allan Moe, Klaus Møller, Stær *Bureaus:* Inga Aistrup Foto, Berlingske Tidene, Nordfoto. *Netherlands:* Werry Crone, Van Dam, Ato Davis, Bart Hofmeester, Rob List, Han Schenk, Paul Stolk, Jan Versnel. *Bureaus:* Algemeen Nederlands Persbureau (ANP), Anefo, Capital Press, Fotobureau Thuring, Koninklijk Huisarchief, Nationaal Foto Persbureau (NFP), NOS-Televisieproduktie, Rijksvoorlichtingdienst (RVD), Vorsten. *Norway:* Bjørn Aslaksen, Nils Bjåland, Knut Falch, Hans-Olav Forsan, Reidar Fure, Furulund, Jan Greve, Pål Hansen, Hender, Erik Johansen, Tore Kristiansen, Campbell Norgaard, Olav Olsen, Åge PedersenTrond Solberg, Bjørn Thunes, O.S. Tøllefsen, Olav Urdahl. *Bureau:* Scan-Foto A/S. *Spain:* Dalda, Angel Millán. *Bureau:* Agencia Efe. *Sweden:* Bobby Andström, Studio Granath, Charles Hammarsten. *Bureaus:* Aller Photo Press, Pressens Bild. *Remaining:* S. Allen, Francis Apesteguy, Jimmy Bolcina, Luc Castel, J. Delorme, Fellens, Jayne Fincher, Mettler, Roemer, Seren, H. Vassal. *Bureaus:* Archive personelle, LAS, Nordfoto, PDV, Photographers International Ltd., Photonews/Gamma.

Illustration on page 6 and 7: Jüri Kann/Penhouse.

Thanks to: the Belgian, the British, the Danish, the Dutch and the Norwegian embassies, to the Dutch Ministry of Foreign Affairs (who gave their permissions), to Protokollen at the Danish Ministry of Foreign Affairs and to the Swedish Court — all for being so helpful with the royal coat of arms.

Edit. coord.: Bodil Andersson, BOA Förlagsservice AB, Bjärred, Sweden

Layout: Hans Christiansen, Informationsgruppen AB, Stockholm, Sweden

Litho: 71 Film Interscan Sweden AB

Printing and binding: Tien Wah Press (PTE.) Ltd., Singapore

ISBN 3-907150-40-6

The European
Royal Families

NORDEN PUBLISHING HOUSE LTD.

The European
Royal Families

Contents

Windsor Castle

Castle of Vaduz

The Belgian Royal Family-tree

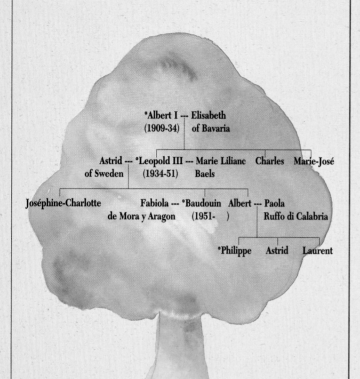

°Albert I --- Elisabeth
(1909-34)   of Bavaria

Astrid --- °Leopold III --- Marie Lilianc   Charles   Marie-José
of Sweden   (1934-51)   Baels

Joséphine-Charlotte   Fabiola --- °Baudouin   Albert --- Paola
de Mora y Aragon   (1951-)   Ruffo di Calabria

°Philippe   Astrid   Laurent

The British Royal Family-tree

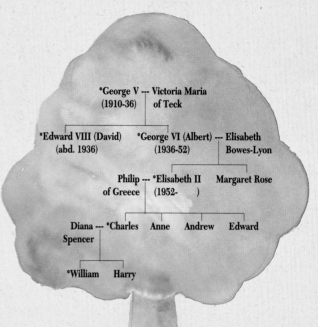

°George V --- Victoria Maria
(1910-36)   of Teck

°Edward VIII (David)   °George VI (Albert) --- Elisabeth
(abd. 1936)   (1936-52)   Bowes-Lyon

Philip --- °Elisabeth II   Margaret Rose
of Greece   (1952-)

Diana --- °Charles   Anne   Andrew   Edward
Spencer

°William   Harry

The Danish Royal Family-tree

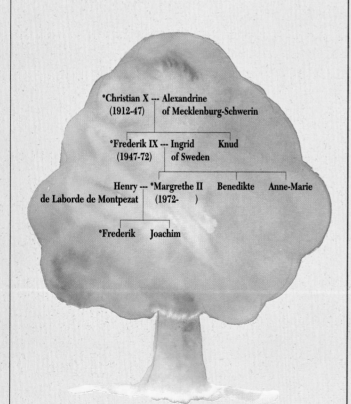

°Christian X --- Alexandrine
(1912-47)   of Mecklenburg-Schwerin

°Frederik IX --- Ingrid   Knud
(1947-72)   of Sweden

Henry --- °Margrethe II   Benedikte   Anne-Marie
de Laborde de Montpezat   (1972-)

°Frederik   Joachim

The Dutch Royal Family-tree

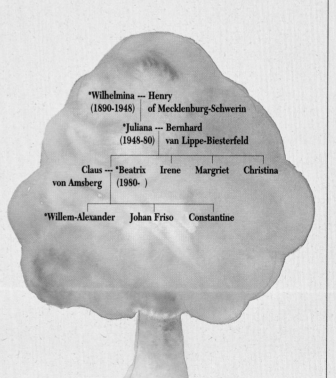

°Wilhelmina --- Henry
(1890-1948)   of Mecklenburg-Schwerin

°Juliana --- Bernhard
(1948-80)   van Lippe-Biesterfeld

Claus --- °Beatrix   Irene   Margriet   Christina
von Amsberg   (1980-)

°Willem-Alexander   Johan Friso   Constantine

The Norwegian Royal Family-tree

°Haakon VII --- Maud
(1905-57)　of Great Britain

Märtha --- °Olav V
of Sweden　(1957-91)

Ragnhild　Astrid　°Harald --- Sonja
(1991-)　Haraldsen

Märtha Louise　°Haakon Magnus

The Spanish Royal Family-tree

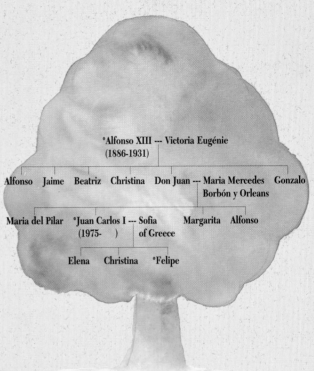

°Alfonso XIII --- Victoria Eugénie
(1886-1931)

Alfonso　Jaime　Beatriz　Christina　Don Juan --- Maria Mercedes　Gonzalo
Borbón y Orleans

Maria del Pilar　°Juan Carlos I --- Sofia　Margarita　Alfonso
(1975-)　of Greece

Elena　Christina　°Felipe

The Swedish Royal Family-tree

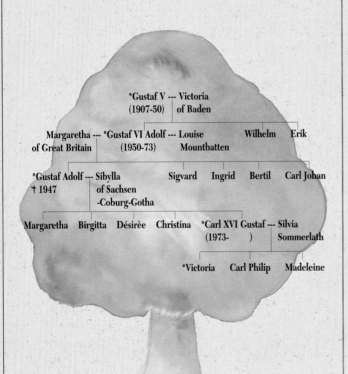

°Gustaf V --- Victoria
(1907-50)　of Baden

Margaretha --- °Gustaf VI Adolf --- Louise　Wilhelm　Erik
of Great Britain　(1950-73)　Mountbatten

°Gustaf Adolf --- Sibylla　Sigvard　Ingrid　Bertil　Carl Johan
† 1947　of Sachsen
-Coburg-Gotha

Margaretha　Birgitta　Désirèe　Christina　°Carl XVI Gustaf --- Silvia
(1973-)　Sommerlath

°Victoria　Carl Philip　Madeleine

The Royal Family trees

*T*he family trees on these pages present four generations of the ruling royal houses of Europe.

The first generation is represented only by the king/queen with wife/husband. In the following you find the king/queen with his/her wife/husband and brothers and sisters.

The years mark ruling years.

Foreword

The history of the royal houses of Europe is nothing if not stirring. More often than not their fates are interwoven. Members of various royal families have intermarried, for one thing, thus assuring the survival of their houses.

No less exciting is the contemporary scene. Though kings and queens no longer have the same degree of political power as before, the on-going story of monarchy is still affected by events within the royal houses themselves.

The growth of the mass media has opened doors into royal houses that were tightly shut until the last few decades. This development is a mixed blessing. The relationship of the public to "their" royal house has become more intimate and personal. At the same time, many royals have been hounded by the mass media.

This book presents the Royal Families of Europe from both the historic and contemporary perspectives. With pictures and narrative we follow them everywhere; Upstairs and downstairs, "on the job" and at leisure, on public occasions and in the privacy of hearth and home.

Belgium

By Philippe Delorme

A deep understanding unites Baudouin and Fabiola.

History

*B*elgium; *"There are Walloons, and there are Flemings, but only one Belgian – King Baudouin".*

This epigram, paraphrase of an open letter from Jules Destrée to Albert I in 1912, expresses a sentiment which is common throughout Belgium. The Belgian king is in fact one of the last living symbols of a fast-decaying national unity.

"There are Walloons, and there are Flemings, but only one Belgian - King Baudouin". This epigram, paraphrase of an open letter from Jules Destrée to Albert I in 1912, expresses a sentiment which is common throughout Belgium. The Belgian king is in fact one of the last living symbols of a fast-decaying national unity. With the Kingdom of Belgium seemingly condemned to fragmentation by irresistible centrifugal forces, it is perhaps appropriate today to

The three children of Léopold I and Louise of France: the future Léopold II, Philippe, Count of Flanders and Charlotte, future Empress of Mexico.

Burgundy sought to promote their dream of a great kingdom of the West by the unification of the "Low Countries". However, after the death of Charles the Bold, his inheritance passed to the Spanish Royal House, then to Charles V.

With the Reformation came fresh rivalries. In the North, the burghers and merchants of Holland embraced Protestantism, and the Calvinist "United Provinces" became independent in 1573. The South, which was still Catholic, remained subjugated to Madrid. This split foreshadowed the present kingdoms of the Netherlands and Belgium. In the 18th century the Hapsburgs of Vienna took over from their Spanish cousins. With the events of 1789 in Versailles and Paris, the winds of liberty swept across Europe. The Austrians were expelled by the Brabantine Revolution. On the 11th January 1790 the Brussels States General proclaimed the independence of the United Belgian States. In 1814, the future Belgium, which had been annexed to the French Republic, then to the French Empire, became part of a great Kingdom of the Netherlands under the crown of William I of Orange-Nassau, along with Holland, the former Austrian possessions and the bishopric of Liège. Powerless to resist, the Belgians could do no more than swallow their anger. Once again it was a revolution in Paris which was to rouse them and give them courage to cast off the oppressor's yoke.

examine the historical origins of the State which emerged out of revolution in 1830.

Before its conquest by Julius Caesar in 57 B.C., Belgian Gaul extended from the Seine to the Rhine. The Treaty of Verdun in 843, where Charlemagne's grandsons divided the territory between France and Lotharingia, established the future Belgium's destiny as a border state at the intersection of Latin and Germanic culture. It meant that throughout the Middle Ages the Counts of Flanders paid homage to the Capetians, while Brabant, Hainault, Limburg and Luxemburg remained within the Imperial orbit. At the end of the 14th century the Dukes of

On the evening of 25th August 1830, the La Monnaie Theatre in Brussels was staging "La Muette de Portici", an opera by Auber based on Scribe's libretto celebrating the Neapolitain revolt against Spanish rule. So similar was the situation depicted to the Dutch oppression of the Belgians, that the audience reaction turned into a riot which soon spread to the streets. The Belgian bourgeoisie, converted to liberal ideas by reading the French press, had long cherished the dream of bringing down King William I, a convinced absolutist. The old religious confrontation between

Protestant Holland and Catholic Belgium added fuel to their political demands.

The heir to the throne, the future William II, with a force of 6000 men, was at once sent by his father the King to restore order. He failed, and a second contingent of 12,000 troops, led by his brother Frederick of Nassau, entered Brussels on the 23rd September. After four days of fighting, the defeated Dutch army was forced to leave the city. The whole of Belgium, apart from the citadel of Antwerp, was soon free. A rebel government proclaimed independence on the 4th October. Several weeks later on the 24th November a National Congress, elected by property holders, voted for the removal of the Nassau dynasty.

At a conference in London the following January the Brussels uprising was approved by the great powers, with the result that Belgium became a nation in its own right. It still remained to the country to find a sovereign. The first choice of the Congress was the 16 year old Duke of Nemours, second son of King Louis-Philippe of France. However, this candidate was withdrawn following a veto by the English, who were reluctant to see the same family ruling in both Paris and Brussels. Then, on the 4th June 1831, 152 deputies out of the 196 present at the Congress transferred their vote to Prince Leopold of Saxe-Coburg-Gotha.

At 41 Leopold was the ideal candidate. He came from a small ducal family from South Germany and was married to the unfortunate Princess Charlotte, heir to the throne of England who died in childbirth in 1817. Her niece was none other than the young Princess Victoria, who was to become Queen of England in 1837. Furthermore, the prince was a francophile who was on excellent terms with Louis-Philippe. After some hesitations - Leopold had already declined the offer of the crown of Greece - he agreed to become the first king of the Belgians.

On the 21st July 1831 Brussels celebrated the "glorious entry" of its new Monarch into the city. An impressive platform had been built in the Place Royale in front of the church of Saint-Jacques sur Coudenberg. Leopold, who arrived on horseback, dismounted, climbed the steps and took his place beneath a canopy by the Regent, Surlet de Chokier. The whole crowd stood for the oath. In calm tones marked by a slight German accent, Leopold swore to "observe the Constitution and the laws of the Belgian people, maintain the nation's independence and the integrity of the territory". The crowd could not retain its excitement. It had just been witness to the birth of a dynasty.

Leopold I could never have expected that the call to honour the terms of his commitment would come so soon. On the 2nd August, two weeks after his accession, the King of Holland's forces invaded Belgium in defiance of the Armistice. Since his army was unprepared, Leopold appeal to France for help, while England intervened by asking William I to end hostilities. The defeat cost Belgium Maastricht, half of Luxembourg and Limburg, and the mouth of the Scheldt. The Dutch, who still held Antwerp, refused to recognise their neighbours' independence until 1839.

The King, who had preserved Belgium's freedom, had his mind on the future of his young dynasty. On the 9th August 1832, he took as his second wife the elder daughter

Léopold of Saxe-Coburg-Gotha at the start of his reign.

of Louis-Philippe, thus consolidating his alliance with France. Princess Marie-Louise of Orleans was 19. The marriage, in which diplomacy took precedence over sentiment, turned out to be a happy one in the end. The first Queen of the Belgians was pious and generous, like her mother Marie-Amélie, a lover of liberty and open to modern ideas. She gave Leopold invaluable support. Above all, she fulfilled her duty admirably by providing the throne with two male heirs - the future Leopold II and Philippe, Count of Flanders - as well as a daughter, Princess Charlotte, who was briefly Empress of Mexico before becoming tragically insane.

The English, reassured by Leopold I's marriage, authorised the French army to retake the citadel of Antwerp. A country still in its infancy, Belgium relied heavily on the statesman-like qualities of its King. "I am the Atlas who must bear my little kingdom on his shoulders", Leopold I often said. He felt that his constitutional prerogatives were too limited, whereas the Chamber sought to keep the royal power restricted within the framework of organic laws. To those who wanted "the king to reign and not to rule", Leopold retorted, "I believe he must do both". In order to develop trade, the King encouraged the creation of a railway network and the development of industry.

In spite of his political activities, Leopold I became bored. Estranged from his wife, he spent his time hunting in the Forests of the Ardennes or travelling. During this period Marie-Louise and her children lived a reclusive life at Laeken Palace, near Brussels. The year 1848 saw the Bourbons finally driven from the French throne. That the

King Léopold II and his morganatic wife, Caroline Delacroix, Baroness of Vaughan

Belgian monarchy survived was entirely to the credit of the King who declared, "I have consistently and conscientiously applied the Constitutional system and do not regret it; for our people say : let others talk of a republic. Our freedom is far greater than that of most republics." The unfortunate Marie-Louise survived her father's downfall and death by only a short time. The old King, Louis-Philippe, died in exile in England in August 1850. His daughter, ravaged by consumption, died three months later. "Her death, like her life, was saintly", cried Leopold, who had hardly been the most constant of husbands. Indeed, the King could not wait long before finding consolation in the arms of Arcadie Meyer, his mistress of many years.

On the 2nd December 1852 France got herself an emperor. Leopold saw Napoleon III as a common troublemaker but feared a rekindling of the old bonapartist ambitions. He called on Parliament to reinforce the nation's defences. And, to make sure of Austria's friendship, in 1853 he married his eldest son to the Archduchess Marie-Henriette, daughter of Ernest, Prince Palatine of Hungary. "It's the union of a stable boy and a nun", said the old Princess of Metternich, adding, "The nun of course is the Duke of Brabant!". This diplomatic coup was to be a complete failure from the human point of view. The future Leopold II

and his wife had nothing in common and very soon led separate lives. In the short term, however, it gave Leopold I a chance to savour his success. On the 21st July 1856, on the silver jubilee of his accession, he paraded proudly through the streets of Brussels in the company of the Princes, his sons. His reign was to last almost another 10 years, and would see the parliamentary system shaken by confrontation between Liberals and Catholics. In 1862 the king was diagnosed with gallstones, and as the attacks gradually became more severe they led to insomnia and re-

Albert I in an aeroplane during the Great War.

Famille Royale de Belgique.

Albert I, Elizabeth of Bavaria and their three children: Léopold, Charles and Marie-José.

quired complex surgery. However, the king courageously continued to direct the affairs of State. On the 10th December 1865, after a final bout of surgery, Leopold I closed his eyes for the last time, secure in the knowledge that he had done his duty.

The new king, also called Leopold, was 30. Commentators of the time described him as astute, patient and given to sarcasm. Possessed of the long Orleans nose, he was a tremendous worker whose upbringing had well prepared him for service to his country. His health, however, gave cause for concern, for he had inherited his mother's pulmonary deficiency and was prematurely lame from sciatica. Here then was a young man of unprepossessing appearance with the pompous mannerisms of an aged sage. While still Duke of Brabant and heir to the throne he had presided over a committee set up to look into smartening the city of Brussels. He was prompted by his visits to the Orient to introduce a project to develop outlets for Belgian trade in the Southern hemisphere. On the 17th February 1860, in a speech to the Senate, he declared: "I believe that the time has now come for us to expand beyond our borders. We must lose no more time, or we will see the few remaining opportunities seized by countries more enterprising than our own." Once he was King, Leopold II worked incessantly to make Belgium a colonial power.

On the 17th December 1865 Leopold II climbed the steps to the Throne in the Palais de la Nation and repeated the oath taken by his predecessor, undertaking to follow his father's fine example. He then recalled that he was "the first Belgian-born King of the Belgians." He went on to say "In my mind, Belgium's future and my own have always been inextricably entwined, and it is a future to

which I have always looked forward with that confidence which the right of a free, honest and courageous nation inspires...". To applause, he gave his definition of his task as a constitutional monarch "set apart from conflicts of opinion, which are matters for the nation itself to decide."

The early days of his reign were overshadowed by disturbing events. In 1866 the Austrian forces were annihilated at Sadowa and the shadow of Prussian domination spread over Europe. In France, Napoleon still harboured ambitions of Belgium possession. Moreover, the Mexican venture was turning into catastrophe. Charlotte, Leopold II's sister, sought aid in vain from Napoleon III while her unfortunate husband, Maximilian, remained doggedly at his post. After his execution by firing squad at Queretaro

Albert I and the French General Foch at the front in the First World War (1914-1918): an image of the soldier king.

Foto: John Stjernström.

927
Ensamrätt: Axel Eliassons Konstförlag,
Stockholm.

The future Léopold III and his fiancée, Princess Astrid of Sweden, on the happy occasion of their engagement.

ary 1885 the General Declaration of the Conference of Berlin recognised Leopold II as sovereign of the Independent State of Congo. A few weeks later, Parliament decreed that "His Majesty Leopold II, King of the Belgians, is authorised to be head of the State founded in Africa by the Congo International Association". The inertia of an entire people had been overcome by the dauntless will of one man.

While the king was carving out an empire in the heart of Africa, Belgium was locked in factional quarrels. Liberals and Catholics were squabbling over the education question until a severe economic depression concentrated the whole country's attention on matters of a rather less trivial nature. In a pragmatic royal address on the 9th November 1886, Leopold II spelled out some general guidelines for a social policy. "The following measures are required : regulation of the employment of women and children ; elimination of abuses in the payment of wages ; con-struction projects for suitable housing for working people ; assistance for the development of provident, mutual benefit, insurance and pensions institutions..."

The King, a man of contradictory personality, was now at the peak of his powers. He came across as an alert sexagenarian, upright despite the stick he carried, sporting a long white square-cut beard. From the privacy of his study, he could ignore his critics while he planned the prosperity of his African kingdom. Although he became a legend in his lifetime, Leopold II was severely criticised both for his shameless exploitation of the Congo and for his all too obvious liaison with Caroline Delacroix, whom he created Baroness of Vaughan and show-ered with riches. The King was very conscious of the dignity of his position, and was wont to refer to himself in the third person. But notwithstanding his shortcomings, he succeeded in transforming Belgium into a thriving state. He used his business acumen to open markets in China and Persia and to make his country the world's fifth largest trading nation.

By the age of 74, Leopold II was increasingly crippled

on the 19th June 1867, Charlotte succumbed to insanity.

Shackled in his ambitions by democratic constraints, Leopold II returned to his project for an African colony. In September 1876 he organised an international geographical conference in Brussels with the object of "raising the flag of civilisation on the soil of Central Africa". The following year, the Englishman Stanley explored the river Congo. Leopold II succeeded in persuading him to set out again, this time in the name of the International African Association of which the King was chairman. The king pursued his dream in great secrecy and against the undeclared hostility of Belgian public opinion. In 1881, the town of Leopoldville came into being. On the 15th Febru-

with rheumatism. In the summer of 1908 he was forced to hand over sovereignty of the Congo to Belgium which, after years of indifference, had begun to covet the wealthy colony's riches. In addition, Leopold II turned over almost all his immense fortune to his country in the form of a Royal gift. But above the venerable king's head, the storm clouds of another war were gathering. In Berlin Kaiser William II no longer troubled to conceal his warlike intentions. Mercifully for him Leopold II died before the storm burst. On the 14th December 1909, he underwent an intestinal operation which exhausted the last of his strength. He hardly had time to initial a final law introducing general military service, before he drew his last breath on the 17th December at the Palmiers Lodge at Laeken.

The marriage of Leopold II had been a failure in more ways than one. Marie-Henriette of Austria had given him three daughters but only one male heir, born in 1859. The death of little Leopold, Count of Hainault, of a heart disorder before his tenth birthday, left his father inconsolable and was to complete the break-up of the Royal Household. The death meant that the King's brother, Philippe Count of Flanders, became Heir to the Throne. However, this prince, who suffered from deafness, was hardly suited to the supreme position. Leopold II then looked to his nephew Baudouin, a light-hearted and energetic youth. But fate seemed to dog the Saxe-Coburg dynasty. When Baudouin was 21, he was struck down on the 23rd January 1891 by pleuropneumonia aggravated by renal haemorrhage. The new heir, Albert, the deceased's younger brother, was a shy, awkward man who was happiest with his own company. To his uncle he would always remain a "closed book"...

In 1909 it was thus Albert who became Belgium's third sovereign since independence. After completing his military training, he had sought to satisfy his interest in science and technology by becoming involved in the world of industry. Unlike his uncle, and to his great good fortune, the introvert prince enjoyed a fulfilling personal life. On the 2nd October 1900 in Munich, Bavaria, he married the lovely Duchess Elizabeth. Two sons and a daughter were soon born of this marriage, which was clearly a love match and was received with affectionate approval by the people of Belgium. On the 23rd December 1909, the day he took the oath, Albert I was heckled by Socialist deputies calling for universal suffrage. Their leader, Vandervelde, however, took the trouble to assure the new king that "It is not you we are protesting against but that pack of rogues in the Government!".

The almost unanimous popularity of Albert I, which was his even before his accession, reached its apotheosis during the First World War. His heroic resistance before the German aggressor earned him the nickname of "soldier-king". On the 28th June 1914 the assassination of Archduke Francis Ferdinand in Sarajevo plunged all Europe into the abyss. With scant regard for its neutrality, on

July 1951, beneath the royal canopy Prince Baudouin becomes King Baudouin I of Belgium.

the 4th August the German army invaded Belgium. That day Albert I, in uniform, addressed Parliament with the words, "I have faith in our destinies. A country which defends itself commands universal respect : this country will not perish!"

In spite of this moving call to arms and stubborn resistance, Belgium was overrun in a few weeks. The Germans advanced as far as the Ijzer. Nevertheless, the King remained at La Panne as Commander-in-Chief of the Belgian army, on the small portion of his country which was still free, and from there kept the flame of hope burning for four years. The Queen remained by his side, forgot her German origin and devoted her energy to assisting the wounded. To all the victims of the war she was, and was to remain, the "Nurse-Queen". And when, on the 22nd November 1918, Albert I passed through Brussels to the ecstatic cheers of his people, it was in the knowledge that from that time forth the very existence of Belgium was bound to that of the Royal Family through a pact of blood.

Strengthened by this revived legitimacy, the King was able to approach Parliament with the major reforms he intended to implement : universal suffrage; equality between Walloons and Flemish; a fairer society, governed by "creative discipline, not imposed by compulsory submission or external constraint, but fostered by a common accord of hearts and minds".

Strobl, 13 mai 1945

13th May 1945, King Léopold III, in exile in Strobl, Austria, renounces his right to return to Belgium.

cord of hearts and minds".

After the war was over, Albert and Elizabeth resumed their peaceful family life. The king practised simple sporting pleasures, and indulged his love of gardening, walking, motorcycling, flying and climbing. When affairs of state got on top of him he would go into the mountains, "to restore the balance between soul and body", as he would say. It was on such an occasion on the 17th February 1934 that he left Brussels in the afternoon to go rock climbing at Marche-les-Dames in the Ardennes. He was hit by a falling rock and fell heavily about 15 metres, fracturing his skull. His body was found at nightfall...

The young man who prematurely assumed supreme responsibility in his place appeared to be equipped with every quality required for success. Certainly, times were not easy. Belgium was still deep in the severe crisis which was ravaging the world economy. Pernicious ideologies were in the ascendancy in Italy and Germany and once again European stability was under threat. Nevertheless, at the age of 32, the king-to-be bore within him the optimism and energy of youth. He had also benefited from excellent teachers who had cultivated in him not only the intellectual capacities, but also the human qualities and

sense of observation. Leopold had spent the early days of the Great War at school in England. But at the age of thirteen and a half, by sheer persistence, he managed to persuade his father to let him take military training. For six months in 1915 he did squad drills and shared the ordinary duties of a soldier.

After this, the Crown Prince crossed the Channel again, this time for the ivied walls of the highly exclusive Eton College. Holidays were spent with the family... and the 12th Regiment ! In November 1920 he joined the Army College, whence he emerged two years later with the rank of second lieutenant. During the post-war years the future king travelled widely, to America, Egypt and to the Congo. His travels in some ways foreshadowed the adventures of another Belgian - Tintin - who was soon to arrive on the scene! His report on the situation in Africa, given at the 2nd Brussels Colonial Congress in 1925, was highly critical. "Our arrival in the Congo has greatly affected the both the traditional customs and state of health of the Blacks. The causes of this are moral as well as physical. Our civilisation's sudden contact with local mores and customs, the break-up and resettlement of tribal groups, has had a profound effect on the native way of life and undermined the foundations of the family ..."

All that was needed for this dashing prince was a beautiful princess. Leopold met Astrid of Sweden in the spring of 1926 during a stay in Stockholm. The third daughter of Prince Carl, Duke of Vestrogothie, Astrid had simple tastes and was training in childcare and domestic economy. She also had a rosy complexion, the most beautiful green eyes and an enigmatic smile, all of which went immediately to Leopold's heart. Their engagement was officially announced at the Royal Palace in Brussels on the 22nd September 1926. Yet Astrid had been sure that she would "never marry a prince. All that matters to me is to marry someone I love". But if both love and realpolitik can be satisfied...

The civil marriage took place at Stockholm onthe 4th November in the presence of four kings, two queens, fifteen princes and ten princesses. Several days later the new Duchess of Brabant made a triumphal entry into the port of Antwerp. Leopold, who had arrived earlier on another ship, defied protocol by rushing onto the bridge of the Swedish cruiser and enthusiastically kissing Astrid, to the great displeasure of his mother, Queen Elizabeth. This spontaneous gesture deeply moved the Belgian people, and from that moment Astrid had a place in their hearts. For the nuptial blessing the next day at the church of Saint-Gudule de Bruxelles, the bride carried a bouquet of lilies and white orchids.

The young couple lived quietly at Bellevue Palace, with Astrid doing the cooking and running the house. Their first baby, Joséphine-Charlotte, was born on the 11th October 1927. "Now I feel like a real Belgian", exclaimed Astrid. Although she showed little interest in etiquette, she took her role as wife of the Crown Prince seriously. She studied French and Dutch with determination and accompanied Leopold on many official duties. Leopold continued to travel, but now in the company of his charming wife. In 1928 the Duke and Duchess of Brabant visited the Dutch East Indies; in 1932 the French colonies in

Asia ; the following year the Congo. In the meantime, Belgium celebrated the centenary of its independence and on the 7th September 1930 the birth of the future King, Baudouin, whom Astrid decided to bring up herself. Her interest in young people extended to all the children of Belgian. Overhearing an obscene remark from some small Brussels street urchin, she retorted, "You should think of me not just as your Queen, but also as your mother!". For by this time Albert I's fatal ac-cident had made Astrid the new Queen of the Belgians.

She worked unsparingly at her husband's side to relieve the misery created by unemployment. Her reputation and grace almost eclipsed those of Elizabeth the "Nurse-Queen". However, Astrid remained discreet and maintained the principle, "The Queen listens to the people, but it is the King who speaks". On the 6th June 1934 a third child, Albert, was born to the couple. Despite her fatigue, at the beginning of 1935 Astrid set up a relief committee, a move which set off a great outburst of national solidarity. During the summer, she decided to spend a few days' holiday with Leopold in Kussnacht in Switzerland. It was there, on the Lucerne road by the side of the Quatre-Cantons lake, that Astrid's reign ended in a simple road accident. The memory of her smile will remain with us forever.

While Leopold III grieved alone, the dangers facing the country became ever more pressing. Belgian Fascists were following Germany's lead and becoming prominent in the form of the Flemish V.N.V. (Vlaamsch Nationaal Verbond) and the Walloon Rexisme, whose leader Léon Degrelle was to earn unenviable notoriety during the Occupation. Another war loomed on the horizon. The king advocated "a policy by, with and for the Belgians". The armaments budget was increased, while Hitler continued to protest his peaceful intentions.

This did not prevent soldiers of the Reich violating Belgian neutrality for the second time in a quarter of a century at dawn on the 10th May 1940. Several hours later the king made a stirring appeal to the Nation: "Belgium today will no more hesitate between sacrifice and dishonour than in 1914." Like Albert I, Leopold III took command of the Army. Soon however, in view of the superiority of the German forces, the King's only concern was to avoid a rout. On the 26th May while his ministers fled to France and then to England, Leopold III decided to remain at his post. There was no going back. Henceforth, history would label him a traitor.

On the 28th May Belgium surrendered. The sad news

was announced by Leopold on the radio with the words: "Exhausted by continuous struggle against a better equipped and more numerous enemy, we have no alternative but to surrender. I will not abandon you in the misfortune which has overtaken us and it is my intention to watch over your destiny and that of your families." From that point on the King would see his captivity under the Nazi occupier as the symbol of his entire nation's imprisonment. Never-

Baudouin based his investiture speech around the themes of social progress and economic development.

theless, his secret morganatic marriage in 1941 to Liliane Baels, who took the title Princess de Réthy, attracted condemnation from many Belgians, who felt that this was not a time for their sovereign to be considering only his own personal happiness.

When the Allies landed in Normandy in June 1944, the King was moved to Germany. When Belgium was finally liberated, Leopold III was still in Germany and prevented from returning to the Throne. His younger brother, Prince Charles, Count of Flanders, who was almost unknown to the Belgian people, was elected Regent. Born in 1903, he had attended several English Naval Colleges and even served as a lieutenant in the Royal Navy. Back in civilian life he avoided honours and sought only to preserve his privacy. His interests were art and driving fast cars, and he had little inclination for politics or the social whirl. During the war he lived quietly in Brussels. In order to avoid arrest by the Germans, he went in 1944 to live near Spa where he took the name Mr. Richard and established contact with the local Resistance.

On the 7th May 1945 the American 8th Army released the King and his family, who were being held in Austria, at Strobl on the shore of Lake Saint-Wolfgang. Three days later his brother arrived with an official delegation and intimated to Leopold III that the situation in Belgium made his immediate return inadvisable. The King accepted this and on the 13th May issued a statement on Belgian radio to the effect that, "The King has written to his brother informing him that, as a result of his captivity, his health does not permit him to continue the task with

A difficult transition skilfully handled by Baudouin: the independence of the Belgian Congo.

which he has been entrusted".

The Socialists - many of whom were pro-Republican - accused the King of collaboration and demanded a formal act of abdication. On the other hand, no politician of the right was willing or able to form a government favourable to Leopold III's return. This unstable situation persisted until 1950. The King set up home in exile at Prégny, near Geneva, awaiting the results of a referendum which was finally held on the 12th March 1950.

The result showed that 57.68% of Belgians were in favour of Leopold III. In Wallonia, however, votes in favour did not reach the 50% mark. For the Monarchy, whose principal function is as a symbol of national unity, such a result was tantamount to rejection. A situation well understood by the elder statesman, Paul-Henri Spaak, when he wrote to the King, "Your Majesty, now that your policy and your conduct have been approved by the majority of the Belgian people, be satisfied with this victory : send us your son".

Ignoring this advice, Leopold III returned to his country onthe 22nd July 1950 after a six year absence. A trial of strength was inevitable. The national economy was paralysed by strikes organised by the Unions and parties of the left. Riots threatened to turn into insurrection. On the 1st August Leopold, abandoned by his Government, threw in the towel. In order to settle what was known at the time as "The royal question", the King decided to hand over his powers to his son, Prince Baudouin. In the King's mind, it was "a necessary stage on the way to a solution which will allow the Crown Prince to succeed when he comes of age if, as I hope and wish, the promised reconciliation around

the person of my son is achieved".

Thus it was, on the 16th July 1951, in the Royal Palace in Brussels, several weeks before his twenty first birthday and ahead of his time, that a shy, short-sighted young man assumed the supreme office. This is how his father addressed the young man who was to be crowned the fifth king of the Saxe-Coburg dynasty: "My dear son, I am proud to hand over to you the noble and onerous task of wearing the Crown of Belgium, a country which, in spite of the most terrible wars and upheavals, is still whole, territorially and morally free, and true to its traditions." The abdication of Leopold III marked a difficult beginning for Baudouin I's reign. What chance had he of preserving such a fragile monarchy ? Yet over more than 40 years, Baudouin has shown himself worthy of his father's confidence and of his subjects' devotion.

Belgium's King for the 21st century: Philippe, Baudouin's nephew.

Official

The Military functions remain an important part of the duties of the Belgian royal family.

*B*efore examining the reign and activities of the present Belgian king, an attempt might usefully be made to define the framework and limits of his prerogatives. For 150 years the powers of the king have been defined by the Constitution of the 7th February 1831. In accordance with its terms, Belgium has been a kingdom and parliamentary monarchy since its foundation. Under the Constitution, an individual who "reigns but does not rule" occupies the position of Head of State, not unlike the way in which the revised Charter of 1830 regulated French institutions under Louis-Philippe. The patriots who had just relieved King William I of Holland of his power, had no intention of entrusting the monarchy to an autocrat by divine right. They wanted a "King of the Belgians", not a "King of Belgium".

The first essential for a divided nation was to have an arbiter, independent of the various factions, who would be able to impose the rules of democracy on every citizen. When the delegation from the National Congress came to Leopold of Saxe-Coburg to offer him the Crown, he said of the Constitution : "You have been harsh in your treatment of royalty !". Nevertheless, he agreed to take up the challenge. Later, his successors' continuing ability to play an essential role in the nation's life rested solely on their moral authority. Notwithstanding these limitations the king retains not inconsiderable powers.

Chapter II of the Constitution, the chapter which concerns us, is headed "Concerning the King and his Ministers" and is divided into sections. The original wording of Article 60, which opens the first section relating to "The King", was as follows: "The constitutional powers of the king are hereditary within the direct, natural and legitimate succession of His Royal Highness Leopold of Saxe-Coburg, from male to male in order of primogeniture with the perpetual exclusion of females and their descendants". Since 1991 the order of absolute primogeniture has replaced the Salic Law, with the result that princesses now enjoy the same succession rights as their brothers.

After Article 61, which deals with cases of inoccupancy of the throne, Article 62 prohibits the king from being at the same time head of another State without the consent of two thirds of the two Assemblies. It will be remembered that this procedure was necessary for Leopold II to become king of the Congo. Article 63 lays down the inviolability of the royal person and the responsibilities of ministers. The next article, which ensues from the theme of ministerial responsibility, is without doubt the most important since it rules out the possibility of arbitrary royal acts : "No act by the king may have any effect unless it is countersigned by a minister who, by so doing, becomes responsible for it".

A perfect couple and the symbol of the Belgian nation: Baudouin and Fabiola.

The king does, however, take part in policy decisions insofar as the Constitution makes him a member - with the Government - of the executive authority, and - with the Assembly and the Senate- of the legislative authority. Does not Article 65 state that "The king appoints and dismisses ministers?" This provision has often given the

king a key role in a regime which in some respects resembles the French 4th Republic. It prompted a journalist to write some years ago that "Baudouin I" had crowned "Martens IV". Martens was the politician who was his own successor as Prime Minister in a whole series of party coalitions.

As Commander-in-Chief of the army the king signs treaties and bestows military ranks. He also makes appointments to administrative and judicial posts. He can make regulations and decrees for the execution of laws, but cannot suspend them. But above all, under Article 69 "The king sanctions and promulgates laws". This is why, in April 1990, Baudouin I was obliged to "vacate the throne" for a few hours in order not to impede the adoption of a law legalising abortion which he did not wish to sign.

The king has the right to adjourn the assemblies for a month and even to dissolve them (Article 71). He also enjoys the main traditional royal prerogatives : the right to grant reprieve, to mint money, to award military decorations and noble titles "without the authority to link them with privileges of any kind".

The Constitution does, however, specify the contractual nature of these royal prerogatives. As a result, Article 78 lays down that "the king has no powers other than those formally granted by the Constitution and by specific laws relating to the Constitution".

As guarantor of the institutions, head of the executive and safeguard of the judicial process, the Belgian Monarch has retained more effective power than any of his European counterparts, apart from Rainier III of Monaco. Perhaps this is because his compatriots, immersed in their squabbles, felt the need for an arbiter of genuine authority.

However, what is set down in the Constitution is not everything. Five reigns and one hundred and sixty years of practical experience have altered the royal prerogatives. The sovereign's personality, precedent and practice are almost as important as legal provisions. In a book dedicated to Baudouin I on the 40th anniversary of his reign, Pierre Wyvenkens emphasised this capacity to adapt to circumstances. "Without a stature commensurate with his

The education of the future King includes military training. The Prince of Liège awarding a medal to his son.

office, a king of the Belgians could easily be reduced to a role more symbolic than real. He could nevertheless constitute no danger to the nation since the Constitution grants him little personal power. On the other hand, if the king's qualities are such that he is able to play a leading role in the nation, that same Constitution allows him to exercise them in a very real way within the framework set aside to that end..."

King Baudouin I.

A sovereign attentive to the needs of his fellow citizens.

King Baudouin, his brother Albert, sister-in-law Paola and second nephew Laurent. The succession of the dynasty is guaranteed.

Princess Astrid and her husband in the company of their three children: Joachim, Amédéo and Maria-Laura.

Still in perfect harmony after more than thirty years of marriage.

Private

On the 16th July 1951, then, Baudouin I became the fifth King of the Belgians. In reply to his father's speech, the new King responded simply : "My dear father, I am greatly moved by the noble sentiment you have just expressed. I promise that I will do my best to prove myself worthy of being your son". It was midday when Leopold signed his abdication and began an internal exile which was to last for more than thirty years. After his demise on the 25th September 1983, several months after another unfortunate king, his brother-in-law Umberto II of Italy, Leopold III, who had sacrificed himself for his dynasty's survival, was to receive unexpected tributes from his people. In death, his self-denial and greatness of spirit finally won their just reckoning from the Belgian people.

Baudouin I, the twenty year old "sad king", kept his oath. Many years later he told journalists that when he became king, he "entered Belgium" as others enter religious orders. The day after his father's abdication he appeared before the Assemblies and said: "It is a precious encouragement to me to see my reign begin in harmony... I will lend my support to all initiatives which favour social progress, scientific advances, economic development and the fulfilment of intellectual and art-istic values".

Baudouin, who was born at Stuyvenberg Chateau on the 7th September 1930 when Belgium was celebrating the centenary of its independence, had not had an uniformly easy life. His grandfather King Albert died while he was still a child, followed by his mother, Queen Astrid, who died in an accident when he was less than five years old. Perhaps that was the day that the Belgian people adopted the little boy whose gaze would always be shadowed by grief at his mother's early death. Brought up with children of his own age from different social backgrounds, Baudouin had a strict but broad education. It included activities like scouting, which taught him the healthy delights of nature, perseverance in the face of adversity and love of life. It provided a solid anchor for the religious which was to guide his actions throughout his life.

The marriage of Baudouin and Fabiola, in 1960, ended a period of sadness in the young King's life.

With the German invasion in 1940, the Royal children and their tutors had to flee Belgium. They went first to Brittany, then to the Lot, and finally to Spain. On their return to Brussels on the 1st August, Baudouin and his brother were sent as a precaution to Ciergnon Chateau where the future king continued his studies under the strict supervision of two private tutors. Lessons were given alternately in French and Dutch, but Baudouin's particular interest was the exact sciences. In July 1941 Baudouin and Albert returned to Laeken. The King had just remarried ; fortu-

Queen Fabiola, her husband's closest aide.

From her first appearance Fabiola won the hearts of her Belgian subjects.

nately, his new wife Princess de Réthy was able to give Astrid's three children all the affection of a second mother.

In 1944 the Royal family shared Leopold III's German captivity in the old castle of Hirscheim-on-Elbe, then at Strobl in Austria. When the King was living in Switzerland, the heir to the throne spent several months at the famous Rosey College, then at Saint-Antoine de Prégny College. To make up for lost time he threw himself into the study of political economy and international and constitutional law. In 1948 Baudouin travelled to the United States and the West Indies. However, the young man's rendezvous with history was not far off. He became Regent for his father on the 11th August 1950 and King a year later.

The new King's first concern was to come to grips with the real undercurrents within his kingdom. On the 19th December 1952, he paid an incognito visit to the Marolles district slums accompanied by Abbot Froidure and the Minister for Public Health. Now the nation's poor could be assured that the King was aware of their plight. Within a few months, he had gained considerably in popularity. Gradually, he freed himself of the influence of his father, the former king, and revealed his own character, a combination of gravity and simplicity.

On the 15th May 1955 he flew to the Congo where he was given a triumphant welcome. In white full dress uniform he was cheered by the native people, who called him "Bwana Kitoko" ("Handsome Master"). When he ended a speech at the Leopoldville Stadium with a few sentences in Lingala, the crowd went wild with delight. Independence was not yet on the agenda, but in his address to the Brussels Royal African Club on his return, the King emphasised the need for change in unambiguous terms : "Then the time will have come - although when this will be we still do not know - for us to give our African colonies a status which, for the good of all, will ensure the survival of a genuine Belgo-Congolese community and guarantee for all people, black and white, according to their merits and ability, an appropriate role in the government of the country ".

Post-war Belgium took a stake in the construction of Europe. 1958 was to be the year when the Common Market opened. It was also the year of the Brussels World Exhibition. This great event provided both Belgium and its

The Royal Family was extended with the marriage of Astrid to the Archduke Lorenz of Austria (far left and right).

Philippe of Belgium on commando training.

Still as much in love as they were on their wedding day.

Archduke and Archduchess Lorenz of Austria and their two eldest children: Amédéo and Maria-Laura.

Princess Astrid and her first son Amédéo, born in 1986.

King with an occasion to set the agenda for the future. "Many years of hard work are required for our institutions and industry to adapt so as to safeguard the country's vital interests while cooperating fairly in the creation of a new Europe."

It was unfortunate for the tabloids that the young king was so perfect, so melancholy, that there was nothing to write about him. Journalists, anxious for something to say, would periodically speculate about his marital prospects. Some, with pretensions to inside knowledge, claimed that the King intended to abdicate in favour of his brother Albert and enter a monastery. At a State Ball given in April 1958 in honour of the Exhibition, the King danced a few times with Crown Princess Beatrix of the Netherlands, and with Princess Isabelle of France, elder daughter of the Count of Paris. But there was still no romance on the horizon. Baudouin would remain an ostensibly confirmed bachelor, even when Prince Albert married a beautiful Italian aristocrat, Paola Ruffo di Calabria, on the 2nd July 1959.

It later became known that Baudouin had already met his soul mate. But, because of the gravity of events in Africa, he preferred to keep his secret and delay his marriage until later. Trouble did indeed flare up in the Congo in January 1959. Riots against the European presence in the country led to hundreds of deaths. The King reacted instantly. On the 13th January he raised the question of independence: "In the civilised world, independence is a status which ensures and combines freedom, order and progress. It can only be acquired through sound well balanced institutions; experienced administrative personnel; an entrenched social, economic and financial organisation in

Princess Astrid of Belgium, Archduchess Lorenz of Austria, is third in the dynastic line.

Prince Philippe on a recent visit to the American base at Cape Canaveral.

Paola, Princess of Liège, carries out a number of representative duties.

Albert, the King's youngest brother, was married in 1959, a year before Baudouin.

Prince Albert, the King's brother, is heir apparent to the throne but will no doubt step down in favour of his son Philippe.

The Princess of Liège.

the hands of qualified people ; and economic and moral education without which a democratic regime is no more than mockery, deceit and tyranny". More than 30 years on, and in the light of the bankruptcy and chaos which continue to haunt the Dark Continent, we can only marvel at the prophetic accuracy of this warning...

Unfortunately, the obduracy of the Nationalist leaders precluded dialogue. On the 30th June 1960 Baudouin I returned to Leopoldville to oversee, with the new president, Joseph Kasavubu, the transfer of power. The great grand-nephew of Leopold II ventured to offer a few words of wisdom and friendship. "Don't be afraid of coming back to us. We are always prepared to remain at your side with help and advice". The Congolese Prime Minister, Lumumba, responded with anger and insult. An outbreak of violence against Belgians in the Congo several weeks later forced Baudouin to send paratroopers to cover their evacuation. The break between Brussels and its colony was a bloody one.

It was the start of a new chapter. Despite the bitterness of the events, at least Baudouin was finally free to express his feelings as a private individual. On the 16th September 1960, the Belgian Prime Minister Gaston Eyskens officially announced the King's engagement. The bride of his choice - Fabiola de Mora y Aragon - was an unknown. Born on the 11th June 1928, she was two years older than Baudouin. Last but one of seven children in a family from the upper echelons of the Madrid nobility, she was stern but majestically graceful in appearance. She had been brought up a strict traditional Catholic and was in perfect

Princess Christine of Belgium.

accord with the king both spiritually and ethically. She and her fiancé had met at a "youth meeting" at the home of her godmother, Queen Victoria-Eugénie, widow of Alphonso XIII. Living in her Swiss exile, the old lady's greatest pleasure in life was to play the matchmaker.

On the 17th September, introducing the future fifth Queen of the Belgians to photographers and cameramen at Ciergnon, Baudouin was wreathed in smiles. It was clear that the "sad King" was sad no more. The religious ceremony took place on the 15th December at Cathedral Saints-Michel-et-Gudule de Bruxelles which was decorated for the occasion with purple and gold tapestries. Before leaving for their honeymoon, the king sent a message to his beloved subjects: "The marriage which has just taken place sets the seal on an alliance not only between me and my wife but between the Royal Family and each of your families. We are now united to serve you and contribute to the best of our abilities to the happiness of each of your homes." To quote Saint-Exupéry: "True love is not two people looking at one other, but two people looking in the same direction".

The new Queen, who within a few hours had conquered the hearts of the Belgian people, added, "Thank you for the warmth of your affection, thank you for your unforgettable welcome. My heart and my life now belong not only to my husband but to all of you." Since that day Fabiola has devoted her life to the King and his people. The vows of marriage are often no more than empty words.

One of the daughters of Léopold III and Lilian Baels, Princess of Réthy: the very beautiful Princess Marie-Christine of Belgium.

But for Fabiola they had the unalterable quality of a commitment rooted in infinite love. Leopold III and the Princess de Réthy left Laeken Palace for the young couple to make it their family home. There, Fabiola created a warm and simple atmosphere, a place of quiet contentment where the King could relax and forget his public duties.

Does this mean that Baudouin and Fabiola sought to avoid their State duties ? Indeed not ; on the contrary, the Queen took on more and more roles. A former nurse who had worked voluntarily in Madrid hospitals, she soon showed that charity was more than just a word to her. Her first act was to assign the wedding presents to a fund which would enable her to engage a private secretary. She refused to surround herself with courtiers. Today she still selects her ladies-in-waiting according to the place and circumstances ; on a school visit, for example, she will arrange to be accompanied by a teacher.

However, fate continues to be unkind to Baudouin. After several false alarms, Fabiola had to give up the idea of providing an heir to the throne. A less united couple might have crumbled before such a trial. But the King and Queen simply drew further spiritual strength from it. The impossibility of an heir of their own blood became for Baudouin and Fabiola a source of deeper compassion for the suffering of others. In 1972, during the Year of the Child, the Queen declared : "You know that we have no children. We have long wondered if there was some meaning in this affliction. Gradually, we have learned that it has made us more free to love all children, everywhere". To love and to serve, this could be Fabiola's motto as she herself recalled on the 11th June 1988 in an admirably high-toned speech on the occasion of her sixtieth birthday. "I believe that there are a thousand ways of loving and that the more we discover of this marvellous and essential art, the better we will understand that to love is to serve, to think of others first, forgetting our own fears, and to share, to give joy without measure. Our love must radiate without bounds and go out to anyone regardless of their age, colour, background, health, or whether or not they are nice. When we experience this internal force, more powerful than force of arms, and which persists beyond death, the meaning of life is within our grasp. The mystery within us emerges gradually into the light and we are filled with joy."

All the affection Baudouin and Fabiola were unable to lavish on children of their own, they thus resolved to expend on all children in need and people in distress. The queen has become Belgium's "number one social worker". Her office recei-

Christine of Belgium, half-sister to King Baudouin.

King Baudouin: the last of Belgians ?

Seventh in line to the throne: Prince Laurent, born in 1963.

events. The interminable squabbles between French and Flemish speaking Belgians is scarcely worthy of note... But the King of the Belgians' job is more of a long term nature. He is discreet but effective. Every morning after breakfast with the Queen at Laeken, and often after attending Mass, the King leaves by car for the Royal Palace in Brussels where he has his offices as Head of State. Between 9 and 10 a.m. he meets each of his officials one by one, asks questions, reads through and signs the documents submitted for his approval - some 20,000 a year! He then gives audiences. He rarely sees more than four people in a morning : ministers, parliamentarians and important individuals from across the socio-political spectrum.

By the nature of his position the King must never take sides. He reads notes carefully. "The king is conscientious to a fault", writes Jo Gérard in a biography of Baudouin. "He is a good listener. He looks you in the eye with a steady gaze and asks questions which are short and to the point. He has inherited Albert I's art of rapidly summing up the key points of a discussion." Following the tradition that "the Crown must not be exposed", those who have an audience with the King must not reveal anything about the conversation.

After lunching with the Queen at Laeken, if there are no official events, the King spends the afternoon on paperwork and on his correspondence. Many of his people write directly to their Sovereign. It is to him that they can go as a last resort. As the supreme mediator between the Administration and the public, he can speed up and simplify certain procedures.

The King does not appear to have extravagant tastes. Like any good hunter, he has a respect for nature. When he was younger, he was keen on skiing and golf. Since he suffers from a heart complaint and sciatica, he has to restrict his physical activities. The Royal couple often spend their evenings peacefully at Laeken watching television or reading and listening to classical music. Every summer the

ves between ten and twelve thousand letters a year. Four full time staff, two French speaking and two Flemish speaking, have the task of writing specific and individual replies to each letter. Fabiola is kept informed of the requests and in some cases answers in person. By becoming a direct mediator between the people and their King, the Queen has in some way taken on the role of principal advisor to His Majesty. What other democracy can boast a better system, the result of 30 years of mutual confidence ?

Apart from the stormy secession of the Congo, the reign of this King has not been marked by any spectacular

Prince Philippe of Belgium in preparation for his future role.

Will Prince Philippe marry the Infanta Cristina of Spain ?

Prince Philippe at the barracks.

Out shopping Philippe of Belgium is just another citizen.

Queen goes back with her husband to Andalusia to enjoy the sunshine at villa Motril, their villa to the south of Grenada.

In his forty years on the throne Baudouin has become the living conscience of the nation. His stance on abortion three years ago indicated the moral dimension of his position. In the early hours of the morning of the 4th April 1990 the Palace announced that the king was "unable to reign" in accordance with Article 82 of the Constitution. This was the only ploy that the King, who strongly opposes legalising the voluntary termination of pregnancy, could use to avoid signing the decree. In the absence of the King's signature, the Government temporarily assumed the royal function in order to ratify the abortion law. Thirty six hours after his "abdication", the King's duties were restored by Parliament.

Some analysts ground their teeth at what Professor Jean Stengers described as a dirty trick. There was talk of modifying the Constitution and depriving the King of his participation in the legislative process. With hindsight, it is apparent that the King's standing was strengthened by this act. By the bold affirmation of his ethical standards, the King had earned the respect of all, including supporters of abortion.

But who now would claim that Belgium could do without its King ? For above all, Baudouin I remains perhaps the ultimate symbol of a national cohesion which is close to breaking point. At a time when there appear to be no bounds to linguistic federalism, he is the only person who remains respected and loved by both the Walloons and the Flemish. The most recent example of this were the mo-

Philippe of Belgium on an official visit.

The Belgian Royal Couple.

ving expressions of affection and sympathy which followed a serious mitral valve repair operation in Paris in the spring of 1992.

For forty years, tirelessly and against all opposition, the King has been the advocate of this "union" which, according to the Belgian motto "makes the strength" of a nation. In his 1986 Christmas message he said, "It is essential that everyone should makes the effort to understand the other community, its history, temperament and language". Several months later he added, "I would like our country to

demonstrate, in the heart of this Europe which is seeking unity in diversity, that it is possible for different cultures to develop side by side within a single political entity".

This consolidation of Belgian identity, both as a blueprint and a constituent of European unity, is the main challenge facing King Baudouin and his nephew and heir, Prince Philippe, in the future. Time alone will tell whether Belgium, which was created five generations ago by the Saxe-Coburgs, will survive intact into the third millennium.

Denmark

By Bodil Cath

Margrethe helps to design her own clothes. Here we see one of the long robes made by Jørgen Bender which she wore for the Silver Wedding celebrations at Kronborg Castle.

Margrethe, Queen of Denmark, inherited the throne — and she was the people's choice

Queen Margrethe II of Denmark is the ruling monarch of the world's oldest kingdom. Her ancestors go back 1,000 years to the time of Gorm den Gamle, who died around 950 A.D. When asked whether she considered herself to be a "chosen" queen, Queen Margrethe quite rightly agreed. "I was actually chosen as queen when the decision was taken in a referendum to allow female succession to the throne," said the Queen.

So Margrethe II feels that she became queen not only as the eldest daughter of the late King Frederik IX, but also because the people chose her. The Danes voted "Yes" to Margrethe in a referendum in 1953 on a new Act of Succession, which was called to decide whether Denmark should allow a woman to succeed to the throne. However, the ruling was that the one to inherit the throne would not necessarily be the first-born - if the first child is a girl, and her parents later have a son, it is the son who will inherit the throne in preference to his sister.

Before this referendum, only men could succeed to the Danish throne. This meant that Frederik IX had no heirs, despite the fact that he had three daughters, the Princesses Margrethe, Benedikte and Anne-Marie. His heir would have been his brother, Prince Knud, who had

A well-known picture of four generations of Danish kings: Christian IX, Christian X, Frederik VIII and at the front Queen Margrethe's father, later Frederik IX.

Christian IX playing cards with his three daughters, Queen Alexandra of England, the widowed Tsarina Dagmar of Russia and Thyra, Duchess of Cumberland.

two sons. The eldest of these, Prince Ingolf, married a commoner, as did his younger brother Prince Christian. Both bear the title Count of Rosenborg.

Prince Knud had been Crown Prince until the new Act of Succession was passed, following the referendum, when he moved to be fourth in line of succession. The result of the referendum was clearly a disappointment for Knud, as he could not but feel that his family had been reduced in status, but this disappointment was not allowed to show. Over the years, there has been public politeness and cordiality between the families of the two brothers, although there does remain a certain distance.

The new Act of Succession meant that King Frederik's eldest daughter, Princess Margrethe, became the fourth generation of her family (the House of Glücksborg) to rule Denmark. Her position was completely changed.

The previous ruling house, the Oldenborgs, died with

King Frederik VII in 1863, and with him the end of an historic era. A new chapter opened when the first member of the House of Glücksborg ascended to the Danish throne - the man who would become King Christian IX was born in April 1818, the son of Duke Wilhelm of Schleswig-Holstein Sonderborg Glücksborg. Christian of Glücksborg, who became King of Denmark, was to father two kings, a queen and an empress, and to become known as the father-in-law of Europe. He had a happy marriage, and he and his Queen Louise had six children, ruling Denmark for 42 years before he died at the age of 87.

The Glücksborg family was a collateral branch of the Oldenborgs, and Duke Wilhelm of Glücksborg, Christian IX's father, was a brother-in-law of King Frederik VI, the Oldenborg King of Denmark. When Duke Wilhelm died, King Frederik VI took Christian in and cared for him as his own son. The guardianship developed into a deep mu-

Christian X loved his morning ride and the King on horseback became a common sight in Copenhagen.

Half a million Danes come out to welcome Princess Ingrid to Copenhagen in May 1935, after marrying the Danish Crown Prince Frederik in Stockholm.

Queen Margrethe was the apple of her father's eye from an early age. Here we see her father, later Frederik IX, as Crown Prince, filming his young daughter in 1941.

tual affection, and Frederik was known to sigh, "If only he were my son!". Frederik VI was a simple, ordinary man, and Christian was a "son" after his own heart.

When Christian was only 19, plans were afoot to marry him to the future Queen of England, Princess Victoria. As events turned out, this was not to be, and both had very happy marriages elsewhere. The curious thing is that two of their children did marry each other - Christian IX's eldest daughter, Princess Alexandra, married the heir to the throne of England, the future King Edward VII, then Prince of Wales.

Christian IX's marriage to his Queen Louise was successful in every way - they complemented one another in public, and loved and supported one another in private. They were married in 1842, and lived to celebrate their Golden Wedding anniversary together. Queen Louise was the daughter of the Landgrave of Hessen, but closely related to the Danish royal family through her mother, who was the sister of King Christian VIII of Denmark.

Christian IX had a reputation for being thrifty, and was definitely not a man to throw his money about. His favourite coffee-coloured overcoat became internationally famous because of its patch on one sleeve - a clear sign of a King who didn't believe in rash expenditure.

The Father-in-law of Europe

The Danish Court was at this time a focal point in Europe. Without any trace of extravagance, the family enjoyed a happy life at Fredensborg Palace, just north of Copenhagen, where daily life was characterised by its simplicity.

Family meals were informal, with everyone helping themselves. Queen Louise loved music, and in the evenings she liked to play quartets in the music room with her three daughters.

In 1889 the eldest son, Prince Frederik, married Lovisa, the daughter of King Carl XV of Sweden. The next son, Prince Vilhelm, was chosen to become King George I of Greece.

The oldest daughter, Alexandra, married the English Prince of Wales. His mother, Queen Victoria, found it difficult at first to reconcile herself to her son's marriage, but soon grew to love her Danish daughter-in-law. The middle daughter, Dagmar, was initially engaged to be married to Grand Duke Nikolaus, heir to the Russian throne, but he died. A year later Dagmar married Nikolaus' brother Grand Duke Alexander (the future Tsar Alexander III). As a Russian Empress, Dagmar took the name Maria Feodorovna. The youngest daughter, Thyra, married the Duke of Cumberland, and before King Christian died he was also to see his young grandson, Carl, accede to the Norwegian throne as King Haakon VII.

Those were the great days of Fredensborg, the time of Christian IX and his Queen Louise. This was when the families from England, Russia and Greece all met at the North Zealand Palace. Most of the palace's vast quantity of rooms were full, and the table was always set for about 100 people. The Danish Royal family alone made up half of this number.

Every summer, the Russian Tsar Alexander and Empress Dagmar came with their children for a holiday. The German Kaiser Wilhelm and

Here we see Queen Margrethe as a 6 year old and star of the Lucia procession, a traditional Scandinavian festival.

In 1952 King Frederik took a long trip to Greenland. Queen Ingrid and the three princesses did not join him, but each of his daughters received a splendid national costume as a memento of the trip.

his family were also guests of King Christian, and the King and Queen of Sweden often sailed across the Sound for a visit. Everyone was careful to avoid political discussions. Alexandra of England loved visiting her parents, and King Christian always referred to her as "my beautiful daughter". His daughter Duchess Thyra of Cumberland was "my good daughter", and the Empress Dagmar said that her father was the wisest person she knew.

Even if King Christian liked a modest lifestyle, there was always room, food and a place in his heart for his beloved family. Once, during the happy days of Fredensborg, Christian was about go out in a carriage with his three daughters - an Empress, a Princess and a Duchess. The King thought a two-horse team quite adequate for driving a short distance, but his daughters disagreed. In the end the King had to give way, and the four of them arrived at the Palace in the style that his daughters felt appropriate - a team of four horses and postilions.

Their network of relations gave the Danish Royal Family a unique position and reputation across Europe - even today Queen Margrethe is related to more than half the royal families of Europe.

She is, for example, related to King Harald of Norway, ex-King Constantine and Queen Anne-Marie of Greece,

King Frederik IX loved his three daughters: (from left) Princess Margrethe, Princess Anne-Marie and Princess Benedikte. Queen Ingrid always dressed her daughters identically when they were younger.

Queen Elizabeth and Prince Philip of England, and King Baudouin of Belgium. The Greek branch of the House of Glücksborg has provided links with the English and Spanish Royal Families, and with the nobilities of Yugoslavia, Italy, France, Romania and Russia.

Christian IX had the joy of living to see the monarchy secure into the fourth generation. In the spring of 1899, then aged 82, he became a great-grandfather, with the birth of Margrethe's father, the future King Frederik IX. Christian's grandson, the future Christian X, had married

the year before to Princess Alexandrine of Mecklenburg-Schwerin.

Christian IX's successor, his son Frederik VIII, was much less conservative than his father. He was king for only 6 years, from 1906 until 1912, when he died suddenly of a heart attach at the age of 68. He was succeeded by his eldest son Christian X - a man with a sense of humour and a quick tongue. He once overheard two ladies speaking in German at a reception, and one of them said "Ja, schön ist er ja nicht" (*Well, he's not very good-looking*), to which the

King replied "Nein, aber er hört gut" (*No, but his hearing's good!*).

Christian X took a firm line with the Germans during the occupation of Denmark, and his people closed ranks around him. There was real concern about the fact that the King, a keen horseman, always rode alone and without protection in the streets of Copenhagen. In 1942, he was involved in a serious riding accident, from which he never really recovered. He died in April 1947, at the age of 76.

Queen Margrethe once said that she does not remember a lot about her grandfather, except that he was an old man in a wheelchair, whereas her grandmother, Queen Alexandrine, had given her a lot of happy memories.

The new King, Frederik IX, Margrethe's father, had done very well at school, particularly at languages. He was involved for a while with Princess Olga of Greece, and they managed to get half-engaged in 1922, when Frederik was 23. Their romance never really received official approval, and before it could do so Frederik and Olga themselves had decided to separate.

It was not until 1935 that the 36-year-old Crown Prince placed his future happiness firmly in the hands of Princess Ingrid of Sweden. They were married on May 24th 1935 in a magnificent ceremony at Storkyrkan, in Stockholm. It was a

There's plenty of bounce in Margrethe - she showed that during training with the Women's Air Corps. Queen Margrethe is known for her elegant leaps as a ballet dancer.

Queen Margrethe at an army training college in 1966.

choice he would never regret. The couple complemented each other superbly, and, as Margrethe herself puts it, during the 25 years she herself has been married she has always had the marriage of her parents as an example.

Margrethe's father was a very popular king. He loved the sea, and his large circle of friends included many sea captains. Inhabitants of Copenhagen, taking an evening stroll past the Amalienborg Palace home of the King, would see a flashing signal light from a royal window, which would then be answered by an enormous bellow from a steamer. This was the King sending a greeting by signal light to one of his seafaring friends, who happened to be the captain of one of the DFDS line of ships. King Frederik made a lot of use of the Royal Yacht Dannebrog, where he enjoyed being hosed down on the quarterdeck - nothing healthier, he reckoned.

Because Frederik loved the sea, and everything to do with it, he got himself tattooed as a young man. The tat-

Elvis Presley kneels before Danish Crown Princess Margrethe when she visited the US in 1960.

toos drew a lot of attention when, as Crown Prince, he visited the USA with his wife. The American press had a field day with the young Danish Prince's tattoos, which came into view when he took off his shirt to do some rowing.

He was also very musical, and loved to conduct large symphony orchestras. It has been said that had he not been king, he could have been one of the best conductors in Denmark.

The world's best-educated monarch

Queen Margrethe is said to be the best-educated monarch in the world. Certainly her record so far seems to prove it.

She was a student at Zahles school, a private institu-

tion, and then at the Danish Women's Air Force College. She took a philosophy course at Copenhagen University, before studying archaeology at Cambridge. She went on to read political science at Århus University, continued at the Sorbonne, and finally at the London School of Economics.

In addition to her education and voluntary service with the Women's Air Force, Queen Margrethe is also an Allied Colonel-in-chief of The Queen's Regiment, the President of the Royal Society of Northern Antiquaries, the Chairman of the Queen Margrethe and Prince Henrik Fund, and the founder of the Queen Margrethe II Archaeological Fund. In addition, Margrethe is the patron of many societies and associations, among them the Royal Danish Scientific Society and the Danish Bible Society. Religion is very close to her heart. The Queen has also received nu-

Margrethe and Henrik were married in a splendid and lavish ceremony in Holmen Church on the afternoon of 10 June 1967. The lace in the bride's veil was also worn by Queen Ingrid at her wedding.

merous honours, amongst them an Honorary Fellowships of the London School of Economics. As recently as 1992 Queen Margrethe became an Honorary Bencher of one of the Inns of Court in England. She has been made an honorary doctor of several foreign universities, and awarded many medals of distinction. Margrethe II has certainly made her mark in the world of art and science.

The Queen's marriage

Queen Margrethe ascended to the throne on January 14th 1972, on the death of her father King Frederik IX. She was accepted as a member of the Statsrad (the Council of State, presided over by the monarch) when she was 18, and in her capacity as Queen she is the Supreme Commander of the Armed Forces. Born during the German occupation of Denmark, the occasion of her birth was a rare ray of sunshine in those dark times.

On June 10th 1967, Margrethe II (Alexander Porhildur Ingrid), Queen of Denmark, born April 16th 1940 at Amalienborg Palace, Copenhagen, daughter of King Frederik IX (died 1972) and Queen Ingrid, married Prince Henrik of Denmark (born Henri Marie Jean-André de Laborde de Monpezat on June 11th 1934 in Talence, Gironde, France), son of Count André de Laborde de Monpezat and Countess Renée de Monpezat, née Doursenot. Twenty-five years later, Margrethe and Henrik celebrated their silver wedding in 1992 with royal guests

Margrethe often wears seal pelts, both because she likes them and also as a way of protesting against wholly unjustified accusations of the slaughter of seals in Greenland being inhumane.

from all over Europe, and a parade through Copenhagen in the state coach.

The constitution

The Danish Constitution says that legislative power lies jointly with the monarch and the Danish Parliament. That may be the formal position, but in nowadays the reality is that true power lies mainly with the Parliament. Margrethe puts her signature to laws, but plays no role whatsoever in drawing them up. The Queen meets the Prime Minister once a week, at a gathering of the Ministers of State, and this keeps her up to date on the work of Government and Parliament.

Streets clear
when Margrethe speaks

Every New Year's Eve, at 6.00 p.m., Queen Margrethe makes a speech to her people. She is well known for the quality and relevance of these annual speeches, which she believes are the most important she makes every year. The Queen's speeches are frequently controversial - they have been much admired, but also much criticised. One for which she certainly had a mixed response was when she reminded her people about the need to "love thy

Margrethe handing over the new standard to the Jutland Transportation Regiment.

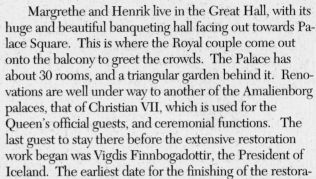

neighbour", and her belief that Denmark should take in more refugees. The Queen speaks on a very wide range of subjects, including philosophy, courage, and morality.

If Queen Margrethe has the opportunity when on an official visit abroad, she will take it to make a point. When on an official visit to Canada, just after the collapse of the Eastern Block Communist regimes, and during a television interview seen by millions, she said "No-one can be happy without freedom". The Queen spoke with enthusiasm on the benefits which would come from the fall of Communism in those countries, explaining that until that time she had seen the Eastern Block countries, metaphorically speaking, as being a deep-freeze with a door no-one could open.

"Eastern Europe was cut off from us, but we knew that its people were suffering. Suddenly seeing the whole thing open up, and finding a wealth of new ideas and human warmth flowing out, was a wonderful experience, and it gave me great joy," said Queen Margrethe.

Money

The Queen of Denmark is by no means a wealthy woman. Although she has the right to use them, most of her residences are owned by the State.

One of her homes is Christian IX's palace, one of the four palaces at Amalienborg, right in the centre of Copenhagen. Queen Margrethe's mother, Queen Ingrid, and Crown Prince Frederik live in two of the other Amalienborg palaces. Margrethe is happy with her Amalienborg home, where her great great grandfather Christian IX lived until his death in 1906. The Palace stood empty for many years after King Christian's death, and it was only in 1961 that preparations began to make the palace into a residence for Margrethe, then Crown Princess.

The Palace was thoroughly renovated by the time that Margrethe and Henrik got married, and Margrethe herself took an active part in the decorations, painting flowers, trees and birds in the bathrooms that were newly fitted for herself and the Prince.

Queen Margrethe has a lively sense of humour and, it appears, a cracking laugh.

Margrethe and Henrik live in the Great Hall, with its huge and beautiful banqueting hall facing out towards Palace Square. This is where the Royal couple come out onto the balcony to greet the crowds. The Palace has about 30 rooms, and a triangular garden behind it. Renovations are well under way to another of the Amalienborg palaces, that of Christian VII, which is used for the Queen's official guests, and ceremonial functions. The last guest to stay there before the extensive restoration work began was Vigdis Finnbogadottir, the President of Iceland. The earliest date for the finishing of the restoration work is 1996, and even then only the front and rear facades may be completed.

The State is footing the bill for these very necessary repairs, with the Royal couple paying for the interior decoration. The Ministry of Housing is, in the main, responsible for external repairs to the Palace.

Amalienborg is the winter residence of Queen Margrethe and her husband, and they live there from December to April. Around Easter, they move to Marselisborg, in Århus, and then in the summer the Royal couple live at Fredensborg.

Marselisborg is their own private residence, and is the only palace which Queen Margrethe herself owns. The Queen does not pay tax on her civil list annuity of DKK 37.4 million per annum, but she does pay a property tax on her own palace of Marselisborg, said to be worth around DKK 47 million. In 1990 this property tax was estimated at DKK 5.5 million.

Marselisborg has a special place all of its own in Queen Margrethe's heart, and there is a tradition of spending all Easter and Christmas holidays here, in addition to the Queen's frequent summer visits. Prince Henrik's vineyard chateau, Caix in Cahors, is also privately owned by the Royal Family, and is used as a holiday home. Once a year, generally in August, Margrethe and Henrik take an extended holiday at their chateau in France.

In 1849, at the end of the absolute monarchy, the King handed over his palaces to the State, which took over the

Queen Margrethe and Prince Henrik are proud of their sons, Crown Prince Frederik (right) and Prince Joachim. Here we see them in full ceremonial dress at their mother's 50th birthday celebrations.

responsibility of managing them. Since then, every time a new king or queen ascends to the throne, a new Civil List Act is drawn up, in which it is decided which palace the ruling monarch will have at his or her disposal. The Queen also has at her disposal the small Eremitage hunting lodge, set in the middle of Dyrehaven, one of the oldest forests in Denmark. The grounds of the Eremitage (seldom used by the Queen) are a popular outdoor retreat for the people of Copenhagen. Until a few years ago, Queen Margrethe used to use another small hunting lodge, Badstuen, at Frederiksborg Palace, for the annual Royal Hunt Breakfasts.

The Royal Yacht

Queen Margrethe and Prince Henrik can really relax on the Royal Yacht Dannebrog, now 60 years old. The Dannebrog is moored at buoy number seven in the outer harbour at Copenhagen, and is something of a floating palace, with all the luxuries that could possibly be wished for. In the early 1980s, DKK 40 million were invested in restoring the Royal Yacht: 140 men were employed for 10 months on painting, varnishing and polishing, putting in the most modern fire control systems, and installing the

very latest of everything to make the Dannebrog the last word in comfort and safety. When at sea, the Royal couple feel they are in their own little world. There are, of course, many royal duties and visits that must be made from the Dannebrog, but there is always time left over for relaxation and enjoying the company of the family in private. Certainly the princes Frederik and Joachim love the Royal Yacht as much as their parents, and as with palaces, the Royal flag flying from the main mast is a sign that the Queen is on board.

The yacht must bring back memories for the Queen and Prince of their first days as man and wife, as it was on the Dannebrog that the newlyweds managed to escape from the press, and get a bit of peace and quiet on their honeymoon.

The Dannebrog, officially Naval Yacht No. 1, is not the private property of Margrethe and Henrik, but a part of the Royal Navy. It is 63m long, 10.4m wide, and can sail at a speed of 14 knots, with its crew of 50 members of the Naval Defence Corps. The Dannebrog has sailed to Greenland, the Faroes, Norway, Sweden, Finland and the Soviet Union, as well as crossing the Atlantic to the U.S.A. It has been on official and semi-official visits to the U.K., France, Germany, Italy, Greece and Iceland.

After four months of marriage Margrethe was able announce the happy news that a new member of the Royal Family was on its way. Only 10 days old, the new prince was presented in public by his proud parents. He was later christened Frederik.

LEFT: A trip through Copenhagen in a horse-drawn carriage as part of the Silver Wedding celebrations turns into a triumphant procession.

The whole of Denmark joined in the Royal Couple's Silver Wedding celebrations in 1992. Here Margrethe and Henrik dance a wedding waltz at Fredensborg Castle.

Each summer the Royal Couple cruise on the Royal Yacht "Dannebrog", Vessel No.1 in the Danish Fleet.

Prince Henrik is not always so happy about his role as Prince Consort: "There are people who look to me as a kind of representative of my sex", he once said.

Queen Margrethe has never been afraid to try her hand at something new. Here we see her riding a camel in Egypt in 1963.

One of the big trips to Iceland was made for the 1000th anniversary of Eric the Red in 1982. On this trip, the Royal Yacht and the Royal couple were involved in a real-life drama, with the old lady of the seas having to fight her way through pack ice around Greenland in order to get to port at Narssarsuag - her passengers had a rough couple of days.

Luckily, Margrethe and Henrik do not suffer from seasickness, and are both renowned for their sturdy sea legs: a definite advantage from time to time on the Dannebrog, as she is known to roll a little when the seas get up. There is a persistent rumour that on one trip to Greenland Queen Margrethe was to be found smoking a cigarette and drinking a glass of port, while many of the others on board were seasick. The Queen appears to be untroubled by really rough seas, and a natural sailor like her father.

Marriage does not entail a right to divorce

Marriage does not entail a right to divorce, reckons the Queen of Denmark. Margrethe has never been afraid of saying what she thinks, especially when she feels the issue is important. The fact that the Queen is very professional in **everything** she does is apparent from her interviews.

Queen Margrethe mentioned the harmony of her family in a conversation with this author:

Many are hoping to see a royal romance blossom between Crown Prince Frederik of Denmark and Princess Märtha-Louise of Norway. The age difference between the 25 year old Crown Prince and the Norwegian princess is ideal. Here we see them enjoying each other's company at Queen Margrethe and Prince Henrik's Silver Wedding celebrations.

"We have a good marriage, I think. We've been married for many years, and we know each other well enough to know where we stand. I **don't** think, though, that we know each other so well that our marriage has become at all routine."

Everyone is allowed to make mistakes. What do you do when you put your foot in it?

"I hurry up and find someone to apologise to, otherwise things stay unpleasant. Of course, the worst thing is putting your foot in it without realising. But if I did that, I hope someone would point it out to me."

What is it that makes Royal marriages seem so much more durable than those of ordinary people?

"It's difficult to understand marriages other than one's own. But in any case royalty should be aware of their responsibility to their country and their position to such an extent that they make an effort with their marriages. This holds true for everyone: those who make most effort with their marriages get the most out of them. In our position, we are extra aware of the fact that we have to think twice. I don't think there's any divorce clause. Anyone who has grown up, as I have, with the opinion that this is the case, then so be it. I don't think that the option of divorce should be part of a marriage, and not only because that marriage is within the Royal Family."

The Queen considered her words, then continued: "However, even if an awful lot of people do split up in

Margarethe is extremely proud of her eldest son, Crown Prince Frederik, who received his military training with both the Royal House Guards and the Hussars of the Household Troop.

spite of everything, then that wasn't their original intention. A couple would surely not find divorce so difficult and distressing if it weren't for the fact that when they got married they believed it was for ever."

What do you think is the reason that so many marriages break up?

"I don't know why some things work out, and others don't. Perhaps it's because people run out of patience with one another, and perhaps they have no patience with themselves either."

Handed equality on a plate

Do you feel that equality of the sexes has been achieved, or does it exist only on paper?

"You should probably ask other people that. It's not something I've been terribly concerned with - it's never been that important to me. It has certainly been of great significance to other people, and perhaps other women have felt that they were under pressure. I haven't. I grew up to a position which is unusual for a woman, but I've never regarded it as something for which I should be especially congratulated. I'm not really a woman who has created her own career. It was, as I usually say, biological fate that my parents weren't blessed with a son. Then you could mention the Act of Succession, but it's still chance that I as

a woman occupy the position that I do.

"You could say that I was handed my equality on a plate. At the same time, I grew up at a time when most girls thought they'd get married and have a husband and children, whether they were educated or not. I myself was certainly prepared to acquire an education - I wanted to go to university, it felt natural to me. I've never been aware of the fact that I didn't have equality, but obviously within the family and our circle of friends there is occasionally talk of equality, and sometimes we tease our three men that they are nothing but male chauvinists. But I've never really thought of them as such." The Queen smiles.

Sexual freedom
- New complications

Do you think we human beings are monogamous by nature?

"To be quite honest, I don't know what we are by nature. I don't have any grand ideas on the subject, but there are hundreds of theories. We really aren't children of nature any longer. People have lived together in communities for such a long time now, and this has been very much the case in this part of the world. So it's not just a case of looking at how things are in the natural world. We've created a model which means that most people, as far as I can tell, have only one spouse at a time."

Queen Margrethe made an official state visit to US President George Bush in the days leading up to the outbreak of war in the Persian Gulf.

Crown Prince Frederik (right) has a good laugh together with his uncle, Konstantin, formerly King of Greece (left) and his aunt, Queen Anne-Marie. In the centre we see Prince Charles, heir to the English throne.

Do you think that we've gained sexual freedom at the expense of romance?

"I don't think it's done away with romance. It's overcome the problem of what's acceptable for "nice girls", but it has also created new complications. And then comes the next problem, which may be invisible but is nevertheless very real, of how to handle this greater freedom in practice. I think this is where we all fall into the trap of thinking that this is easy. But it isn't."

Your husband, the Prince, once said that you're the General and he's the Colonel, and that created an imbalance right from the start. How do you feel about that?

"It's not as simple as that. It's not generally the case that the female partner in a marriage has the best job, although you can talk about equality as much as you like. One day, it may be normal for this to happen, but it's certainly not so in the age group to which my husband and I belong. My husband was almost 33 when we got married, and I was 27. Obviously it hasn't been easy for my husband, who was a Frenchman, to come to terms with this. None the less, when we're at home we're probably - how should I put it? - a traditional couple."

Prince Henrik has been quoted as saying that you're perhaps not very organised, as is the case with many other women. Do you agree?

"I don't know whether that many other women are lacking in that respect, but it's true that I'm a bit untidy. That much is obvious - he's quite right. It's probably because it's beyond my capabilities to keep a diary. I think the two are linked. People who are methodical keep diaries, and less methodical people seldom do. Of course, this isn't always true either," smiled the Queen cheerfully.

The Queen says of her sons, Crown Prince Frederik and Prince Joachim, "I hope both my boys meet the right women. A really good wife will support her husband not only in their domestic life, but also, to a large extent in their public life and activities as well. In other words, the Crown Prince as King, and Prince Joachim as a landowner." The Queen paused for a moment, then emphasised:

"This is very important. I hope the boys have seen and felt this from their home and family. It's terribly important that couples can support each other. I think they've considered this carefully, and it is possible to consider things, when you're in love."

Did you do that?

"Yes, of course. Yes, just before I was that much in love, I knew I ought to think carefully. Someone once said that you can't stop the lightning, but it's quite simple to prevent the whole town from burning down. You can fall in love, but it's always possible to prevent there being more fire in the whole affair than is good for you."

We get so much pleasure from our boys

Are you afraid that the things the press write about your sons will tag them with a playboy image?

"I find it tiresome that the press pursue everything down to the tiniest little detail. Sometimes they're interested in things which, as far as I can see, exist only in their imaginations. I think this is very unfair on two youngsters. Why do people try to apply double standards? My sons are like everyone else, and yet they have to be hounded in a way that other people aren't. Can you see the logic in that?" asked the Queen.

"I can't, and neither can the boys. But this is a side to their existence which they have learned to know and expect. Therefore I believe they will find a way to live with it. They do know that a certain amount of responsibility goes with their jobs - I believe they're quite well aware of that. I don't nag them, that's not my job, and it's not the way I am. It's not a virtue! I think Frederik and Joachim handle their lives properly and sensibly: our boys are healthy and happy, and we're extremely pleased about that. Now that they're really on the point of becoming adults, I think we have such a pleasant family life together. We don't always get to see each other as much as we would like, but when we do get together we always talk about everything under the sun, and tell each other what we've been doing, and discuss what's going on. It really is a pleasure to have grown-up sons.

Would you have liked another child?

"Well, it just didn't happen, and that was that. That's the way things go sometimes."

If you ask Queen Margrethe if there is anything she has ever regretted, she will say that she was probably not a perfect mother to her two now-adult sons, when they were babies.

"If I were to regret anything regarding my boys, it would probably be the fact that I didn't allow myself more time with them when they were small."

Designs her own wardrobe

Were you once voted the best-dressed monarch of the year?

"Yes, I was. I was very surprised about that."

Do you sketch your clothes yourself?

"When I'm having clothes made for me, I always discuss

Queen Margrethe is happy to get down on her knees in the name of Art - here she is designing for the ballet "Hyrdinden og Skorstensfejeren" [The Shepherd Girl and the Chimney Sweep]. On the right we see Tina Lauritzen, head of special effects at Danish TV.

things down to the tiniest detail with my fashion designer, Jorgen Bender. It's interesting to follow fashion, and to follow my own taste. It may well be that what I draw and paint is reflected in my clothes - that happens without thinking. We talk, and it's quite true that you talk best with a pencil in your hand."

Do you ever feel you're on dangerous ground in your working life, or in other areas of your life?

"Everyone feels that way at one time or another. It's not possible to keep such a tight grip on existence that you never have any problems: that much is obvious. At one point in time, something may seem to be a problem, but a little later a solution is found, and you discover that it wasn't such a problem after all. Or even if it was a problem, it still resolved itself one way or another."

Margrethe doesn't want to be a tailor's dummy

You said once that you had no inclination to be seen as a romantic figure, viewed through rose-coloured glasses.

"I'm reluctant to be seen as a tailor's dummy, but people do still look at my outer appearance rather than towards the person inside."

Do you think that it can be difficult at times to differentiate between superficial praise and true warm-heartedness?

"I fluctuate between happy naïveté and chilly scepticism about people in general. There are times when I do doubt whether someone's interest is genuine, and feel they may be being superficial, but it's very easy to mis-interpret. There is no list of answers to life, and we learn this gradually as we become more mature. Everything has its price, and most things entail some sort of risk.

"I once heard something that was quite amusing. A long-dead senior civil servant had his motto, his device, on a shield hung up at Frederiksborg Palace, when he was

Queen Margrethe's cover illustration for the book "Alle mennesker er dødelige" [All Men Are Mortal] by Simone de Beauvoir which Margrethe and Henrik translated together.

awarded the Grand Cross of Dannebrog. It read 'He who achieves nothing will never make mistakes'. That was very well put," smiled the Queen, and continued: "The idea behind this was purely and simply that we shouldn't imagine that we can do things without ever making mistakes. We need to realise this, in order that we avoid doing nothing at all, because we're so nervous of doing things wrong."

The Queen of Denmark is not afraid to admit that she

at alt dansk er godt ... ubetinget.

Each year Queen Margrethe gives her eagerly awaited New Year speech. In 1992 she warned against nationalism which can lead to xenophobia and racial hatred.

gets cross with herself. "It's the obvious things that I get irritated and annoyed about. This is worst when I've done something which wasn't terribly successful, or said something foolish."

Margrethe has this to say of her friends: "I have a fairly large circle of friends, and this is made up partly of people I've known for a very long time, and partly of people I've met more recently. Most people have a mixed circle of friends, some whom they know very well, and others less well. It's true that we can't always see as much of our friends as we'd like, but we do know each other well, and so can always pick up the telephone and call."

Is it true that you dance ballet in the winter?

"Yes, it's the only exercise I take. I'm really quite lazy. I've not enough patience to take part in sport in a more systematic manner."

Happy to receive criticism

You've received a lot of praise as an artist, but you've also received criticism. How do you feel about that?

"I'm very happy to receive criticism. I think it shows that

people understand that I take my art seriously. At the same time, I do realise that art will always come second to my real job. This doesn't mean that I don't want to do the best I can as regards my art. I don't handicap myself, I don't try to paint left-handed!"

The Queen thinks her husband, Prince Henrik - a very artistic man himself - is an excellent critic.

You've been a popular model for caricatures on television and in revues and newspaper cartoons. What do you think of that?

"I've seen quite a few of them. They're certainly nothing new in Denmark. My father has been depicted hundreds of times in caricatures, and in his time he was quite amused by them, as I am now. In any case, this is a thing which surprises non-Danes more than it surprises us. Even the way in which we move has been picked up. That's the cleverest part - that it's possible to pick up not only what's typical about a person's looks, but also the way they move. That's really the art of representation, found in revues, satires and caricatures."

The Queen is not particularly interested in television. Margrethe herself says that she only watches it occasionally, apart from the news. Soap operas and the like do not interest her in the slightest: she finds them far too tiresome.

Queen Margrethe's sketches for a television production of Hans Christian Andersen's famous fairy tale "The Shepherd Girl and the Chimney Sweep" were also used as the basis for figurines made by the Royal Copenhagen porcelain factory.

The writer Bodil Cath in conversation with Queen Margrethe and Prince Henrik.

Stress

"I don't think about stress from day to day. It may be, though, that other people think I'm tense."

You've been quoted as once saying that you would probably end up being some sort of eternal student. Has that turned out to be the case?

"I don't study actively any more. However, I'm always interested in learning more than I already know. Most people think, when they've grown up a bit, that they've missed the boat. They no longer have the time to go into depth on the things which they would perhaps have liked to study."

What about your epitaph? How would you like to be remembered in your role as Queen of Denmark?

"I'd really like to be remembered for the fact that people realised fully that I took my work seriously. Even if what I achieved wasn't good enough, I'd like to be remembered for the fact that I did the very best I could."

Literature

Queen Margrethe and Prince Henrik are very keen on reading. They both read all the daily newspapers first thing in the morning: they are brought to them along with their breakfast tray.

" I skim through the papers. Some things I read

thoroughly, and others I leave until later in the day," says Queen Margrethe. The fact that both Margrethe and Henrik are fond of words was displayed by the fact that they translated Simone de Beauvoir's novel, *Tous les hommes sont mortels* together under the pseudonym H M Vejerberg. Queen Margrethe has also singlehandedly translated a trilogy by the Swedish author Stig Strömholm: *Dalen*, *Markerne*, and *Skoven*. The Queen speaks Swedish almost as fluently as she speaks Danish. Prince Henrik is the poet of the family. The Prince's poetic talents have been displayed, for example, in a book on Fredensborg, which was a Silver Wedding Anniversary present to the Royal couple from the municipality of Fredensborg Humlebæk. Henrik wrote a poem in French for the book, and this poem pays homage to Fredensborg. The Queen helped the Prince to translate it into Danish.

Prince Henrik reads a fantastic amount of French literature. The first the public knew of Henrik's talent for poetry was in 1982 when he had 150 copies of a book of his poems in French, entitled *Chemin Saisant*, published for his family and closest friends. The book also contained a poem entitled *Les Filles de Copenhague*, in which Henrik praises the girls of Copenhagen. In addition, in the first years of his marriage Prince Henrik wrote passionate love poems to his Daisy, but these are treasures which Margrethe keeps for herself.

Margrethe demonstrated that she is fascinated by languages, be it Danish, Swedish, French or English, with her new translation of her favourite book from her childhood, *The Wind on the Moon* by Eric Linklater, which in Danish was entitled *Det blæser på månen*. The rhyme in the book, "Remember that honey is better than money, and friends are the sweetest of all", had to be rewritten by the Queen in her own style, and the translation turned out like this: "Husk på børn, at honning kan fryde en Dronning- men sværest er venner at få" [*Remember, children, that honey may please a queen, but friends are much more difficult to find*].

Queen Margrethe reads a great deal, but at the same time says she has never entirely come to grips with contemporary Danish literature. She is comfortable with her collection of books in English. The Queen's luggage is always full of new English books when she has been on her Christmas shopping trip to London. For example, Margrethe likes Karen Blixen's works, Tolkien - whose work the Queen herself has illustrated - H C Andersen, and we must not forget to mention all the books she reads on history such as World War II. She very much likes Sigrid Undset's *Kristin Lavransdatter*, and she has read the "Olav Audunssøn" books several times. Margrethe thinks Lawrence Durrell's book *The Alexandria Quartet* is quite exceptional. Books by authors like Charles Morgan have been read from cover to cover. Her Majesty also thinks that works by Kipling are not to be sneezed at. In addition to illustrating Tolkien's *The Lord of the Rings* in 1977, the Queen has also produced drawings for *Historien om Regnar Lodbrog*, *Bjarkemål* and *Komedie i Florens* by the Danish author Poul Ørøm.

Art - Margrethe's alter ego

Art is Queen Margrethe's *alter ego*. Margrethe has been holding more and more exhibitions both in Denmark and abroad, and constantly amazes the world with her artistic talents.

For example, in 1993 Margrethe will be exhibiting 12 pieces of Royal art in Denmark which anyone can buy for just DKK 100. The Queen helped the Third World by painting the National Church's Emergency Aid calendar. The money raised will go towards the emergency aid programme of the organisation. Using a limited palette of colours, Her Majesty has painted 12 beautiful watercolours with a biblical theme which illustrate texts from the Third World. The Queen makes it quite clear that she finds painting art from the Bible very revealing.

"There's so much in each subject which means a lot to the person painting it, and from time to time I also feel that the whole thing is very personal, however I choose to illustrate a passage from the Bible," says the Queen.

"I didn't dare to tackle that job before I knew whether I'd have time to do it as well as I am now able. I've never before attempted seriously to understand the motifs in the Bible, even if they must have been behind a great deal of my previous work. There's something very difficult about having to draw pictures on a subject which means so much to so many people," says Queen Margrethe.

"One thing I did consciously: I kept to a very strict

A lithograph of Queen Margrethe sold in aid of the Danish Red Cross.

range of colours in order to add a little distance to the subject and for the calendar to give an overall impression of pleasantness to anyone standing and leafing through it, and also because I find it more exciting to work with a more limited palette."

Margrethe loves her art, and she paints using materials such as acrylics more than she uses oils. "I simply can't wait for oils to dry," she reveals.

Queen Margrethe has exhibited her paintings in Norway, Sweden and the USA as well as in Denmark.

Margrethe feels that the Danes have

The Queen of Denmark painting with quick-drying acrylic paints. Her paintings were first shown at an exhibition in Køge in 1988.

accepted her as an artist. "It's happened without any great fuss, and that makes me very happy," she says.

The Queen of Denmark may well be afraid of receiving reviews which are a little too positive. On this subject, she says, "When I hold an exhibition, I'm always a little afraid of what the public might think. This can often be hard to bear, and I also get nervous when it comes to the professional art critics. I'm more afraid of receiving reviews which are too positive due to the fact that I'm also the Queen.

The critics owe it to themselves to be honest, and that goes for work that a queen has signed, too," thinks Margrethe. She now has a certain amount of experience on the subject. The Queen believes that she can somehow read between the lines and see when the critics are being too servile.

The art of the Queen of Denmark, which covers everything from sewing, sketched embroidered chasubles and episcopal cloaks, paintings and watercolours, is partly inspired by the scenery of Greenland, just as some of her pictures have motifs from Norway. More than 100 watercolours, Indian-ink drawings, paintings and various church cloths have been on display at Her Majesty's exhibitions. Queen Margrethe is primarily fascinated by landscapes in all sorts of weathers. Several of the Queen's works have been presented to members of the family and close friends, but otherwise the Royal art is not for sale, with the exception of the Queen's work, for example for calendars, pictures or

Queen Margrethe also enjoys embroidery. Here she has embroidered two seat covers for the Danish Needlework Association's 60th birthday exhibition.

Even if you have been married for 15 years, you can still hold his hand in public. "And it's not just for the sake of the press", says Prince Henrik.

Queen Margrethe curtseys to the audience after the premiere of "Et Folkesagn" [A Folk Tale] in 1991, for which she was scenographer. The applause seemed never-ending and her work was highly acclaimed.

Queen Margrethe on her way to a gala banquet at Christianborg Castle in her new silver fox pelt, a 50th birthday present.

lithographs, which are numbered and sold for charity. Margrethe is acutely aware of her situation in this context. She herself says, "The prices could easily be raised artificially, regardless of quality. My paintings are never exhibited commercially. I've considered that quite carefully. I've also sought the advice of others on this matter. The fact that a Royal exhibits paintings. watercolours and other art is in itself a sensation. I'm quite aware of that," says Queen Margrethe.

Curtsied to the people

It was the first time a queen staged an entire ballet, sets and new costumes as Queen Margrethe did for that piece of our Danish heritage, Bournonville's 1854 ballet, *Et Folkesagn*. At the première in September 1991, an obviously self-conscious 51-year-old Danish artist came forward to receive the applause of the audience in a manner quite different to that which she displays as our Queen. Her Majesty seemed to be quite overwhelmed. The whole theatre was roaring with enthusiasm. People went wild, and they gave the Queen a standing ovation. There seemed to be no end to the applause. The Queen curtsied three times to her audience during the first curtain call. "Bravo! Bravo!" came the cheers, while everyone clapped and stamped. Margrethe brushed away a tear of happiness brought on by the reception which she as an artist received for her colourful stage revival of *Et Folkesagn*. Crown Prince Frederik, who sat in the dress circle, was obviously very proud

Margrethe and Henrik both love dachshunds and have one each. Like a true Royal Hound, Margrethe's always likes to trot along in front.

Each year Queen Margrethe takes a skiing holiday, normally in Norway. However, here we see a shot of her in Megève in Switzerland.

of his mother. This was an evening when Royal history was made even before the ballet began. *Et Folkesagn* is the story of trolls, elf girls and babies being mixed up. The ballet is an adventure which happens in the real world, but it is also a romantic picture of the Danish summer, and at the same time it is a cheering sight in the grotesque world of trolls. The Queen's stage production has also received excellent reviews on an international level.

Scandals?

When I was a journalist and an authorised member of Queen Margrethe's official tour party, a Canadian TV journalist asked me whether I could honestly say there were absolutely no scandals surrounding the Queen of Denmark, as there are in the British Royal Family. I could only reply that we Danes had never witnessed our queen behaving in a scandalous manner at all, but we were quite aware of the fact that, according to the Canadian newspapers, the Canadians find it incredible that the Queen of Denmark smokes so much.

Queen Margrethe does not wish to discuss her smoking habits. "It's perhaps not very good for some people, but I don't think it has any effect whatsoever on my life," the Queen is quoted as saying. The Queen has also remarked, "I don't smoke outside. That's never been regarded as a

particularly ladylike thing to do. It's not a courtesy which people observe nowadays, but I'm very old-fashioned in some respects."

The Queen ends by pointing out that smoking is not such a big issue in Denmark as it is in other countries.

Margrethe and Henrik in full ceremonial dress, each bearing Denmark's highest honour, the Order of the Elephant.

Great Britain

By Judy Wade

The history of the British Monarchy

Queen Elisabeth II celebrated 40 years on the throne 1992.

The British monarchy is a living link with the past. Queen Elizabeth II can trace her ancestry back to King Egbert, who first turned England into a united kingdom in A.D. 829.

She is also a descendant of Mohammet II, King of Seville in the 11th Century, whose heirs ruled Castile and Portugal.

Through Edward II of England, who married Isabel of France in the 14th Century, her family counts among its ancestors Rurik, Grand Prince of Novgorod from 862-79, who was the founder of the Russian monarchy.

But the history of the monarchy in England begins with the Saxons. These invaders from Germany and Frisia arrived in the fourth century, and their conquest of England was complete within 150 years.

The first kings were tribal chieftains who dominated their neighbours by force. The principle of hereditary succession was followed with rare exceptions. The Crown was handed down from fathers to sons in order of seniority, then to daughters in the same way. If a monarch died without heirs the kingdom passed on to his eldest brother. But no woman became a sovereign until Tudor times.

The Saxon kings loosely followed this hereditary rule. Quite often, the Witan, a council made up of bishops and major land-holders, did not electthe true heir but another relative preferred for his experience or wisdom.

This is how Alfred (849-899) the greatest of the 17 Saxon kings came to the throne. His youth might have ru-

led him out. He was only 22 when his elder brother Ethelred I died. But Alfred had proved himself in battles against the Danes. An enlightened ruler, often compared to Charlemagne, he was a scholar who had been partly educated in Rome.

Henry VIII (1509-1547) the most-married monarch, had six wives.

Catherine Howard, fifth wife of Henry VIII was executed in 1542.

Windsor Castle has been a home for British monarchs for 900 years.

Elisabeth I reigned from 1558 until 1603 and died childless.

father's estates and rapidly lost Normandy and Anjou in battles with the King of France. His misgovernment and extortionate taxes led to a revolt by the English barons. On the 15th June in the year 1215 they forced him to sign the Magna Carta, which ended the unlimited power of the king. And in every century after that the sovereign's authority was steadily reduced.

Two hundred years later the Plantagenets' reign came to an end when the two powerful houses of Lancaster and York began the War of the Roses. This was a struggle for the crown among Edward III's heirs. But the Welsh prince Henry Tudor married the heiress Elizabeth of York and united the opposing forces.

After he defeated the last Plantagenet monarch Richard III at the Battle of Bosworth in 1485, Henry claimed the crown and the Tudor dynasty began.

His victory brought peace to the war-torn nation, although he was not universally welcomed because he had only a weak claim to the succession. Henry's grandfather Owen Tudor had married Queen Catherine, the widow of Henry V.

He was succeeded by his second son Henry VIII, best known for his six wives. Desperate for a male heir he divorced his wife Catherine of Aragon, which led to a break with the Pope in Rome. He then declared himself the head of the Church in England.

King Alfred founded more towns in three decades than the Romans had in three centuries. He established schools, restored monasteries, designed houses and invented a candle clock.

But William the Conqueror (1027-1097), who was distantly related to one of the last Saxon kings, Edward the Confessor, changed Britain forever when he led the his army across the channel from Normandy and defeated Harold II at the Battle of Hastings. He fortified a castle above the Thames at Windsor, which Queen Elizabeth II and her family still live in almost a thousand years later.

Military might kept two of the Conqueror's sons followed by a nephew on the throne for almost a century. Then his great-grandson Henry II became the first of the Plantagenet kings. After marrying Eleanor of Aquitaine his kingdom stretched from Ireland almost to the Mediterranean.

The most notorious of the Plantagenets was King John known as Lackland. He inherited none of his

Victoria's love of family life set a style followed by monarchs ever since.

William had military power and his wife had a legitimate claim to the throne. Parliament swiftly decided to offer them the crown and they reigned jointly from 1689. From then on the monarchy became constitutional and Britain was spared the battles between Crown and Parliament that divided many other European nations in the Nineteenth Century.

Their successor Queen Anne had seventeen children, all of whom died. But the 1701 Act of Settlement ensured that the throne would go to her nearest Protestant relative. This was Sophia, wife of the Elector of Hanover, who was James I's grand daughter. As she died two months before Queen Anne the crown passed to Sophia's son George.

Despite speaking no English at all he arrived in London in 1714 to become the first Hanoverian king of England. The 1701 Act is still in force, preventing any Catholic or anyone who marries a Catholic, from enjoying the right of succession to the throne.

George I and George II were absentee kings who spent a great deal of time in Europe, and therefore, the balance of power gradually shifted further on to the side of Parliament.

It was not until George III was born in London in 1738 that the nation once again had an English king. A victim of a much misunderstood blood disease which caused wild outbursts, he was considered deranged and spent the last nine years of his life locked up.

Queen Victoria inherited the throne in 1837 at the age of 18.

It is ironic that the greatest of the Tudors was Henry's daughter Elizabeth I. Noted for her learning, she spoke nine languages and after her navy defeated the Spanish Armada, she left England secure and peaceful.

As she never married the crown passed to James I, the son of her half-sister Mary Queen of Scots. He was also James VI of Scotland and so the first of the Stuart kings united both nations.

He believed that kings ruled by Divine Right, but support for this idea waned when his son Charles I tried to govern without Parliament and was executed by it. Eleven years later the Restoration brought his son Charles II to the throne.

His Catholic brother James II succeeded him and became deeply unpopular. When the Dutch prince William of Orange, whose wife Mary was a grand daughter of Charles I, arrived with an army to start the Glorious Revolution it did not take long before James fled the country leaving the throne vacant.

Victoria developed a love for the Scottish Highlands still shared by the Royal Family.

Victoria and her German cousin Albert were married in the Chapel Royal, St. James's Palace in 1839.

The newly-weds had only a two-day honeymoon at Windsor.

Prince Albert died in 1861 at Windsor, leaving his wife desolate.

In later life Victoria became known as "the grandmother of Europe".

In 1897 Victoria celebrated her Diamond Jubilee with a parade through London.

George V changed the royal family's German name to Windsor during the first World War.

His grand daughter Victoria restored the prestige of the monarchy with her strong sense of duty and domestic virtues. During her reign the British Empire became the greatest on earth as it added territories in India, Africa and the Pacific. Peace and prosperity kept her people content as new laws guaranteed greater liberties. She was related by blood or by marriage to many other royal houses and became known as "the Grandmother of Europe."

Victoria and her husband Prince Albert of Saxe-Coburg had nine children and their obvious enjoyment of family life set a style that has been generally followed by monarchs ever since.

As British sovereigns

George V and Queen Mary celebrated 25 years on the throne in 1935.

George became heir to the throne after his older brother Albert died young.

George and his six children enjoyed country pursuits at their Norfolk home Sandringham.

George V's four sons and daughter grew to adulthood. A fifth son John died aged at 13.

follow the rule of primogeniture which allows male heirs to take precedence over females, Victoria's second child, her son Edward VII inherited the throne rather than her first-born, a daughter.

During the reign of his son George V the royal family decided when World War I broke out that it would be wise to shake off its former German connections and change its name. An adviser suggested Windsor after the castle which had been the family home for a thousand years.

The abdication of his eldest son Edward VIII brought his reluctant second son George VI to the throne. The House of Windsor has now been in the capable hands of his daughter Elizabeth for more than 40 years. And despite minor setbacks recently it seems set to continue into the 21st century.

Queen Elisabeth II wearing the Imperial State Crown for the State Opening of Parliament.

The Queen as Head of State

Queen Elizabeth II reigns but does not rule. She follows the example of Queen Victoria who realised that to survive the industrial revolution the monarchy had to adapt to a less potent but still useful role.

The function of the monarchy in Great Britain is to be a symbol of unity and continuity. Almost everything official is done in the Queen's name. The government's correct title is "Her Majesty's Government", not the British Government. Criminals are not simply sent to prison but sentenced "to be detained at Her Majesty's pleasure". The postal service is known as the Royal Mail.

Almost every public institution from the armed forces to the police force functions is in the name of Elizabeth II.

No Act of Parliament is legal until it has the sovereign's signature, although today, this is little more than a formality.

Ever since the Middle Ages the power of British monarchs has been slowly diminishing. As a 20th century constitutional monarch her only rights are to advise and be advised. The historian Walter Bagehot summed up the limited powers of a British sovereign as "the right to be consulted, the right to encourage, the right to warn."

In theory, the Queen still summons Parliament. But the actual ability to do so was eliminated by the constitutional struggles of the seventeenth century culminating in the 1689 Bill of Rights. This finally abolished the idea of the Divine Right of Kings.

At the end of the 20th century the Queen's constitutional duties are severely limited. Traditionally, she opens Parliament and neither the House of Commons nor the House of Lords can proceed with its business until after the Queen's speech.

But this is written for her by the Cabinet and sets out the government's policy for the coming session including proposed legislation.

Taking the salute at the annual Trooping the Colour ceremony in June.

Trooping the Colour marks the sovereign's official birthday.

On a state visit to Washington in 1991 the Queen addressed both houses of Congress.

The Queen greeted the Soviet President Mikhail Gorbachev in a colourful ceremony at Windsor Castle.

The Queen and Prince Philip visited the Great Wall of China in 1986.

The Queen welcomed Pope John Paul II to Buckingham Palace, 1982.

The state opening of Parliament is the ceremony which superbly sums up the role of the constitutional monarchy in Great Britain. It is a royal occasion celebrating the orderly process of government. Carried out with all the pageantry for which the British monarchy is renowned, it demonstrates the importance of the sovereign's position. .

The Queen drives from Buckingham Palace to the Palace of Westminster in the Irish State Coach. Her carriage is preceded by another carrying the royal regalia including the Imperial State Crown, and the Sword of State. This display is a reminder of the sovereign's lawful authority as Head of State.

The Queen was greeted by President Mitterand on a state visit to France in 1992.

On her arrival the Queen puts on the crown and the crimson robe of state made for Queen Victoria then proceeds to the House of Lords. Here certain customs are maintained to show the restrictions placed on a constitutional monarch in Britain.

The Queen is not allowed to enter the House of Commons, a tradition introduced after the reign of Charles I who abused its privileges. And when the Lord Chamberlain sends a messenger called Black Rod to summon members in the Commons, the door is at first symbolically slammed in his face.

Although the Queen cannot summon Parliament in any real sense, she can dissolve it. This has not happened since 1818 when the Prince Regent acted for George III. Today, dissolution occurs by Royal Proclamation at the request of the Prime Minister. But according to constitutional experts one of the few remaining royal prerogatives is the right to dismiss Parliament. This is only likely to happen in rare and unusual circumstances. If, for instance, the government unexpectedly introduced a bill which had no popular support, such as abolishing the monarchy, the Queen would be permitted to dismiss Parliament. Then a General Election could decide the will of the people.

A prime minister with a working majority was dismissed in 1975. But this was done not by the Queen, but in her name. The Governor General of Australia Sir John Kerr dismissed Gough Whitlam, the Australian prime minister, after the Senate or Upper House failed to approve his budget.

The Queen was totally ignorant of all this. In fact, she was sound asleep on the other side of the world when the decision was taken to "sack" the Australian leader. This incident illustrates the Queen's dual role. She is not only Elizabeth the Second, by the grace of God of the United Kingdom of Great Britain and Northern Ireland and Defender of the Faith, but also the Head of the Commonwealth of 50 nations around the world.

The Queen holds weekly meetings with Prime Minister John Major, here with Foreign Secretary Douglas Hurd.

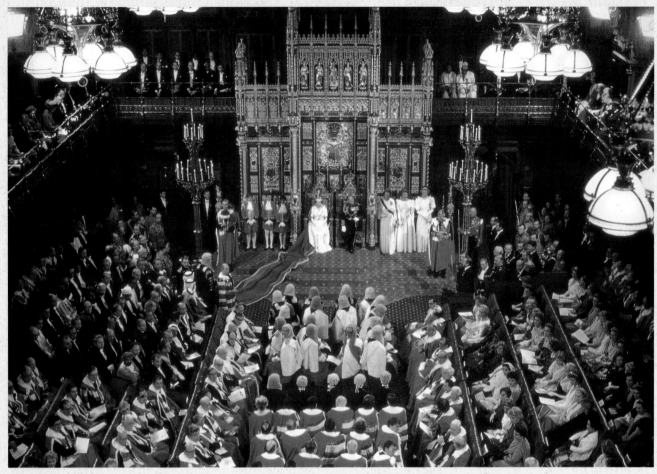

The Queen's presence at the State Opening of Parliament is a reminder of the sovereign's authority.

The Queen's devotion to the idea of the Commonwealth, formerly known as the British Empire is not always shared by her government.

As the author Alan Hamilton explains: "Politicians may see it merely as a means by which Third World nations increase their share of British aid, but the Queen believes it can and does have a higher purpose in the constant search for world order."

The only other important prerogative the Queen retains is the right to refuse to dismiss Parliament. if she felt that the existing Parliament could still do its job, or that a General Election would be detrimental to the nation's economy, and believed she could find another Prime Minister capable of carrying on, she could legitimately refuse a dissolution.

Her powers may be restricted but her influence is great. In 40 years on the throne she has been served by ten prime ministers ranging from Sir Winston Churchill to John Major. Each prime minister has followed the custom of briefing the Queen on current issues at a weekly meeting normally held on Tuesday evenings at Buckingham Palace. As a result she has a unique experience and knowledge of the workings of government.As the noted writer Antony Jay observes: "It is hard to believe that any prime minister would not find it useful from time to time to talk things over with an adviser with these qualifications."

The Queen in the red robes of the Order of the British Empire.

Red boxes crammed with Cabinet papers and Foreign Office telegrams are delivered to her each night. Government departments also despatch frequent reports to the Queen. Despite or perhaps because of this, the Queen does not have a vote. Her role forbids her to demonstrate support for any political party. This rule also applies to every member of her family. The monarchy must remain above politics.

The Queen has lost the ability to choose her Prime Minister, as all leaders of political parties are now elected. She could only use her discretion to appoint a new Premier if a general election produced a hung parliament. Even then no one has any doubt that she would act without consulting the Prime Minister of the day, whoever that may be.

More proof of the official bond between the government and the sovereign comes when the Queen travels abroad on state visits. She is always accompanied by the Foreign Secretary or another Foreign Office minister to advise on any political problems that may arise.

"The whole idea of such visits is to increase goodwill between Britain and the country being visited", a Buckingham Palace spokesman explains.

Many of these official trips are arranged to mark significant turning points. The Queen's 1992 tour of Germany was her first to the newly re-united nation and the high point of her visit was a walk through the Brandenburg gate.

She took only a few steps through the great stone columns on the "death strip", the

Laughing in the rain with the Life Guards at Windsor.

With King Birendra on a state visit to Nepal in 1986.

former border between the democratic West and the totalitarian East. But this short stroll by the world's most famous monarch became a symbolic gesture appreciated by all Berliners. As one man who travelled for three hours from his home in the East to see her said: "When I see the English queen walking here now I really know I am free."

The Queen also invites foreign Heads of State to Britain two or three times each year. This follows a custom begun around 1520 when Henry VIII invited Francois I of France to seal a treaty of friendship between their countries.

The Order of the Garter procession en route to St. George's Chapel, Windsor Castle.

Crowned Heads and Presidents from all over the world are given a formal welcome on arrival in London and travel in a carriage procession with the Queen and other members of the Royal Family to Buckingham Palace. Later they attend a banquet she hosts in their honour at the Palace or Windsor Castle before holding talks with the Prime Minister.

When she opens Parliament, welcomes state visitors, or confers honours, the Queen may seem just an outdated tourist attraction to republicans. But repeated opinion polls show that the majority of the British people value their monarchy. To them and to millions more in many Commonwealth countries Elizabeth II is not just another occupant of a high office. Over 40 years on the throne she has won the respect and affection of her subjects by her extraordinary devotion to duty and moral propriety. Few people do the same job for such a long time. And as she is firmly opposed to abdication, the Queen can never retire as most of her subjects do.

Perhaps the best indication of how closely the monarchy is intertwined with the State is the British national anthem. "God Save the Queen", a 17th Century tune, once used in Russia, Denmark and Sweden, among others, is still performed on all state occasions.

Private

The Queen is an expert on bloodstock and breeds champion dogs at her Sandringham kennels.

Elizabeth II is the most publicised, scrutinised, criticised monarch in history. To tens of millions of people around the world she is not the Queen of England, but simply "the Queen".

Her family's joys and misfortunes attract manic media interest and fascinate a worldwide audience. Their most famous homes Buckingham Palace and Windsor Castle lure thousands of tourists every day, and their triumphs are causes for national celebration.

The Queen's reign began in 1952 on a tide of optimism. The worst days of postwar austerity were over. Britain was still one of the Great Powers. Independence had not yet robbed it of many of its former colonies. Winston Churchill was Prime Minister, and a young, smiling queen seemed a hopeful sign of better days ahead. When a British mountaineering party became the first to conquer Mount Everest the day before her coronation on the 2nd June, 1953 Britain seemed set for a glorious new Elizabethan era.

These hopes were dashed as things began to go wrong. The former African colonies replaced British rule with civil wars and military dicatatorships. Closer to home terrorism turned Northern Ireland into the British government's insoluble problem.

Britain today may no longer be a dominant world power, but the House of Windsor has retained its status as the last surviving major monarchy on earth.

Its glamour and sheer power to dazzle is in part due to the wealth of the Royal Family. The Queen has the greatest private art collection in the world, owns the most valuable stamp collection, wears the most fabulous jewels on earth, and her palaces are crammed with the finest furniture still in private use.

But the British royals' ability to command worldwide respect and interest is mainly due to the personality of the Queen herself.

It may seem puzzling to avowed Republicans that this middle-aged grandmother, with a fondness for flowery hats and unfashionable handbags, and gifted with no special talent, can inspire such loyalty and affection.

Born on the 21st April, 1926 she had a sheltered, secure childhood and was poorly educated at home by governesses. No one expected that she would ever become a queen as her father was King George V's second son. It was hoped her uncle David, later Edward VIII, would marry and produce heirs.

The searching spotlight of the media, now relentlessly focussed on her family, rarely intruded on the private life of the young Princess Elizabeth and her sister Princess Margaret Rose. In the 1930s British newshounds were so effectively muzzled that the public did not learn until almost the last moment about the royal calamity that was to change her life forever.

Her uncle David decided to abandon his throne to marry a divorced American woman Wallis Simpson. Elizabeth's father came reluctantly to the throne as George VI and she became heir presumptive.

She was exposed briefly to a simulation of the ordinary working world when she trained during the closing days of World War Two as a subaltern in the Auxiliary Territorial Service. At the age of eighteen she was driven each day to

The young Princess Elisabeth photographed in 1945 by Cecil Beaton at Buckingham Palace.

Princess Elisabeth outside Y Bwthyn Bach the thatched cottage given to her by the people of Wales in 1931.

Elisabeth and her sister Margaret with their parents King George VI and Queen Elisabeth.

Aldershot in Surrey, where with a hand-picked team of the right sort of young women, she did a course on vehicle maintenance. Shortly after she finished training the war ended and so did her glimpse of the real world.

On her 21st birthday she made a broadcast in which she vowed to serve the people for the rest of her life. Speaking from South Africa where she was on a tour with her father, mother and sister she declared: "I declare before you all that my whole life, whether it be long or short, shall be devoted to your service and the service of our great Imperial Commonwealth to which we all belong."

She has carried out that vow with exemplary dedication. She was married at a comparatively young age, had a family soon afterwards and became Queen at the age of twenty-five. With the birth of three sons Charles, Andrew and Edward and a daughter Anne, she ensured the line of succession and set an example of happy family life to the nation.

Her image has always been that of a hard-working, reserved woman with simple tastes. An ordinary person born into an extraordinary position.

She doesn't smoke like her sister Margaret, or swear like her husband Prince Philip. Despite her great wealth she is frugal by nature and constantly recycles her clothes. "It's my Scottish blood", she explains.

Her day clothes are as simple and unostentatious as it is possible for a royal wardrobe to be. She is happiest wearing tweed skirts and woollen twinsets with her trademark Hermes scarf covering her tightly permed hair.

Edward VIII abandoned his throne to marry divorcee Wallis Simpson, making Elisabeth heir presumptive.

Bertie, later Edward VII, used to moan: "I am cursed by an eternal mother."

Victoria's influence was still evident when her grandson George V's consort Queen Mary became the dominant personality in the family. She believed all her family should make any sacrifice in the name of duty.

Her inflexible attitude led to a rift with her eldest son Edward VIII who abandoned his throne in 1936 to marry the American divorcee Wallis Simpson.

Her place was taken by the next Queen Consort Elizabeth, mo-ther of the present Queen. Her support and encouragement turned her shy, unprepared husband George VI into a much-loved king who reigned from 1936-1952..

Now this great-grandmother still wields great influence over her family. In particular, she has often been more of a mother to her grandson Prince Charles than her daughter had time to be.

The Queen sticks rigidly to the principles followed by these powerful, positive women. In particular, she has been slow to adapt the monarchy to a changing world. Britain has been utterly transformed in the four decades since she became queen. Its social,and ethnic composition has altered as much as its economy. Yet there is little sign of this behind the walls of Buckingham Palace. There are no black or disabled people, and no women in top positions at Court. A 1990 survey revealed that of 891 royal employees only nine came from ethnic minorities.

But the Queen is exempted from racial and sex discrimination acts of Parliament. The result is her subjects are bound by laws passed in her name which she ignores.

The landed aristocracy which was once the Royal Family's chief support is now fading from the forefront of British society.

Most of all, the Queen and her relatives, unlike other major British institutions, have neglected to pay enough attention to public relations.

The Queen still draws her friends and advisers from a small circle of dull, upper class courtiers, once described by the critic John Grigg as "a tweedy, tight little enclave of English ladies and gentlemen," who were, he said "second-rate" and "lacking in gumption."

But even more unimpressive, according to royal com-

In all her years on the throne she has never had a real holiday. Every morning when she is enjoying a break at her Highland retreat Balmoral or her Norfolk estate Sandringham, she works on boxes of state papers.

Her husband Prince Philip calls her Lilibet, her friends call her "Ma'am" and her grown-up children still refer to her as "Mummy".

Her passions for dogs and horses are ordinary ones shared by many of her subjects. Her staff always know when she is near because a pack of snappy little corgis waddle ahead of her like an early warning system.

Her dignity is legendary and when she is in a bad mood her family say she is having "one of her chinless days". People steer clear when she tucks in her chin and frowns.

For more than a hundred years the Windsor dynasty has been a matriarchy. The last woman to reign in her own right, Queen Victoria, celebrated sixty years on the throne before she died at the age of eighty-two in 1901. Her son

Elisabeth was 25 when she succeeded her father George VI.

mentators are the Queen's staff. There are no high-flying civil servants among her advisers, says David Robertson, Fellow in Politics at St.Hugh's College, Oxford. "No one in the royal household has the slightest experience of ordinary life, and they have precious few technical skills," he observes.

The Queen was particularly ill-served, according to such critics when her family encountered well-publicised personal difficulties in the Eighties and Nineties. The most damaging of these setbacks was the break-up of the Prince and Princess of Wales's marriage, which occurred amid astounding revelations about their private lives.

The consequence of these family troubles has been a gradual decline in the Windsors' overall popularity. During the 1991 Gulf War they were accused of gross insensitivity for enjoying holidays and frivolous pastimes while British troops were risking their lives.

Another public outcry broke out when it was learned that the Queen, believed to be Britain's wealthiest woman, did not pay tax on her private income.Rather reluctantly and far too late to appease her critics, she caved in under the pressure and agreed in 1992 to pay some taxes, not necessarily at the same rate as her subjects.

Until then Elizabeth II had always escaped censure. Things started to go seriously wrong when the royal children grew up and began to marry and have families of their own. Unhappily, not one of the Queen's children appeared able to maintain a good relationship.

Princess Anne, the first to wed, also became the first to divorce. In 1992 her marriage to Captain Mark Phillips formally ended after a two-and-a-half year separation. The

The Queen, her children Anne and Charles with the Queen Mother at the Highland Games, Braemar.

The Royal Apartments in the Quadrangle of Windsor Castle.

Queen's sister Princess Margaret had already divorced her husband Lord Snowdon 14 years earlier.

For several years these troubles were forgotten as the world became entranced by the appearance of a dazzling new star on the royal stage.

When Prince Charles announced his engagement to Lady Diana Spencer in 1981 she seemed to be Heaven sent. This blue-eyed blonde was not just gorgeous, but suitable as well. Her family had served his for centuries. She was "the girl next door", born on the royal estate Sandringham at Park House, which her father, a former royal equerry, leased from the Queen.

To the public she seemed the perfect choice for a future queen.

The Queen, Prince Philip and their children relaxing at Balmoral.

The marriage of Charles and Diana was the culmination of a storybook romance and the whole world rejoiced with the British people when the handsome prince walked down the aisle of St. Paul's Cathedral with the new Princess of Wales.

Many people closely connected to the Royal Family had privately doubted that the union between the charming but immature Lady Diana and the sophisticated, solemn Prince would work out.

She was barely twenty when she married on the 29th July, 1981, but Charles, who was thirty two, seemed far older. As well as this yawning, twelve-and-a-half year age gap, the couple seemed to have little in common. He was a history graduate who enjoyed opera, architecture, the

Buckingham Palace, the official London residence of the sovereign since Queen Victoria's reign.

company of worldly women and the conversation of deep thinkers. His wife's main interest seemed to be shopping.

Interest in the Prince's bride developed into a stampede for news about her all over the world. At first, the royal household mistakenly believed interest in her would abate when the newlyweds settled down to married life.

They were unprepared as Diana-mania steadily in-

creased, especially when three months after the wedding of the century, she delighted everyone again with the announcement that she was expecting a baby.

But the transformation from an unknown nursery school assistant to a future queen simply proved too much for a girl so young and inexperienced. She had given up a job she enjoyed for a far more demanding one. Engaged, married and pregnant within nine months, she had the unsettling experience of living in four different places in that period while her first married home Highgrove became ready for occupation.

At first the Queen sympathised with her new daughter-in-law's struggles to adapt to life at Court. "She is not like the rest of us", she explained when Diana rebelled against stuffy dinner parties and gatherings with elderly courtiers.

The concerned mother-in-law even called the editors of national newspapers together in an unprecedented plea to give her son's wife more privacy.

At the same time, the new star in the royal firmament was outshining all the others. Suddenly, a

Built in 1677 it was enlarged by the Duke of Buckingham in 1702.

The Imperial State Crown (left), St. Edward's Crown, with the symbols of the sovereign's power, the Orb and Sceptre.

younger, prettier woman had upstaged the Queen and all her relatives.

Her husband had also noticed that his beautiful wife grabbed more attention than he did. Although at first proud that she was so popular and that the public clearly approved of his choice, he seemed rather miffed when she was cheered more loudly than he was.

Diana had at first seemed to be the answer to the Royal Family's prayers. With the birth of their son Prince William in 1982 she had given the throne a new heir and changed Prince Charles from a crusty bachelor into a happy family man. But the Princess seemed to have difficulty coping with her pressurised palace life, and developed the eating disorder Bulimia. The illness began to affect her seriously after the birth of her second son Prince Harry in 1984.

The young couple gradually grew further and further apart. They made little effort to disguise that they were leading separate lives, which quickly became reported by the ever-vigilant tabloid press.

Meanwhile, the Queen's second son Prince Andrew, who distinguished himself by serving as a helicopter pilot in the Falklands Conflict, became romantically entangled with a number of unsuitable girls. The most serious of these involvements was with the American soft porn starlet Koo Stark.

His days as a playboy prince finally ended when he fell in love with Princess Diana's best friend Sarah Ferguson, an attractive redhead. They were married in 1986 but after the birth of two little daughters Beatrice and Eugenie, their union also became beset by problems.

Although at first admired for her breezy personality and zest for life, Sarah was unfavourably compared with her sister-in-law, the paragon of princesses, Diana. "Fergie", as she became known, was neither as slim nor as elegant. More sophisticated and ambitious, she hoped to con-

The Round Tower with the Royal Standard flying indicates the Queen is in residence at Windsor Castle.

tinue working in the publishing world but this soon became impossible. Prince Andrew, whom his mother had created Duke of York on his marriage, was away at sea for long stretches serving with the Royal Navy. His lonely wife found the restrictions of court life unbearable without the

Windsor Castle is the only royal residence in continual use since William the Conqueror built a fortress on the site.

support of her husband.

Her only chance to escape from the stifling world she had married into was to take holidays abroad with old friends. But this produced headlines screaming: "Freebie Fergie."

After months of wild allegations in the press about her private life, the distraught Duchess opted out of royal life altogether by leaving the Duke in March, 1992.

The Queen's third son, Prince Edward, had also encountered difficulties. He dropped out of the Royal Marines half way through his course amid much critical publicity. He then joined the West End office of the music mogul Andrew Lloyd Webber. After rising to become an assistant producer he too met failure when he left to start an independent production company with friends. After one or two productions they went out of business.

The Queen sympathised with her children's attempts to make their own way in the world. As she revealed in the BBC TV documentary Elizabeth R, they

found it difficult to cope with the rigid way of royal life.

She said: "If you live this sort of life, which people don't very much, you live very much by tradition and continuity. As far as I'm concerned I know exactly what I am going to be doing two months hence or even beginning to know about next year.

The State Bedchamber at Windsor Castle decorated in 1855

The Queen's only daugther Anne dancing with her second husband Tim Lawrence at the Caledonian Ball.

opinion polls quickly proved. And it was the final blow in a disastrous period for the Royal Family.

Within twelve months two royal couples had separated, another had divorced, and recordings of embarrassingly private telephone calls made by both the Prince and Princess of Wales and the Duke and Duchess of York had been leaked to newspapers.

The Queen had been pelted with eggs by anti-royal demonstrators during a visit to East Germany. Another tour of Australia was marred by the broadest hint from the Prime Minister in Canberra

"This is what the younger members find difficult - the regimented side of it.Most people have a job and then they go home. In this existence the job and the life go together. You can't really divide them up."

But her loyalty to one member of the family firm was tested when the Princess of Wales gave a few close friends the go-ahead to assist author Andrew Morton with a book that revealed the full misery of her marriage, There had been other desperately unhappy royal marriages but none had been so devastatingly exposed from the inside.

The Princess wanted the world to know that her husband neglected his family to spend much of his time with an old friend Camilla Parker-Bowles, who was married with two children. Prince Charles was depicted as a selfish, cold man, who drove his unhappy wife to attempt suicide.

Diana's action spelled out her determination to escape from her unhappy situation. Although the Queen hoped that for the sake of the monarchy and the children Prince William and Prince Harry, that her son and his wife might find a way to stay together, it soon became obvious that this was not possible.

The end of the fairytale romance plunged the monarchy into the greatest crisis it had faced since the abdication of 1936.

Despite assurances from the Prime Minister in a statement to the House of Commons that the separation would not affect the Princess of Wales's position as Britain's future queen, the people plainly rejected this idea.

Dozens of politicians and other pundits came forward to declare that the country would not tolerate a separated King and his consort on the throne. Some even speculated that Charles would never become king, although Buckingham Palace claimed his "lifelong commitment" to his public duties as the Queen's heir remained undiminished by the break-up of his marriage..

The painful and humiliating split from his wife definitely damaged his standing with the British people, as

Princess Anne, here in Bangla Desh, tours the Third World visiting Save The Children projects.

that the country would soon dispense with the monarchy and become a republic. This followed protests on a 1990 visit to Canada when Quebec separatists turned their backs on her.

It seemed that all she had achieved in forty years on

Queen Elisabeth the Queen Mother attending the Derby at Epsom.

the throne was fast disappearing.

And when fire broke out at Windsor Castle the blaze that destroyed the royal apartments seemed to symbolise the damage done to the fabric of the monarchy. Even this traumatic disaster did not attract much support from the Queen's subjects. A cabinet minister announced that the goverment not the monarch would pay for all the repairs to the Castle, infuriating most taxpayers, who would eventually foot the bill.

This flagrant example of royal privilege had a souring effect on a nation hit by a lengthy recession and soaring unemployment.

But the Queen managed to deflect this criticism when she voiced her deep unhappiness in an uncharacteristically personal speech. Describing 1992 as an "Annus Horribilis" she touched many hearts as she described the difficulties her family had encountered in a year that should have been one long celebration of her 40 years on the throne. Many people, nevertheless, felt that the Royal Family had brought their troubles on themselves.

For a mother of four to see the marriage of one son break up is probably not unusual in modern Britain, wrote the best-selling author Julian Barnes. Then he added: "Two looks like positive misfortune. Three begins to argue that there is something seriously wrong with the family it-self. "The fact that her only other child seems uninterested in marriage suggests an even deeper malaise."

One in three British marriages ends in separation, mak-ing the Royal Family above average in disfunctional rela-tionships. Was the Queen to blame for the unhappy unions

The Queen Mother and her favourite grandson Prince Charles at the Garter ceremony.

Prince Charles in full dress uniform attending Founders' Day at the Royal Hospital, Chelsea.

of her children?

Did she devote too much time to royal duties and too little to her sons and daughter?

The private suffering of the nation's most privileged family will perhaps allow them to seem human like the rest of us, rather than remote figureheads. And this unhappy chapter in the Queen's life may yet have a beneficial outcome, as it has sparked a re-examination of the monarchy's role in a modern society.

Jack Straw, a Member of Parliament who is the Labour Party's spokesman on the Environment, expressed the thoughts of many when he observed that the Queen's family had lost a lot of their respect and mystique. He asked if the time had come for them to be scaled down into "a much tighter and more limited constitutional monarchy" such as exists in the Netherlands or Sweden.

The Queen and her children gather at Clarence House to celebrate the Queen Mother's birthday.

Once it was fashionable in Britain to jeer at "the bicycling Royals", as the crowned heads of Scandinavia are known. Now there is a growing recognition that their decorous sovereigns are more respected than the tarnished

The Prince and Princess of Wales leave St. Paul's Cathedral on their wedding day in 1981.

The Duke of York distinguished himself as a helicopter pilot in the 1982 Falklands Conflict.

Prince William and Prince Harry attended Wetherby School in London.

Charles and Diana's last tour together was a visit to Korea in 1992.

Windsors.

If our battered royal family can take such condemnation to heart and emerge from this unhappy period stronger and wiser, then its survival seems assured. From the time of King John's Magna Carta, through the 1688 Glorious Revolution, to the present day the British monarchy has demonstrated a great talent for self-reformation. That is undoubtedly what it needs to continue in the Twenty-First Century.

Many royal critics feel one cause of the Royal Family's dwindling public esteem is its size.

When it was limited to just the Queen, her husband Philip, their four children, as well as the Queen Mother and Princess Margaret it had far more appeal and did not seem such a burden on the taxpayers.

There are now around 30 of the Queen's relatives featuring in official life. And the national reluctance to support so many in such privileged positions forced her to reduce drastically the number on the Civil List. The Queen has now suggested that only the monarch, her spouse, and her mother should be funded by taxpayers. Her eldest son, the next king, is supported by his income from the Duchy of Cornwall.

Once again in taking this action to appease public opinion, the Queen reacted to disapproval voiced by her critics, rather than forestalling it.

As the Twentieth Century nears its end the British monarchy is in a mess, and the woes of the Windsors seem certain to worsen unless something is done quickly.

Another solution to their many problems could be a split between Church and State. The disestablishment of

Happier times — on honeymoon at Balmoral in 1981.

Princess Diana at a women's health centre in Jaipur, India.

The young royals appeared for charity in the much-criticised Royal Knockout TV special.

The Prince of Wales could then divorce his wife, remarry and find new happiness with a woman he could legitimately make his queen.

The upheavals of recent years must have left the Queen disappointed and disheartened. But there is no reason to suppose now that this great institution has lost any of its resilience. By her recent actions Elizabeth has shown a determination to put her unruly house in order.

It is well known that she has no plans to abdicate in favour of Prince Charles. And while this sober, steadfast sovereign remains on the throne any gloomy talk about the Fall of the House of Windsor seems premature.

the Church of England would mean the monarch and her heirs were no longer forced to abide by the Church's rules on divorce and remarriage.

When she recently congratulated a serviceman on his

The wedding of the Queen's second son Andrew to Sarah Ferguson in 1986.

The Duchess of York on a winter holiday with her children Beatrice and Eugenie.

gallantry as she awarded him a medal he replied by saying: "Och, it's all in the training."

Looking back on her life the Queen revealed in the BBC television documentary Elizabeth R that those few words summed up what she believed was the secret of doing her own job well. "I have a feeling that in the end training is the answer to a great many things," she told television viewers.

"You can do a lot if you have been properly trained. And I hope I have been."

The Queen presents Prince Charles with a prize after a game of polo at Smith's Lawn, Windsor.

The Netherlands

By Mirjam J. Spiering

History

Queen and Prince in their garden at Palace Huis ten Bosch.

Queen Beatrix is descended from the German aristocratic family of the Counts of Nassau, whose ancestor Walram I Van Nassau is mentioned for the first time in a document dating from 1160. In 1255 the county was divided. From Walram II there descended the Walram line – the grand-ducal house of Nassau – and from Otto I, the Ottonian line which developed into the Dutch royal house of Orange Nassau. The most famous hero from this family was Count William, Prince of Orange and Count of Nassau, born in Dillenburg in 1533. Notably enough, his great service lay in the failure of his efforts to maintain his late-feudal rights and expand them as much as possible. Unintentionally he played a decisive role in the establishment of the Republic of the Seven United Netherlands, the world's first civil republic. A kind

Willem van Oranje

"The water and the dykes and moles are still an integral element in the picture of our society. But the Netherlands are so much more. Perhaps the most important aspect is that the Netherlands is a country of toleránce. Our national history began with it. The ideal of William of Orange, the Founder of our Fatherland, was a country where people would not accuse each other of heresy nor persecute people for their convictions, but be tolerant and have respect for others. He envisaged a country where living in freedom and the pursuit of happiness were essential values. We must not idealize the past, but it is nevertheless true that, in the seventeenth century, greater tolerance developed in the Low Countries than elsewhere in Europe, to say nothing of the rest of the world."

This is what Queen Beatrix had to say in a speech to the University of Princeton, United States, on the 22nd April 1982.

of confederation of states in which religious freedom reigned. William of Orange certainly did have the latter in mind. He himself gave up everything which he held dear,

Willem van Oranje

Dillenburg castle where William of Orange was born.

even his life; but his conscience left him no choice.

A great influence on the course of his life was the inheritance which his nephew, René de Chalons, left him on his death in 1544. The princedom of Orange in France and large estates in the Low Countries made the insignificant young Count one of the richest aristocrats in Europe. The sovereign rights over Orange offered his family the chance to develop into a royal house.

The Dutch provinces were under the rule of the Hapsburgs at this time. Charles V took William away from his parents and had him raised at his court in Brussels in keeping with his new rank. The intelligent Prince became the apple of Charles V's eye. A glittering career awaited him. He was already the Commander-in-Chief of the army of the Meuse at 22 years of age and a member of the Board of State; four years later followed his appointment as Governor of Holland, Zeeland and Utrecht. He strove for political freedom and religious tolerance for all the seventeen Dutch regions, under the supreme authority of the King.

The Hapsburgs, however, led an antinational, centralized regime and oppressed the growing protestantism in the Low Countries with brute force. Prince William was ambitious enough to join the union of nobles, known as 'The Compromise', in resisting royal absolutism. He regarded having to conform to the will of a foreign overlord as an encroachment of his rights, but the burning of heretics he found intolerable. Influenced by the humanist Erasmus and by his association with scholars who were advocates of freedom of conscience, the Prince expressed the view: "I cannot allow a monarch who wishes to rule the conscience of his subjects. The freedom to think and to believe in what he wants to is the inalienable right of every man."

The fleet of stadholder Willem III departs from Hellevoetsluis to England to free the Protestants (1688)

His identification with the people's uprising made William of Orange a rebel leader who destroyed his own career. In vain he sought support from abroad and his army was too weak to drive out the Spanish crack troops. After a desperate struggle, partition occurred in 1579 between the southern Roman-Catholic provinces, present-day Belgium, and the northern Netherlands, the United Republic, which declared itself independent two years later. From that moment the Prince of Orange was a declared rebel outlaw. The second assassination attempt on him succeeded: Balthasar Gerards murdered him at his house in Delft in 1584.

The Prince's sons Maurits and Frederik Hendrik continued the struggle for freedom, which only came to an end in 1648 with the Peace of Munster. The republic then developed at a fast tempo into a great power surrounded by states under absolutist rule. In France and England, absolutist authority was to be maintained for around another hundred years, and in Russia and Germany even up to this century.

The name of Orange has become synonymous with tolerance for the Netherlands. Although there have been strong and weak personalities among the descendants of William of Orange, freedom and tolerance remained the highest ideals to inspire all of them.

The Princes of Orange served the republic as Governors for two hundred and fifty years. From 1814 they were kings in a monarchy, the form of state chosen by the great powers at the Congress of Vienna, about which King William I was more enthusiastic than the Dutch themselves. Their spirit and traditions have always remained republican. Even now in the Netherlands there are very few monarchists to be found; the great majority of the people support the monarchy only because it is fulfilled by the Orange dynasty.

Freedom stimulated the spirit of enterprise, business instincts, science and the arts in this small country by the sea. In the 'golden' seventeenth century there was an unsurpassed period of development into the most important trading power in Europe and, due to its strategic position, the country would have to continually defend its independence against the great European powers.

There was a long struggle in the republic for sovereignty. Abroad, the Governors were regarded as monarchs, at home they contended with the growing resistance of the merchant princes. These achieved their wealth in the United East India Company, which had built up a colonial and commercial empire in Asia. The people focused their hopes on the Governor to control these powerful regents.

Thanks to Governors Maurits (1567-1625) and Frederik Hendrik (1584-1647), both great Generals, the esteem for the House of Orange rose to such an extent that William II (1626-1650) was able to marry none less than Mary, the daughter of Charles I. This was, of course, also thanks to the powerful financial support his father, Frederik Hendrik, granted to the British king, who needed to finance a war. William III (1650-1702) lay in a black-draped cradle: he saw the light of day eight days after his 24 year old father died of smallpox. He too was to marry a British Princess, Mary, the eldest daughter of King Charles II's brother James. In the meantime the republic took advantage of the Orange prince's minority to abolish the Governorship. But when in 1672 they were attacked by England, France, Munster and Cologne, it was the young Prince who had to bring help. His military and diplomatic talents made him the most successful and the most powerful of all the House of Orange. He vested the hereditary governorship in the male line, was able to acquire for himself a constitutional monarchy, but William III fostered higher aspirations. He, with his balanced politics, would go on to play the leading role on the European political stage.

After his father-in-law became King of England in 1685, the Protestant opposition in this country continuously and ever more forcefully pressed him to make an end to the Catholic absolutist rule of James II. After careful preparation William III led an invasion in 1688 which would not have been out of place in the twentieth century. With a fleet of 308 ships, 15,000 men and 4,000 horses, he made the crossing in a few days, thanks to a favourable wind, to

The first Orange king, Willem I, reigned in the Netherlands, Belgium and the Grand-Duchy of Luxembourg.

south-west England from whence he began his "Glorious Revolution", a peaceful revolution due to James's most important generals and troops changing sides. Nothing now stood in his way of his triumphal march on London; James fled to France. This meant more than a palace revolution: William and Mary were crowned King and Queen of England and ruled jointly, subject to acceptance of the Bill of Rights – constitutional law which extended parliamentary control over the kingdom. Governor-King William's goal was thereby achieved. He wanted to use the English struggle for freedom in his own struggle against the European power politics of France.

After the childless deaths of Mary (1694) and William (1702), John William Friso, of the Frisian branch of the Nassau family, appeared to be designated as the universal heir. Claims to the inheritance, however, came from many sides. On the way to The Hague in 1711, where he hoped to reach a definitive settlement with the Prussian king, John William Friso was drowned when a ferryboat capsized. Five months later his son William IV (1711-1751) was born. As Governor of Friesland and Gronigen he did not succeed in bringing the other provinces under his rule, al-though he did gain some influence through his marriage to the British king's daughter, Anna of Hanover. Just after the threat of a French attack, William IV was offered the general hereditary governorship of all the provinces. The mild-mannered, sickly William IV proved, however, not to be a powerful political leader, and nor did his ostentatious successor, William V (1748-1806), who preferred to occupy himself with architecture, music and his collection of paintings. He allowed his duties to be taken away from him and had to be helped back into the saddle with the assistance of the Prussian King, his wife's brother. In 1795 there was no saving him: the governor's family fled before the French revolutionary troops to England and thence to the dynastic lands of the Nassaus. The Netherlands became a satellite of France, and Louis Napoleon, brother of the French Emperor, held the monarchy from 1806-1810.

It was eighteen years before the House of Orange returned. Meanwhile, times had changed. They were offered complete, hereditary sovereignty. William I, installed as sovereign Prince in 1813, avoided the appearance of wanting the kingship, because prejudice against the title had existed for so long in the Netherlands. Thanks to a secret plan of the great powers who were deciding the fate of Europe at the Vienna Congress, he was able to take the title of king in 1815. They conceived a kingdom of the Netherlands that, increased by the southern Netherlands and Luxembourg, could serve as a buffer state against expansionist France. William I reigned as the Grand Duke in Luxembourg. It was on the new state's territory that the Battle of Waterloo took place in June 1815. Hereditary Prince William (II), a fearless but also reckless soldier, held supreme command over the Belgo-Dutch division and played a not unimportant role alongside the British General Wellington and the Prussian Blücher in the final reckoning with Napoleon Bonaparte. It won him the title of "Hero of Waterloo", as well as his bride, the Grand Duchess Anna Pavlovna, sister of the Czar Alexander I. Napoleon had sought her hand in vain.

extremely short temper also had another side. For the people he fostered a great affection: "Orange can never, never do enough for the Netherlands," was his famous comment. Marriage to the erudite Princess Sophia of Württemburg ended in 1851 with a secret divorce and William III outlived his three sons.

The dynasty was continued on his death in 1890 by his second wife Princess Emma of Waldeck-Pyrmont (1858-1934), who acted as regent for the ten-year-old Wilhelmina (1880-1962), their only child. Luxembourg, however, had to be relinquished. Salic law was enforced, according to which a woman cannot succeed. The Walram branch of the House of Nassau, the present ruling family, took over the rule.

Emma appeared to be an outstanding regent, who won over the ministers with tact and dignity. With her daughter she travelled throughout the country to allow the people to get to know her, bringing mother and daughter great popularity. On her eighteenth birthday, Wilhelmina took up her reign, which was to last for fifty years. In 1901 she married Duke Hendrik van Mecklenburg-Schwerin. Their only child Juliana was born in 1909. Due to the financial independence of the Queen and the lack of any practical duties, Prince Hendrik felt "just like the luggage" when he accompanied his wife. He and Queen Emma both died in 1934. Again, the House of Orange consisted of only two women, but in 1937 Juliana married Prince Bernhard van Lippe-Biesterfeld. During the German occupation in the Second World War, the royal family stayed in England and in Canada. The loss of parliament strengthened Wilhelmina's position considerably. She be-

Queen Wilhelmina, ten years old, the youngest queen in Europe.

The authoritarian, energetic William I provided for a tremendous economic recovery with a number of initiatives. In the Protestant North they called him the "Merchant-King", in the Roman-Catholic South he was ridiculed for his copper crown with artificial gems and hated for his decisive government. 1830 saw the start of an uprising which ended in 1839 with the definitive partition, under which Belgium became an independent kingdom.

William II reigned from 1840 to 1849. He lived continuously in greater luxury than the treasury warranted and ran up so many debts that, after his death, Queen Anna Pavlovna had to sell Rembrandts and other old masters to the Russian Czar. These pictures are still in the St. Petersburg museum. His greatest service was in 1848, when a revolutionary storm shook many a throne in Europe, when within one twenty-four hour period he made a U-turn from being very conservative to being very liberal, and agreed to a new constitution. The introduction of ministerial responsibility for the transactions of the king thereby became a fact. His son, the subsequent William III, declared that he would never ever be a "cipher king" and tried to abdicate. In 1849, however, he succeeded to the throne, having never hit it off with his parliament, composed of liberal critics and violent socialists, let alone with ministers who were no longer accountable to him. His rough treatment of cabinet and court personnel, and his

Queen Wilhelmina, Prince Hendrik and Princess Juliana dressed in Rembrandt's 17th century style.

came the boss. Ministers recognized that the Queen as it were stood over them and that their continuance in office was dependent on the question of whether or not she still had adequate confidence in their policy! With great force of will, the Queen inspired the resistance from her place of exile; she made Prince Bernhard supreme commander of the Underground Forces. After the war, she abdicated in 1948 in favour of Queen Juliana (1909), whose reign started with the transfer of sovereignty to Indonesia, followed by the independence of Surinam in 1975.

Queen Juliana's reign was characterized by humanity. She pertinently refused to sign the death sentence of war criminals. Juliana democratized the monarchy and dedicated herself to social justice. Right up to her abdication she promoted the emancipation of women and the position of the poor in society. After his important role in the resistance, Prince Bernhard developed his multiple abilities in the service of Dutch business life. Also, he was one of the founders of the World Wildlife Fund and the initiator of the Bilderberg Conference, where the heads from the worlds of science and politics met. In 1976 he was compromised by his involvement – never proven for that matter – in a matter of bribery by Lockheed, the American aircraft manufacturers. He resigned from his military duties and commissions, but in resistance circles, the army and business people stood loyally behind him. Bernhard is the only member of the Orange family who, during his lifetime, already had a statue of himself erected. Both Princess Juliana and Prince Bernhard, now well advanced in age, still continue to fulfil a number of official duties.

In 1980 Juliana abdicated in favour of Queen Beatrix, born at Soestdijk Palace in 1938. She obtained a Doctorate

Queen Wilhelmina speaks to the American Congress during World War II.

of Law and on 10th March 1966 married Claus von Amsberg, a German diplomat. Although smoke bombs were let off around their wedding carriage, due to anti-German feelings, the Princess's husband was quickly accepted due to his congenial manner and valuable contribution to Dutch society. He has developed into an expert in the sphere of North-South relations.

Queen Wilhelmina, in exile in England during World War II, welcomes the plane from Canada with her daughter Juliana (1943).

The Royal House of Orange regulary visits the Netherlands Antilles, where it is enthusiastically welcomed by the population. Here the three sons of the Queen are swinging with the Rainbow Dancers on the island of St. Eustatius.

Official

*I*n the land of Van Gogh, no larger than 41,000 square kilometres, the presence of the House of Orange means reassuring security for the fourteen million inhabitants, who seldom stand still.

The exception is the Queen's Birthday, on the 30th April. On the Queen's official anniversary, the nation throws itself into a frenzy of flags, triumphal arches, aubades, traditional games and free markets. Every year Queen Beatrix chooses two places where she and her family go to join in the people's festivities. If Heads of State in other European monarchies are honoured with a march-past, a parade or palace reception for the 'establishment', the Dutch television cameras record hours of 'live' coverage of the warm-hearted contact between the Royal House and the people.

This celebration characterizes the reigning style of Queen Beatrix, as well as her walk-abouts alongside the public, a fixed item on the agenda for her working visits. She shakes the hands held out to right and left, accepts the flowers or children's drawings offered and it does not escape her when someone in a wheelchair looks hopefully in her direction.

The modern monarchy demands of the Queen that she be ordinary and royal at the same time, a difficult task affording chances for integrating the paradoxes successful-ly in her duties.

She observes the constitutional rules of the game. She is also grateful for her popularity, however, for it allows her to hammer home the subjects close to her heart: European integration, the environment and the Third World. The old aristocratic court has made way for a modern business court with about three hundred highly qualified staff.

Official birthday of Queen Beatrix 1992.

This professionalism contrasts again surprisingly with the elegant style of her official duties.

The 'function which no-one should question', as she called her office in her accession speech, gradually became 'a task in which I can find pleasure from the fact that I am allowed to do something'.

About the obligations of the present day monarchy, the Queen says: "It is only worthwhile if it is supported by a large part of the Dutch people. If people do not want it any more or if they should no longer feel it belonged to them, then it would not work well. Of course, I am only human with limitations and I will obviously never be able to represent the whole of the Netherlands, but I do think that the monarchy can indeed be a focus of identity for many Dutch people."

Beatrix now enjoys a broad consensus of confidence. If in 1980 she still had some leeway in popularity due to her image of being self-willed, arrogant and domineering, now she is generally admired for her great dedication, professionalism and dignity. At her copper/brass official jubilee – celebrated modestly so as not to waste taxpayers' money – Prof. E. H. Kossmann, a prominent historian, said: "It is particularly exciting to see how, even in our times, such an old institution in the Netherlands appears to acquire fresh meaning."

Queen Beatrix has never striven for popularity anyway. "A much greater concern has always been: am I doing it well, can I do it better, am I doing what is expected of me, am I hurting anyone, can I really say that?"

The Dutch monarchy has a role all to its own when

Official birthday of Queen Beatrix 1986.

compared with the monarchies in Belgium, England and the Scandinavian countries, where there is much more ceremony. Beatrix does not figure as the representational top of a ceremonial structure. The Governors were the first servants in a republican government, the kings and queens are the sounding board of the social groups among the people and in the cabinet.

The House of Orange has always known when it must

The Queen with family visits unexpectedly Amsterdam on her official birthday, 30th April, 1988. She makes her triumph-tour by boat through the canals.

Mariage of Princess Beatrix and Prince Claus on March 10th, 1966 in Amsterdam.

choose a party, but it remains popular by never doing this in public. There is a growing tendency in European countries to regard the monarchy as a fairy tale or a kind of entertainment. Queen Beatrix lays rather more emphasis however on the aspect of the content of her task and interprets it in contemporary ways. She is no tinsel queen, nor is she an ornament. Consistent with her abilities and character, she is like an ambitious manager at the head of her efficient court business, in which a shift system of seconded officials have to prevent the formation of any coterie. Her Majesty, herself a 'workaholic', demands a great deal from her employees. Her perfectionism is (almost) dreaded.

Whenever ambassadors come to Noordeinde Palace by royal carriage to offer their credentials, they are surprised by the state protocol for which usually the larger countries hold the patent. Prior to every meeting the

Queen learns about everyone's role and background thoroughly. Being well-informed has always traditionally been among the features of royal excellence. The Queen takes masses of notes, reads stacks of reports and every year signs almost twelve thousand statute laws and royal decrees, and never without not knowing what they are about. Prince Claus, himself a perfectionist, sometimes even says: "Must you really read all that? A minister doesn't read it!" But of course, the sense of duty is enormously developed!" And on top of that there are still the fourteen thousand plus petitions which the Dutch send to their head of state every year.

Every Monday morning the Queen, in the presence of her husband, discusses the coming week's agenda of visits, openings, appointments and requests with her closest members of staff. Monday afternoon is reserved for an audience with the prime minister. With a member of the pol-

Queen Juliana, just abdicated, is proposing Beatrix as the new queen to the people on the balcony of Palace op de Dam in Amsterdam. April 30th, 1980.

Inauguration of Queen Beatrix in the New Church in Amsterdam, April 30th 1980.

icy staff the Queen regularly consults a map of the Netherlands, on which flags indicate where members of the Royal House have been in the past and where planned visits are to take place, so that no regions or areas of special attention are forgotten. Every year there are two State visits, around fifty working visits and a similar number of official receptions.

The Queen has a great need to direct her attention to the pressure points in society. Nobody deceives her, since she has been everywhere: with minority groups, refugees, drug addicts, the unemployed, the homeless, with the S.O.S. telephone service and to the prisons. She has accompanied the Amsterdam dustmen on their rounds and listened to the problems of families from agricultural areas. She, and her husband, Prince Claus, make time available within their schedule to chat to people about their occupations and concerns, and also about their plans and successes. "It is a wonderful feeling when people you do not know at all want to say hello. I find meeting such completely divergent groups of people so extremely valuable," says the Queen.

Inauguration of Queen Beatrix in the New Church in Amsterdam, April 30th, 1980.

Amsterdam spoiled her wedding day with smoke bombs and her investiture with serious riots by squatters – the latter were however not directed against her but against the monarch as the exponent of the establishment. This left the Queen 'certainly not unmoved, on the contrary' and she made the pledge in her accession speech: 'I have no aspirations other than to do my best for you. The new Queen kept her word. Precisely eight years later came the response: Amsterdam entertain-ed the Royal Family, who unexpectedly appeared among the merrymakers for

the Queen's Birthday, with great en-thusiasm. Her Majesty even collected a spontaneous kiss in the street from a young man. Even the demonstrators who had thrown smo-ke bombs ended up by publicly regretting their actions.

The obvious respect for the monarchy, on which Queen Beatrix's three predecessors – Emma, Wilhelmina and Juliana – could still count, no longer existed on her accession. In the sixties and seventies, leftism was on the move. Republicanism, however, remained a marginal phenomenon and nowadays both fierce royalists and fiery

The Queen meets her staff on Monday morning.

republicans are found equally laughable.

Relations with the House of Orange became less emotional during the eighties as a result of the businesslike, functional make-up of the court. This does not stand in the way of respect and esteem. The Oranges appear valuable to the Netherlands; they know what service is. That the younger generation of the Royal Family seldom appear in public and no bond can be built up with them, is less appreciated.

The Dutch monarchy does however have one ceremonial function: the day of the Queen's Speech, the opening of the States-General – the Dutch parliament – on the third Tuesday in September. Then the Golden Coach, made in 1898 from teak and gold leaf, rolls out of the Royal Stables and the Queen, Prince Claus and their eldest son William-Alexander ride in it to the mediaeval Ridderzaal in the heart of The Hague. In the royal procession, watched by hundreds along the route, the Princes Johan Friso and Constantine follow in the Glass Coach with the Queen's sister Princess Margriet and her husband

Mr. Pieter van Vollenhoven.

Apart from a glittering display, each year it is the solemn renewal of the mutual pledge which the Queen and parliament gave on her investiture – there is no coron-

A crashed El Al-plane in the Bijlmer near Amsterdam sweeps away an appartment building and killed many people. The Queen looks with horror at the ravage.

Enthusiasm for the Queen during a working visit in the province

ation in the Netherlands. Seated on the throne the Queen reads out the address from the throne, in which the government announces its most important policies for the coming year. People attend the Queen's Speech Day, travelling to The Hague from all over the country, mainly for the finale of the festive ceremony. Their hours-long wait by the gilded railings of Noordeinde Palace is rewarded when the members of the House of Orange appear on the balcony for the traditional ovation on their return.

Working visits, official visits, State visits, lightning visits, audiences, diplomatic corps receptions, concerts, staff meetings. A full agenda. None of the members of the government would want to change places with Her Majesty. Particularly on State visits the Queen and Prince do a great deal of work. From the schedule the programme appears regularly overloaded. The Queen and Prince do not go to

take part in banquets but to see a great deal of the country and to make many contacts. They have converted the ceremonial State visit into a Netherlands promotional tour. As a reciprocal service they offer a cultural evening with Dutch music and ballet companies, followed by a buffet supper with Dutch specialities such as seafood dishes, appetizing croquettes and 'Hollands' gin.

The greatest impression, however, is made by the Queen's politically-charged speeches. She finds State visits a good means of identifying the great world problems and encouraging joint action to do something about them. She does not skirt round differences of opinion as they do in America; in Japan she pointed out the suffering inflicted on her countrymen during the Second World War and she thanked President Von Weizsäcker when he had the courage to publicly acknowledge the collective guilt of Ger-

The Queen travels by helicopter for her working visits.

Prince Claus, promoting the Dutch mill, is handed over a bag and kissed by a three year old boy.

The young people are Queen Beatrix' greatest love and care.

Prince of Orange salutes passing ships when he sails with his mother, father and uncle Pieter van Vollenhoven on the royal 'Groene Draeck' (Green drake).

On January 31st, the real birthday of the Queen, she only receives a deputation of The Royal Marechaussee, her lifeguard. Their bouquet gets a place of honour.

Working palace Noordeinde in the left wing, on the first floor, the Queen's offices.

many. At her own request, after the fall of the Berlin Wall, Queen Beatrix travelled to the former DDR as the first of the crowned heads of state, in order to give heart to the people. Confrontation, but also reconciliation.

The Queen's office in Palace Noordeinde in 's-Gravenhage.

The Royal couple receives at Huis ten Bosch the Oranje team after winning the Europa football cup.

Beatrix's international prestige has been confirmed by the award of some of the highest honours. The Spanish King awarded her the Gold Fleece, Queen Elizabeth II enrolled her in the Order of the Garter.

Prince Claus gives his wife a great deal of support in her task and helps her bear the heavy responsibilities. "We do of course have our separate duties, in the sense that my husband has his own tasks, but he does give me a great

Princes' day, the only royal ceremonial, is the traditional opening of parliament on the third Tuesday in September in 's-Gravenhage.

deal of support with his advice and his often very good ideas. We complement each other very well, even as regards our interests. He is the one who, shall we say, "coaches me," says the Queen. "You have to do this together. I do not believe that this is a task which one can do alone. And I am therefore very fortunate that I share my life with someone who is also prepared to take this on."

How great is the Queen's influence on the government? As in most European monarchies, Beatrix operates under ministerial responsibility. What a monarch can make of 'the right to be consulted, to warn and to encourage', as formulated in the last century by the English economist and writer Walter Bagehot, depends on the elbow-room and the confidence he or she receives from the cabinet. The royal head of state does, however, have her

Dutch prestige-project number 1: the Deltaworks in Zeeland with the stormbarrier, one of the modern wonders of the world.

Queen Beatrix and Prince Claus on a state visit in India.

In France with President Mitterrand.

own political responsibility. The weight of her official machin-ery and her interpretation of the task leave no doubt that Queen Beatrix utilizes her possibilities within the constitution to the utmost. Prime Minister Lubbers, with whom the Queen has worked for many years, lifted a corner of the veil when he stated that 'a royal, anxiety-free interpretation of ministerial responsibility appears worth-while. This has become obvious to us in innumerable speeches. It is fascinating that the ministers are still re-sponsible, how-ever noticeable it sometimes is, that the Queen and the Prince manage to slip just that extra some-thing into their speeches'.

It is not surprising that Beatrix has built up personal authority by this style of regality. Her reign is so profes-sional that it is attracting attention as the modern formula for monarchy even from abroad.

The Queen at the important EEC-TOP in Maastricht, December 1991.

The Queen with German Chancellor Kohl at Huis ten Bosch.

The Royal Family. Queen Beatrix, Prince Claus, Prince Constantijn, Prince Johan Friso and Prince Willem–Alexander.

The private life of The House of Orange

Beatrix spending her free time in the gardens of Paleis Huis ten Bosch.

The European dynasties are doing what they can to protect their private lives, but few are as successful as the House of Orange under Queen Beatrix and Prince Claus.

In a country where personal freedom and mutual tolerance have been the feature of the social climate for centuries, one would expect that the privacy of the Royal House would also be guaranteed – even though the multi-ethnic society of 1993 is not without tension. With the advent of the mass media, however, the popular House of Orange has, if anything, even less privacy than ever. Juliana – so ordinary, human and accessible – was more or less the 'property' of her people. In the seventies a contrasting development came about. It is in particularly due to Claus, the commoner who became a prince, that a public discussion was held, on the one hand about the extent of ministerial responsibility for the lives of the Royal House (according to Claus nothing other than legal conjecture), and on the about the space they should be allowed as private individuals on the other.

Prince Claus appeared in a TV debate on behalf of the Royal Family and appealed to the universal rights of man. The fact that the House of Orange does not look on passively when its private interests are harmed is demonstrated by the several occasions when legal steps have been taken to prevent publicity in the gossip columns. Sensational reporting about the Royal House is not appreciated anyway by the majority of the Dutch people. The people have no reason to doubt their respectable Royal Family. Since her accession, Queen Beatrix has been actively concerned with media policy, which is generally reticent, but sometimes remarkably open in order to prevent undesirable speculation. The Queen once remarked:

"We cherish our privacy as something valuable of our own. Because we have the right to it. We need it to be able to live a live a life which presents enough difficulties as it is."

Compared with their European counterparts, the members of the House of Orange have certainly nothing to complain about with regard to privacy. Apart from their official duties, they can go and do what they want. And the Crown Prince is quite at liberty to pop round to the corner shop to stock up on coffee for his bachelor pad.

Hermetically sealed private wing

In contrast to the time of popular Queen Juliana, when the press literally came 'to the door' of the Soestdijk Palace to see the 'Mother of Holland', the private wing of Queen Beatrix's residential palace 'Huis ten Bosch' in The Hague is hermetically sealed from the media. Practically nobody in the Netherlands has any idea about the home lifestyle of the Queen and her husband. Even less is known about how the Queen, with her great interest in interior design, has fitted out the restored mediaeval manor house 'Het Oude Loo' in Apeldoorn or about what happens at her hunting parties there. Whilst she is fulfilling her public duties, the Queen is kind and sympathetic towards the photographers, since she considers it important that her work as Head of State be reported. The media, however, are not permitted at family gatherings. Nothing at all leaked out about the gala reception for European royalty on the occasion of the Queen's Silver Wedding anniversary.

Yet the Queen and the Prince do try to give the image of their House a more realistic basis. So far, the medium of television has proved to be the most suitable for this. In occasional TV interviews, the Queen and Prince have come over as approachable people. Amongst other subjects, they spoke openly about the symptoms of depression suffered by Prince Claus, who was ill for quite a while in 1983 and 1990. He has also been suffering for a number of years from Parkinson's disease. "We would like to make it clear to people that we too are just ordinary people. These things can also happen to us. It is better to be honest about it", they said. In the same interview, Prince Claus reacted to the question as to whether he can indeed identify with

Private-session of the royal family at Palace Soestdijk at the occasion of the Golden Wedding of Princess Juliana and Prince Bernhard.

Own work

Queen Beatrix's most private room in the Noordeinde Palace in The Hague where she works is, of course, her study This is situated on the first floor directly overlooking the street, from where she can watch the public going about their shopping. Her Majesty has furnished her study with modern Dutch furniture and contemporary art, but on the wall there hangs a large portrait of William of Orange in later life. This is a present she received on her accession from her mother, in whose study at the Soestdijk Palace it also used to hang.

Like all the resident members of the House of Orange since 1591, when William of Orange's widow Louise de Coligny came to live here, Queen Beatrix has also made her mark on the interior, like many of the former residents of the palace. She has added some provocative modern art: fabric sculptures, pictures, even computer art.

There even lurks within her an artist, although she would never admit to it. But she does try to keep Thursday afternoons free for sculpting in her studio at her home in the 'Huis ten Bosch' Palace in The Hague. She produces handsome portrait busts, but rarely displays any of them. There are some statues in her garden, which also contains a collection of modern sculpture. The Queen, like her forebears, is eager to promote art and makes grants available to young artists. She knows a great many 'craftsmen', visits their studios and receives them at home. A category of people outside any hierarchy with whom she gets on well.

the Netherlands by saying, "I feel most at home in this country, where everything is regulated in a very special way, quite differently from other countries. The result is that the prosperity and well-being of the people are very important to the rulers and everyone who holds responsibility. It is a thoroughly democratic country. I always tell foreigners that we are a republic by tradition, with a bond with one particular family from which we choose our president. But we leave the choice to the laws of nature."

In many countries, such an interpretation of the monarchical constitution would be amazing, and would inevitably provoke criticism, but Claus simply demonstrates his understanding of the historical Orange-Netherlands relationship.

Inspiring predecessors

Like her Danish contemporary Queen Margrethe, Queen Beatrix co-operated in the production of a TV documentary about her life and the royal cultural heritage to celebrate her 50th birthday. She took the viewing public with her to one of the favourite palaces of many generations of the House of Orange, the stately hunting lodge 'Het Loo' in Apeldoorn. This was built between 1686 and 1694 by the famous Governor-King William III and his British wife, Queen Mary. ('Loo' is the equivalent of the English 'lea', meaning a clearing or glade in the woods.) There she drew on memories from her own youth, when she and her sisters used to spend the summers with her grandmother, Wilhelmina, and played in the woods. Beatrix greatly admired the Queen who, when she was exiled during the Second World War, became the commanding figure of the resistance, and who spent the last years of her life in this historic house, living among her ancestors, the great figures from her House of Orange, as if they were still present and of consequence. "I myself grew up with the perspective of the future and the changes in the world", explai-

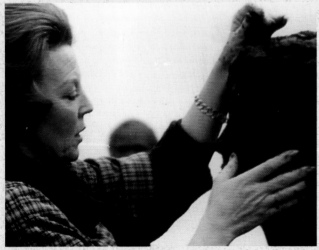

The Queen who is a talented sculptor, here working on the portrait of her son Constantijn.

The Dutch Royal Couple loves classic music, here with soprano Charlotte Margiono.

ned Queen Beatrix. "It was much later before I got engrossed in historical personalities." Queen Wilhelmina had a studio installed in the palace. Sometimes she drove to the woods where she sat for hours painting, sensing an inner bond with nature, just as she had captured the Norwegian landscape during her many summer visits.

After about eight years' restoration work, 'Het Loo' became the museum of the Orange dynasty in 1984. With its reconstructed baroque gardens, it is one of the most important tourist attractions in the Netherlands. The Queen regularly loans items from her house and the royal art collection for the exhibitions held there.

The Queen and Prince not only form an excellent working team, but privately they also share many interests and complement each other very well. The Queen involves her husband in her interest in modern art, while he teaches her the appreciation of classical music. Both are eager for far-reaching discussions and include scientists, politicians and artists among their acquaintances. The Queen is spontaneous while the Prince is circumspect. But both have a sense of humour and they hold very lively conversations, in which the passionate Prince Claus is likely to 'explode' when fired by inspiration.

Does the Royal Couple, with such a full agenda, still find time for each other? The Queen had the following to say, "My husband and I find that we have to catch up on the gossip now and then. Without anybody else about and without the disruptive elements of modern living, such as the telephone. I can picture the little chamber in 'Het Loo' palace, where Queen Mary used to sit at the end of the day and talk to her husband, the Governor-King, although three hundred years separate us. I can understand her feelings, and how they sat and talked to each other there and both knew they were responsible for the things for

which they stood and for which they had been appointed. This is indeed something which appeals to me when put in the context of the times in which we live."

Few members of the House of Orange live in palaces

Dutch palaces have been the property of the nation since 1972. Only the Royal couple and the former Queen Juliana and Prince Bernhard live in a palace. The other members of the family live in country houses or cottages.

The move in 1981 from the country mansion 'Drakensteyn' in the province of Utrecht to the centre of government in The Hague radically changed the life of the Royal Family. Gone were the fourteen happy, carefree years centred round a delightful family life. Beatrix did not leave her sons to the care of nannies and governesses.

Since her official accession, the Queen has used Noordeinde Palace in The Hague as her place of work and the 'Huis ten Bosch' for her home. Both have been renovated at a cost of several million pounds and are among the most modern equipped in Europe. The Queen was involved in the renovations right down to the details. Silk fabrics, colours, furniture all required her sanction.

'Huis ten Bosch' (1647), a splendid example of Dutch classicism, has a domed hall in the centre with eight metre high walls, all covered with allegorical representations of the triumphs won by the great strategist, Governor Frederik Hendrik, a son of William of Orange. This 'Orange Hall', on whose walls the great Dutch painters such as Jacob Jordaens indulged themselves, was then intended as a

The portrait gallery of Museum Palace Het Loo with the ancestors of the Queen.

Exterior Huis ten Bosch where the Queen and Prince Claus live.

mausoleum for the Orange hero.

The famous French architect, Daniel Marot, who has done a lot of work for the Orange family, designed a number of living rooms in this very small but elegant palace with its numerous art treasures. The private rooms of the Royal Family are in the East Wing.

In front of the steps stand the royal cars in Nassau blue. No Rolls Royces. Following the oil crisis in 1973, Queen Juliana had the whole fleet of cars replaced by economical models. Many famous personalities have ascended the grand stairway of 'Huis ten Bosch'. These include Pope John Paul II, President Vaclac Havel, President Mitterand, Federal Chancellor Kohl, Nelson Mandela and the cellist Rostropovitch. The footmen on duty in their Nassau blue uniforms also undertake other duties as necessary, since Her Majesty requires her staff to be versatile.

Royal Family
with three students

The Queen and Prince reserve their Satur-
days as often as possible for their three sons
whom they call 'the focus of our happiness'.
Even though their sons now live among the
people in the university towns, the bond is
still close.

There used to be repeated criticism of
their liberal upbringing, but the royal parents
kept them away from representative duties
and publicity. Even now when they are studying, they enjoy considerable freedom.

The youngest, Prince Constantine (born
in 1969), a multi-talented law student at Lei-
den and artistic like his mother, is completely
accessible to his fellows. Prince Johan Friso
(1968), the intellectual of the family, is known
as an ambitious, hard worker, who has taken
on a double range of studies: Aviation and
Space Travel Technology at Delft plus Economics.

The heir to the throne, William-Alexander, Prince of
Orange (1967), is being educated at the University of Lei-
den, founded by William of Orange. He chose history and
is following a course specially adapted for him. He is prep-
aring himself for his future task with dedication and ser-
iousness. Besides that, he has just as great a passion for flying as his grandfather, Prince Bernhard, a pilot with more
than fifty years' experience. The Prince of Orange has a
private pilot's license and is able to fly transport planes including multi-engined jet aircraft. Were he not in line for
the throne, he would prefer to spend his life as a pilot.

He has worked as a volunteer for the Flying Doctor
organization in Africa and he regularly acts as co-pilot
when his mother goes travelling.

Willem-Allexander, Prince Johan-Friso and their uncle, Mr. Pieter van Vollenhoven, are diving after rubbish in the Dutch Lakes during the action "Dive the Netherlands clean".

Prince Willem-Alexander is an excellent pilot.

The Queen, active and very keen on sport, enjoys
horse-riding along the beach. She also plays tennis, skis,
swims and sails exceedingly well. Summer weekends will
find the Royal Family out on the 'Groene Draeck', the sailing yacht which the Queen received from the Dutch-
people on her eighteenth birthday. Even during the holidays, Her Majesty is up early and ready for a game of tennis by seven o'clock. She is furious when she cannot find
anyone to join her before eleven o'clock.

The Prince, a thinker, plays golf, enjoys photographs
and does what he can to appease his intellectual hunger.
Quite often he sends off for books to read in order to understand other people's opinions.

As is the case with many Dutch people, the Royal
Family takes great pleasure in gardens. At 'Huis ten Bosch'
the display of summer flowers includes the amazing
Orange collection of roses. And the Queen is as delighted
as anyone else with new garden furniture.

Prince Konstantijn and Prince Johan Friso.

The annual ski-vacation in Lech (Austria).

The House of Orange popularized Porto Ercole and Lech

Besides being a break from work, the holidays offer the chance for the family to be together on their own. Since the '60s the Orange family have gone skiing to Lech in Austria and spend their summer holidays in Porto Ercole, Italy, a hundred and fifty kilometres north of Rome. Both places have the Dutch Royal Family to thank for their popularity as tourist centres. The sunny spot on the river Lech, where people still primarily come to ski, despite the luxury and the 'après-ski', has in the meantime also been discovered by the royal families of Norway, Sweden, England, Monaco and Liechtenstein. To avoid the high season crowds, the Royal Family nowadays visits in the low season. Their holiday address is invariably 'Gasthof Post',

whose owner is a personal friend. Residents of Lech talk with great respect of the skiing ability of the royal 'lowlanders'. Even in their eighties, Princess Juliana and Prince Bernhard used still to venture on long treks with their attendants. Lech is so keen on its exalted clientele that sometimes snow ploughs are in action for days on end when the Oranges have announced their imminent arrival.

The Dutch Royal Family enjoys equal popularity in Porto Ercole on the azure blue Tyrrhenian Sea. The white villa 'Elefante Felice', owned by Princess Juliana and Prince Bernhard, numbers eight austerely appointed rooms but, alas, has never offered any appreciable privacy. Since 1975, the art-loving Queen Beatrix has owned an old Tuscan farmstead with twenty-two rooms at Tavernelle, a twenty minutes' drive from Florence. With its citrus and olive trees, this is a fortress not to be taken even by the paparazzi.

Princes Margriet's family during their vacation in Porto Ercole (Italy).

Usually tirelessly energetic and very rarely ill, the Queen has sometimes had problems with her health whilst on holiday. In the summer of 1987 she had to be flown back urgently to the Netherlands due to meningitis. Four years later, whilst in Portugal, she broke her right fibula. The Queen reacted according to the Orange motto 'Je maintiendrai' (I shall uphold) and on her return performed her official visits on crutches and with the aid of a motorized golf buggy.

Measured frugality

Apart from the regal state which the Royal Couple hold because of their high position, their personal lifestyle is characterized by frugality. Not for them the expensive powered yacht, Paris couture and costly hobbies. They have almost ascetic preferences, do not smoke and drink one glass of wine at the most.

The Queen has for years been dressed by the Amsterdam fashion house, Theresia Couture. Her striking hats are likewise 'made in Holland'.

Her Majesty's appearance is based not on fashion but on a carefully-cultivated, personal style. The broad-shouldered coats, wide sleeves and strong colours give her an imposing silhouette which accentuates her gestures. Beatrix prefers modern jewellery. The famous historic Orange jewels only appear for special occasions, such as a state visit or a special banquet at the palace. Although the collection includes some valuable large sets, the value and extent of the jewels is usually over-estimated. The legendary pearls and gems brought into the family by the Russian Grand Duchess Anna Pavlovna (1795-1865), the wife of King William II, have been broken up through inheritance.

The Queen, known for her generosity, enjoys shopping. In the immediate surroundings of the Nordeinde Palace, at Harrods in London, and in Italy, she chooses her presents, varying from art, books, porcelain, crystal and silver to original gadgets. Once during a quick stop-over at Bangkok airport, the shops were opened especially for her and her retinue in the middle of the night.

Around the feast of St. Nicholas (6th December) and Christmas, the Queen distributes her presents throughout the world. She places great value on maintaining friendships and sacrifices her night's rest in order to provide the recipients of her presents with an appropriate poem as well.

Birds of diverse plumage

Queen Juliana and Prince Bernhard were already of the opinion in the '60s that 'the time when parents stipulate who their children must marry is past'. Their four daughters followed their hearts, with the result that the 23 members of the Royal Family fairly reflect Dutch society in the matter of variety and non-conformity. There are Oranges with and without membership of the Royal House, with and without a title, with and without a state income; their religion is Protestant or Roman Catholic. One notable point of agreement – the Oranges are strongly influenced by the dynastic tradition. Although they have sometimes experienced great resistance, they have all endeavoured to lead useful lives and make a contribution to Dutch society. The Princesses, who went to live abroad because of their marriages, came back to the Netherlands later. Nowhere is it better than under the Orange sun!

The free marriage choice of the Princesses appeared in practice to have unforeseen consequences. None of them came to Soestdijk Palace with an 'ordinary' Prince. Only two obtained parliamentary approval for their marriages.

Princess Juliana (1909) still going strong and active for the Netherlands.

Prince Bernhard, co-founder and president of World Wildlife Fund for almost half a century, still in his eighties visits projects like here in Indonesia.

Crown Princess Beatrix pressed ahead with her marriage in 1966 to the German diplomat Claus von Amsberg (born in 1926), who as an adolescent had served in the Wehrmacht. After a very lengthy debate, parliament agreed to the alliance. Von Amsberg became naturalized and took the title Prince of the Netherlands. Later he said that he had been too optimistic about his task of convincing the whole country of his integrity: "Without my wife, being just as she is, I would not have survived." The Prince is now one of the most valued members of the Royal House.

The second Princess, Irene, renounced her rights to the throne and in 1964 in Rome married Prince Karl Hugo of Bourbon-Parma, the eldest son of the Carlist pretender to the Spanish throne. Dutch Protestants did not like her conversion to the Roman Catholic church. The couple had four children – Carlos, the twins Margarita and Jaime, and Maria-Carolina, and lived in France and Spain. After her divorce in 1981, the Princess returned to the Netherlands with her children. She is a well-known feminist, advises on multi-cultural communications, lives in a villa in the village of Wijk near Duurstede and wants to go through life known as Mrs. I. van Lippe-Biesterfeld. Prince Karl-Hugo teaches economics in the United States.

In 1967, and subject to parliamentary approval, Princess Margriet got engaged to her fellow countryman, Mr. Pieter van Vollenhoven (born in 1939), to whom no princely or noble title was given. "If my choice had not

been accepted, I would not have gone through with the wedding. Following the departure of my sister Irene, I had become the second in line. I did not want to leave matters in the lurch", revealed the Princess at her Silver Wedding. With a great deal of difficulty, Mr. Van Vollenhoven has won himself a place in business life as the 'husband of the Princess'. He has seen his career blocked many times due to the fact that he is a member of the Royal House. His work includes road safety, the environment, conservation and sport for the handicapped. As a creditable amateur pianist, Van Vollenhoven took the initiative with a number of well-known Dutch pianists to give concerts for the benefit of the Victims Support Fund.

The Princess and her husband carry out dozens of official engagements every year for the House of Orange. On her fiftieth birthday, the Queen rewarded her sister for her devoted service with the award of the Grand Cross of the Order of the House of Orange. The Van Vollenhovens live with their four sons, Princes Maurits, Bernhard jr., Pieter-Christiaan and Floris, in a villa near 'Het Loo' Palace in Apeldoorn.

Princess Christina did not ask for parliamentary approval for her wedding in 1975 to the (Roman Catholic) stateless Cuban Jorge Guillermo (born 1946). Three children have been born to this oecumenical marriage: Bernhard jr., Nicholas and Juliana. The family lived in New York until 1985 and moved that year to a country home at Wassen-aar near The Hague. Art historian Jorge Guillermo publishes books on his special field. The Princess, who

Prince Willem-Alexander in action on the Antilles. His family is not as rich as always has been suggested.

has impaired sight, trained in singing in Canada and now and then gives concerts. The family lives in a 17th century style country house in Wassenaar.

William-Alexander and his "upsetting example"

Queen Juliana's first grandchild, which the then Crown Princess Beatrix brought into the world in 1967, was the first male offspring for 116 years. The female Orange dynasty (there has been Emma, Wilhelmina, Juliana and Beatrix since 1890) has the highest reputation. "I find it almost upsetting when I see what an example my mother

The Royal Couple plant a tree on the occasion of their Silver Wedding. Their countrymen followed this example to make Holland 'greener' and more beautiful.

gives. Anyway to try to equal it will be a complete job in itself", acknowledges the present Crown Prince. His father calmly tells him : "But you should get fairly close."

Prince Claus, not a sportsman, but curious enough to enjoy this adventure on his way to Australia for a State visit. He is being sandwiched between two Dutch ships.

The training of the Prince for his future task began when he was eighteen. He became a member of the Council of State, the highest advisory board in the government and, after ample discussion in the Second Chamber, received a state income of 900,000 guilders (about £350,000), twenty per cent of which is personal income. The Prince did his national service with the Dutch Royal Navy where he reached the rank of Second Lieutenant. After his university studies, he is expected to have closer ties with the armed forces.

A Crown Prince needs to have a positive profile. William-Alexander achieved this when he was about 19 by taking part, without any preparatory training, in the 'Elfstedentocht', the famous long-distance skating race over the Friesian lakes.

In 1991 he trained for months to be able to do well in the New York City Marathon, in which he covered the 42 kilometres in four hours and thirty-three minutes. Along the way the Prince had 'aches in parts I didn't know I had'.

Six in line for the throne expect to follow an ordinary occupation

Apart from the Crown Prince there are still six young Princes in line to the Dutch throne. The two brothers of Prince William-Alexander and the four children of Princess Mar-

The Queen goes for a bicycle ride through the Waterland, north of Amsterdam.

griet. All heirs to the throne require parliamentary approval for their marriages. Much to the displeasure of the former Queen Juliana, the sons of Princess Margriet will lose their membership of the Royal House, thus their rights to the throne, as soon as the Prince of Orange succeeds Queen Beatrix. These Princes, who are 'only' Highnesses – and not Royal Highnesses – and bear the personal title of Prince of Orange-Nassau, will however then be subjected to no further restrictions regarding their marriages or careers. Their future will be an ordinary career in Dutch society and their children will bear the name 'Van Vollenhoven'. In future, the Royal House will therefore be limited to the direct descendants of Queen Beatrix and Prince Claus.

Seven princes seeking suitable marriage partners

Although they can never 'shake off' the bodyguards, the student lives of the Dutch Princes closely resemble those of ordinary students. They are members of the Students' Union, drink beer in the local pub and enjoy themselves at the disco. Prince Bernhard jr., an economics student, is co-director of a courier service. The circle of friends of the young members of the Royal House consists mainly of young people of middle-class extraction.

None of the Princes, not even the Crown Prince, is obliged to marry a Princess or an aristocrat. Although the names of various girls have been linked with the Prince of

Orange, there has so far been no engagement. According to an opinion poll, it appears the Dutch people do not begrudge the young Princes the woman of their heart, providing she is fits in with the royal lifestyle.

Belief based on free will

William II, who was greatly influenced by the thinking of Erasmus, and his family, always considered spiritual life to be of great importance. For a long time dynasty, state and Protestantism were intertwined, but the Orange Princes tried many times to break through the exclusively Protestant character of the national consciousness. They wanted religious tolerance which embraced all persuasions. Although they adhered to the Protestant state church, their personal beliefs were for the most part not bound by church walls and dogma.

With the exception of the Queen, who, according to the Constitution, must be a member of the Dutch reformed church, the religion of the members of the Royal Family is not officially known. They are for the most part Protestant. In conformity to the pattern which has developed nowadays in many families, free will and room for personal choice governs the relationship with religion and the church. Only Princess Juliana goes to church regularly. The Queen and Prince belong to an ecumenical religious community in The Hague, where the liturgy, contemplation and education occupy an important place. The Royal Couple seldom miss the monthly Bach cantata service. Princess Margriet and Mr. Van Vollenhoven are members of a Bible group not affiliated to any church. Princess Irene and her children Carlos, Jaime, Margarita and Carolina profess the Roman Catholic faith, as do Princess Christina and her family. Whilst Princess Irene's conversion to Roman Catholicism resulted in a real storm in 1964. The conversion of Princess Christina in 1992 occurred without any comment from the Protestant population.

The House of Orange is dedicated to nature and the environment

The Dutch feel strongly involved with environmental problems and the Royal House has taken the lead in this. All are inspired by Prince Bernhard, who, as a co-founder of the international organization known as the World Wildlife Fund, has already been dedicated to the conservation of nature and the environment for more than half a century. Long before the public at large became interested in this development, Bernhard's reports and films of his in-

The Queen makes an inspection visit in a boot of the Natural Monument Garde.

vestigative travel made his family aware of its importance. The majority of the members of the Royal House have personally come to know the African jungle and various Asiatic countries. Princess Margriet and Mr. Van Vollenhoven, strongly orientated towards Canada, conducted an expedition and collaborated on a TV film and a book about the Eskimos. The huskies fascinated them to such an extent that they took some of these polar dogs back with them to the Netherlands to breed. A great wish of Princess Juliana to visit the Galapagos Islands with her husband could only be undertaken after she had abdicated. It was an exciting experience.

The House of Orange is indeed dedicated to the conservation of nature and the environment. In her speeches, the Queen always emphasizes man's responsibility for nature. "The earth is slowly dying and the inconceivable – the end of life itself – has actually become conceivable." Her Christmas message of 1988, completely dedicated to environmental matters, even caused an uproar because the Queen's vision sounded noticeably more pessimistic than that of the government. Prince Claus harped on the same theme and warned: "The world will not come to grief, but it is indeed being poisoned!" This is not just lip service. Claus takes part in cleaning up woods and parks and his two eldest sons go diving with their uncle, Mr. Pieter Van Vollenhoven, at the end of the water sports season, for a big clean up of the Dutch lakes. Such environmental action meets with great sympathy.

In the Netherlands hunting is practised with discretion and the Royal House no longer wears fur, because it is no longer socially acceptable. To the alarming death of the

woodlands, the Queen reacted spontaneously with: "What we can do is plant an enormous number of trees." The largest 'Green action' took place on her Silver Wedding anniversary. As a national present, the couple wanted a greener Netherlands and the people gave them a massive response. The hundreds of thousand of trees then planted should ensure that every spring becomes more beautiful and greener in the kingdom of the House or Orange.

Culture blooms under Beatrix's governance

Queen Beatrix and Prince Claus, living in splendid cultural monuments and devotees of art and culture, have given cultural life in the Netherlands a powerful impetus. 'Het Loo' Palace Museum, already mentioned, is devoted to all the Orange Governors and Monarchs and is visited by hundreds of thousands of tourists every year. Queen Elizabeth II, who in 1988 visited this mansion of Governor King William III, her predecessor, was so enchanted by the flower arrangements à la Queen Mary, that she directed her own flower arrangers to familiarize themselves with this art.

Queen Beatrix has led the public to still more treasure houses. The Mauritshuis in The Hague, the city palace built in the centre of The Hague by Johan Maurits van Nassau-Siegen (1604-1679), nowadays houses the royal collection of paintings. It was here the Queen displayed for the first time her House's imposing collection of miniatures.

Opening of the Van Gogh-exposition in the Stedelijk Museum in Amsterdam.

the world's greatest flower and vegetable exhibition, 'Floriade' in Zoestermeer.

Prince Claus was the pace-setter for the rebuilding of the Amsterdam Concertgebouw and the orchestra of that name has a Royal prefix. It travels with the Royal Couple on state visits, as does the National Ballet. Culture is, without doubt, flourishing under Queen Beatrix's governance.

But what does she do when she wants to attend a performance quietly and unobserved? She sends for tickets and unobtrusively takes her place. Too bad that when the auditorium lights suddenly go up again, everyone stands and welcomes her with deafening applause. However warmly meant, the Dutch still have to break the habit.

The Queen is pleased to encourage her people to enjoy the traditions and the art treasures of the House of Orange. These include paintings, porcelain, lace, thrones, investiture accoutrements, costumes and the insignia of the Order of the Garter.

The Oranges reopened the shipping museums in Amsterdam and Rotterdam after they had undergone a fundamental 'face-lift'. They stood on a restored 17th century ship of the Dutch East India Company and took part in the five-yearly international sailing festival, 'Sail Amsterdam'. Many millions of visitors from all over the world followed in the Queen's footsteps after she had toured the Van Gogh and Rembrandt exhibition in Amsterdam and

The Queen is very fond of ballet. Here she visits the performance of the Foundation Dancers Funds in Amsterdam.

Norway

By Annemor Møst

At home - an informal family portrait from the large drawing room at Skaugum Palace, later known as "Crown Princess Märtha's drawing room" after King Harald's mother. "As far as possible we try to live like other families", the Royal Couple often say.

"The Queen is extremely capable, almost a perfectionist, both in private and in public", stated King Harald.

"The King has an amazing ability to see the funny side of things, and to get through to people. He has a very good sense of humour and is extremely witty", said Queen Sonja.

This is how the King and Queen of Norway described each other at their first, and to date only, press conference since their marriage. They also took the opportunity to announce that, although they are in no way planning a "palace revolution" in any manner or form, the people of Norway will gradually see a change in the role of the Royal Family - and that a press conference at the Royal Palace in Oslo on that autumn day in 1991 was just one example of the changes in store.

It is only natural that a new King and Queen with young adult children should introduce new ways of doing things when they take over from an elderly widower king. But King Harald and Queen Sonja are taking things slowly; changes will be made gradually and go almost unnoticed. Ancient traditions will be upheld, such as the consecration of the new King and Queen a few months after ascending to the throne: On the 23rd June 1991, on midsummers day, King Harald and Queen Sonja of Norway knelt at the high altar in the ancient cathedral dating back to the Middle Ages in Trondhiem and received the Church's blessing on their royal acts. It was solemn, religious recognition of the fact that a new King and Queen had taken on the mantle their predecessors.

Kings of Norway are no longer crowned, but King Harald chose to celebrate his succession to the throne in the same way as his father had 34 years previously with a church ceremony in Norway's ancient coronation church. In the same church, on almost the same date, Harald's grandparents, King Haakon and Queen Maud, were crowned the first King and Queen of independent Norway.

The consecration on that midsummer day was to become one of *the* dates in the history of the Norwegian monarchy. More than 2,000 Norwegian representatives from public life filled the cathedral, tens of thousands of Trondheim's citizens greeted the Royal Family outside the church, and the entire nation sat glued to their televisions. It was evident confirmation of the Royal Family's standing in a country where nearly 90 percent of the nation is in favour of the monarchy.

On this occasion the Norwegian Royal Family - the King and Queen, Crown Prince Haakon, Princess Märtha Louise and the King's two sisters (both of whom have married commoners) - was at its most formal, with full formal dress and medals. Their sense of design and style is pronounced. However, you are just as likely to see this sporty family in track suits, on board their yacht, or on long walks in the mountains. "We need the opportunity to unwind - sailing for me and mountain hikes for the Queen", says the King.

King Harald V and Queen Sonja are newcomers to Europe's royal couples. Harald V became King on the 17th January 1991 when his father Olav V, who was much loved by the people, died.

Many had doubted whether the new King would achieve the same standing with the people as his father - but in a very short time indeed it became obvious that he would. The support which the Royal Family enjoys is greater than ever before - quite a contradiction in a country where equality is given more emphasis than almost anywhere else in the world.

When Harald V became King, Norway also gained a Queen - the first for more that fifty years. King Harald's own mother, Swedish-born Crown Princess Märtha, died in 1954, three years before King Olav succeeded to the throne and King Olav chose to live the rest of his life alone. King Haakon, Harald's paternal grandfather, also lost his wife at an early stage; Queen Maud, Norway's first Queen in modern times, died in 1938. A King and a Queen is therefore something new and rather unusual to Norwegians.

There has never been much distance between the Royal Family and ordinary people in Norway. Indeed, many are of the opinion that it has almost been too little when Crown Prince Harald insisted in 1968 on marrying the girl he loved - his long-time friend Sonja Haraldsen, daughter of a businessman in Oslo without a drop of blue blood in her veins. They had known each other for nine years and had agreed that there was little possibility of their spending their future together. But time passed by and it gradually became clear that there was no other option for them - if the Crown Prince was not allowed to marry his Sonja then he would not marry at all. And that would have been the end of the Norwegian monarchy as there were no other heirs to the throne. The Crown Prince's two elder sisters had long since married commoners and, besides, women do not hold the right of succession in Norway.

Time has shown that the Crown Prince chose well and that Sonja Haraldsen was well qualified to fulfil her duties as Crown Princess and later as Queen. The most important argument against royalty marrying commoners was that such a marriage would "dilute" the monarchy and would create a new nobility of families and friends in Norway - a worry which was ultimately unfounded. Throughout her 25 years as Crown Princess and Queen, Sonja has managed a difficult juggling act and has used all her energy to live up to the expectations that people have of her.

Crown Prince Harald was asked on his 50th birthday what he thought was the reason for the Royal Family's strong position in Norway. "It's because the two most recent kings (Haakon and Olav) got most things right." he replied without a moment's hesitation. We could add that he himself has lived up to this tradition as both Crown Prince and King. At a time when the media is always ready to pounce upon the slightest royal irregularity, there has rarely, if ever, been any hint of scandal surrounding the Norwegian Royal Family.

Young dynasty with historic roots

The present dynasty in Norway is very young - King Harald is only the third king in the line. He is also the first of the three monarchs to have been born in Norway. At birth, 21st February 1937, he was the first prince to have been born in the country for almost 600 years.

However, his roots go deep into the old European royal families, and deeper still to distant links with the Norwegian kings during the Middle Ages, and even back to the first king of Norway, Harald Hårfagre in the ninth century. King Harald also has close family ties with the other royal families in Europe, primarily in Denmark, Britain and Belgium.

The royal family from the Middle Ages died out on the male side in the fourteenth century and for 400 years, until 1814, Norway was united with Denmark. After the Napoleonic Wars, when Denmark was on the losing side, Norway was relinquished to Sweden. But the Norwegians, who had long dreamed of freedom, rebelled. A national assembly was called at Eidsvold, a small town north of Oslo, and a constitution was drawn up and ratified in record time. The constitution has been called the world's

The new King of Norway, Haakon VII, arrives in the country with his young son, later Olav V, on his arm. Prime Minister Christian Michelsen was the first to greet them.

freest and was strongly influenced by the new constitutions in France and the USA. But the national assembly wanted to keep the country as a kingdom with a royal family, and on the 17th May 1814 it elected the young Danish Prince Christian Frederik as the new King of Norway. 17th May is still Norway's national day celebrated across the country with the Royal Family as a focal point.

However, it became obvious that the young nation was not really strong enough to stand on its own two feet. After a difficult summer and autumn, the dream of independence was put to one side and Norway entered into a union with Sweden, although it now had a great deal more independence than under Danish rule. The Union lasted over 90 years but came to a definitive end in 1905. On the 7th June the Norwegian Parliament declared the Union dissolved and that the Swedish King, Oscar II, was no longer the King of Norway. In reality it was a revolution, but a very peaceful one.

Many thought that Norway should go the whole way and become a republic, but the monarchists won.

A new Royal family

To cut a long story short, the Norwegian throne was offered to Prince Carl of Denmark, aged 33, grandson of King Christian IX and younger son of the Danish Crown Prince, later Frederik VIII. Quite apart from his personal qualities, which to be honest very few Norwegians knew anything about at the time, he had two invaluable advantages on his side: he was the son-in-law of the powerful King of England, King Edward VII, a valuable support for

a young nation in a world where the great powers made all the decisions; and he had a small son aged two who would grow up to be "totally Norwegian".

Prince Carl was interested but was adamant that he would only come to Norway if he could perform some kind of service for the Norwegians, not just on account of his personal vanity. He also insisted that a referendum should first be held on the constitution in Norway. On this point he was immovable. However, the referendum produced an overwhelming majority in favour of the monarchy, with the result that the elected king Prince Carl came to Oslo, then known as Kristiania, on the 25th November with his wife and son.

In the meantime he adopted the old Norwegian royal name of Haakon and changed his son's name from Alex-

A popular family - this picture of King Haakon, Queen Maud and the young Crown Prince Olav was soon to be found in homes all over Norway.

ander to Olav. Only the English-born queen, Maud, Edward VII's youngest daughter, retained her original name.

The family received a very warm welcome at the small Norwegian capital, despite the falling snow. It was an unkind beginning with a new mother country; all the same, Queen Maud's first words on Norwegian soil were "I like the air here".

Little Prince Olav became the darling of Kristiania from the moment he was carried onto land whilst energetically waving his little Norwegian flag. As an adult the Prince was to ski at Holmenkollbakken - a great achievement in the Norwegian skiing world, and to win an Olympic gold medal for sailing.

King Haakon had laid down certain conditions before becoming king. He wanted a simple court and he wanted the chance to live privately and to be able to take a walk around town with his queen if he should so wish. The present royal family does to some extent enjoy these privileges, although their freedom is more limited on account of the constant media interest in the Royals' private lives. Proximity to the people and the Royal Family's down-to-earth ways have contributed more than anything else to its unique position in Norway.

The new Royal Family arrived at a run-down and impractical palace with very little in the way of furnishings. It was built in the 1840s in the German empire style but the Swedish Royal Family had only lived there sporadically during the Union. Much of the furniture and valuables had been taken back to Sweden when the Union was dissolved. Gradually however the young couple changed the Palace into a home by rebuilding and buying new items - it became a kind of tradition that they would receive silver and other furnishings and fittings as gifts at celebrations with the result that the royal palace in Oslo compares favourably with other royal residences in Europe although it is much bigger than most others.

King Haakon set himself early goals of getting to know his new country and its people. As early as the summer of 1906 the family travelled around southern Norway with the coronation in Trondheim (the last in Norway) as a magnificent high point. The following year they took a similar trip in northern Norway, right up to the Russian border, a very tiring and difficult journey in those days. Travelling around their own country is a very important part of the Royal Family's life, as Norway is extremely long - there is more to Norway than its capital.

The family quickly became popular with the people. The King's sociability and simple ways made it easy for him to get to know people. However they were a little more reserved with Queen Maud who never really mastered the Norwegian language and who spent much of the year with her family in England for health reasons.

As had been hoped, Crown Prince Olav became a "real Norwegian lad" who took part in sports competitions together

Family connections - the new Royal Family was closely related to the old European dynasties, and here we see Crown Prince Olav sitting on the lap of his grandfather, King Edward VII of England.

BELOW: Royal Wedding - Crown Prince Olav married his cousin, Princess Märtha of Sweden, in 1929.

A new generation - that is how Norwegians viewed the Crown Prince's family. Here we see Crown Prince Olav and Crown Princess Märtha skiing with (from left) Princess Ragnhild, Princess Astrid and Prince Harald, only three years old in this picture.

with other competitors and was the first European heir to the throne to go to a state school and also undertook normal military training without any special concessions - all of which held the Royal Family and the Norwegian people together. The relationship with Sweden was strained after the dissolution of the Union in 1905 but on the 14th January 1925 the flag was raised on both sides of the border - Crown Prince Olav had become engaged to Princess Märtha of Sweden the granddaughter of King Oscar who had been deposed by the Norwegians less than 25 years previously. The engaged couple were cousins (Princess Märtha's mother was King Haakon's sister) and had known each other since childhood.

Even if it seemed, at a superficial level, to be a marriage of convenience, there is no doubt that they really loved each other. King Olav confirmed this several times in interviews when he was much older and the world had changed so that even kings were allowed to express their thoughts and feelings. More than fifty years after the

wedding in 1929 he referred to it in a television interview as the happiest event of his life.

The newly married couple moved in to the Skaugum estate 20 km west of Oslo. The property was a gift from a Norwegian diplomat which solved a difficult problem for both the Royal Family and the government - politicians had been unable to agree on the construction of a residence for the Crown Prince. Skaugum later became the scene of happy royal family life for three generations and is still home to a Royal Family which has still (1993) failed to move into the Palace in Oslo and the King's Manor House just outside the capital, both of which belong to the state.

The 1930s saw the birth of three children, Princess Ragnhild in 1930, Princess Astrid in 1932 and finally the heir to the throne Prince Harald in 1937. Even before he was born the Norwegians had discussed the idea of introducing female succession to the throne. However, discussions came to an end with the birth of the little prince and the reform was eventually made in 1991. The reform will not be valid for the next generation as Crown Prince Haakon, born in 1973 will succeed his father although he has an elder sister two years older than he is. In the following generation, the throne will go to the King's first born, male or not.

Symbol of resistance

Both kingly rule and King Haakon's personal authority had deep roots in Norway when the country was occupied on the 9th April 1940 by Nazi Germany. Hitler's plan was to take the country while the Norwegians were in their beds and to depose both the Royal Family and the government with one swift coup. However as the battle ship "Bluecher" was on its way into the Oslo Fjord to occupy the capital and imprison the King and government, it miraculously sank at Drøbak, about 30 kilometres south of Oslo. Thus the Royal Family, the national assembly and the government managed to escape to safety.

Crown Princess Märtha and the three children (Prince

In exile - during the German occupation of Norway, Crown Princess Märtha and her children stayed in the USA. From their temporary home near Washington they sent Christmas greetings by radio to their countrymen back in Norway.

Harald was only three years old) drove over the border to Sweden and later travelled on to the USA after receiving a personal invitation from President Roosevelt. They lived in the USA, near Washington, for the duration of the war.

King Haakon, who repeatedly refused to give in to the Germans' demands including that the traitor Quisling be appointed Prime Minister, chose to remain in Norway together with Crown Prince Olav and stay with the troops for the two month duration of the military campaign in Norway.

It quickly became clear that the Germans were conducting a witch hunt for them - towns and villages where they were staying were brutally bombed to the ground. Keeping their location secret became a matter of life and death and King Haakon was disturbed that his presence would result in disaster for innocent civilians. Southern

Norway was surrendered and in the final weeks before the capitulation the King and Crown Prince stayed, amid total secrecy, in a cabin in northern Norway, several kilometres from Tromsø where the government had sought refuge.

By the 7th June it was obvious that Norway could hold out no longer and the King, Crown Prince and government left the country on a British cruiser headed for Great Britain, to continue their fight outside Norway. It was a difficult decision for the King to make, he was afraid that the Norwegians would not understand his actions and that he would be accused of fleeing, and that German propaganda would exploit the "flight" for all it was worth (he was right about the latter). Crown Prince Olav shared his worries and offered to return to Norway and become a prisoner of war. However the government managed to persuade him that he could do a great deal for the cause in London.

Their exile was to last five years and the King and Crown Prince became symbols of Norwegian resistance both in Norway and abroad. Occupied Norway looked forward to "the day when the King would come home" and Haakon VII's monogram was secretly drawn on walls, in the streets and in the snow with skis alongside ski tracks. On the 3rd August, the King's birthday, people in Oslo spent the day with flowers in their button holes, which made the Germans so angry that they started making mass arrests. But the Norwegians had a better idea, they protested by walking along King Street instead, and it is very difficult to arrest someone for that....

Crown Prince Olav, who was now Norwegian Head of

Defence in London, was the first member of the Royal Family to return home to Norway. On the 13th May, just five days after the Germans capitulated in Europe, he arrived in Oslo in battle dress and the welcome was so great that he sat on the collapsible hood of the open top car to see and be seen. This worried his security guards as there were still a good few Germans and Nazis with weapons in the city.

On the 7th June, exactly five years after leaving Tromsø, King Haakon returned to Norway as did Crown Princess Märtha and the children who had flown over the Atlantic to travel home to be with the King. This was to

Jubilant homecoming - 7 June 1945, the day King Haakon and the Crown Prince's family returned to Norway after five years in exile, has been called the happiest day in Norwegian history.

be the happiest day in the history of Norway to be celebrated by many with coffee made from their last real coffee beans which they had saved during the strict rationing for this very day.

The Royal Family's standing and efforts during the war had done away with the last of those in favour of a republic. In the years which followed the King and Crown Prince travelled far and wide in the country - as early as 1945 King Haakon was on the move to see with his own eyes what had been devastated during the war.

A welcome guest - Queen Elizabeth II's first state visit outside the Commonwealth was to Norway in 1955. It was the last time Haakon VII, then Europe's oldest monarch, was seen in public - a few days later he fell to the bathroom floor and broke his neck, and spent the last two years of his life an invalid.

King Haakon died on the 21st September 1957 at the age of 85 after a reign of almost 52 years. His last two years were rather withdrawn after a serious leg fracture sustained in 1955. The last time the Norwegian people saw their beloved old king was on the 1st June 1955 when young Queen Elizabeth of Great Britain and her husband Prince Philip made their first ever state visit outside the Commonwealth to Norway and "uncle Charles" which was the family's pet name for him.

His son became King Olav V and ruled very much in the vein of his father. He even chose the same motto as his father had chosen in 1905 "Alt for Norge" [Everything for Norway], a motto which King Harald took into a third generation. All three kings have proved that this motto means more to them than empty words, it is a code of conduct for their lives.

King Olav was a widower when he became king. Crown Princess Märtha died in 1954 after a long period of illness. The King's eldest daughter, Princess Ragnhild, had married a Norwegian businessman in 1953 and had moved to Brazil, where she still lives. The marriage was

A new Royal Family - King Olav V is blessed in Nideros Cathedral in Trondheim in 1958, and greets the crowds together with his family (from left) Princess Astrid, Princess Ragnhild and Crown Prince Harald.

extremely popular in Norway, even though the bridegroom, Erling Lorentzen, was a commoner. Some of the popularity can be attributed to the fact that he was a prominent member of the Norwegian resistance during the war and was thus chosen as part of the group representing the resistance which was given the honour of escorting the Royal Family that first summer. And that was how he met the princess, just a few days after her return on the 7th June 1945.

For some years Princess Astrid, King Olav's other daughter, acted as Norway's first lady, as she had done during King Haakon's final years. She accepted her many duties with youthful enthusiasm, but married in 1961. Like her sister before her she chose a commoner as a husband - Johan Martin Ferner. Although she still performed official duties, these dwindled as her family grew to five children in all.

Triumphant - Crown Prince Harald and Sonja Haraldsen knew each other for nine years before they were allowed to get engaged. Beaming with joy, the two meet the crowds and photographers in front of Oslo Castle in March 1968.

"Norway's best kept secret"

*I*n the footsteps of his father, Crown Prince Harald did military service and then studied at Oxford for two years. This was in the 1960s when the world was full of young unmarried princesses, and the Norwegian Crown Prince was married off to most of them - in the headlines at least. Very few people actually knew that he had met a young lady in the summer of 1959. Her name was Sonja Haraldsen and they spent a great deal of time together; however it was unthinkable at the time that the heir to the throne should marry a commoner. In retrospect it is difficult to

understand that the Norwegian media failed to report on the Crown Prince's romance. This formed the run-up to national speculation in 1964, when rumours were rife, which was silenced with an official denial from the Palace. Most people were satisfied with this and the Norwegian press manifested almost unbelievable restraint in the years that followed. It is not surprising that one headline after the engagement was announced read "Norway's best kept secret". "Those years were not exactly the easiest of my life", said Crown Prince Harald. Nor were they easy on King Olav. On the one hand his greatest wish was to see his son happy, and on the other he was worried about what this marriage would mean for the monarchy in the long term. The constitution dictates that the king and the king alone shall approve the marriage of the heir to the throne, even if it is understood that the government shall

History in the making - the newly-wed Crown Prince and Princess emerge from Oslo Cathedral. For the first time since the Middle Ages an heir to the Norwegian throne had married "a common girl", one he chose himself.

Their very own kingdom - Crown Prince Harald and Crown Princess Sonja at Skaugum Palace. We can see a little of the large the park and, in the background, the wonderful view out over the countryside and the Oslo fjord.

be in agreement. In 1967 Crown Prince Harald celebrated his 30th birthday and it became clear to everyone that it was to be Sonja or nobody. King Olav thought long and hard before making his decision. He discussed the matter with the government, with the opposition, with the political leaders in the national assembly and with his advisors, all in utmost secrecy.

It was therefore a great surprise to the public when it was announced on the 19th March 1968 that Crown Prince Harald had become engaged to Miss Sonja Haraldsen. However, the vast majority of Norwegians were enthusiastic about the announcement, and the few protesters were silenced by the general celebration. "We were expecting much more trouble" commented Crown Prince

Officer - King Olav was actively interested in all aspects of the defence of Norway, and whenever he inspected an honorary company he took it very seriously.

white main building built in 1932, a glimpse of

although she knew that it was the right solution for both herself and the man she loved.

They had only been engaged an hour when they stood on the Palace balcony to accept the congratulations of a handful of people who had heard the news on the radio and had hurried along to the Palace. It was the first glimpse the Norwegian people were to have of their future Crown Princess. In all the nine years the pair had known each other, there had hardly been a single picture published in any of the Norwegian newspapers. Dark, slim, smiling and well-dressed - people approved. They also approved of the happy, smiling, and very much in love Crown Prince Harald - he hadn't been seen smiling or happy for several years.

The engagement was brought forward a week as some

King of Skis - King Olav was the guardian of all Norwegian sport, and was an untiring spectator at all the major sporting events, particularly in the winter. Here we see him congratulating the Norwegian winners of the World Ski Championships in Oslo in 1982.

Harald many years later.

How does it feel to be a young woman suddenly snatched, so to speak, from anonymity and to become a member of the Royal Family, constantly in the limelight? "It was like being thrown off a precipice without a safety net" explains Queen Sonja thinking back to that eventful spring and summer. And she makes no secret of the fact that she had some doubts about what she was taking on,

of the newspapers had begun to note that something was brewing. The Crown Prince had not even had a chance to buy a ring for his fiancée. That same afternoon the couple appeared quite informally in Oslo's largest jewellery shop to order the rings; traditional Norwegian simple plain rings. One for him and one for her.

So who was the young lady who had conquered the Crown Prince's heart and outdone all the other princes-

Popular - King Olav was King of Norway for 33 years, and over the years was loved all over the country. This much was obvious when he made a trip around the country on his Silver Jubilee in 1982 to be greeted by huge crowds. This picture was taken in Trondheim.

Family excursion - Crown Prince Harald and Crown Princess Sonja often took their children for trips in the country when they were small. And a packed lunch and a thermos flask are an important part of a good walk in the forest.

ses in Europe? Sonja Haraldsen was born in Oslo in 1937, just a few months after Prince Harald was born at Skaugum. She was the youngest of three and grew up in one of Oslo's western suburbs, an ordinary little girl and nothing special - at the time. When she finished school she did think about carrying on with her education, but eventually decided to train in cutting and sewing, an obvious choice since her father ran one of Oslo's well known women's clothes businesses. She took a one year course at a technical college in Oslo and went to Switzerland to continue her training.

However, her interest in more formal studies returned and she took her A levels in one year (three years are normal) and began her studies at the university in Oslo, first English and then French. She spent some time in France (which is still her favourite country) before her final examination in French. She then began to study the history of Art, which she gave up when she became engaged to the Crown Prince. However, she did complete all her studies a few years later when she was pregnant with her first child. Her knowledge of Art and culture has been invaluable to her both during her time as Crown Princess and as Queen - she is often referred to as Norway's leading cultural ambassador.

Crown Prince Harald and Sonja Haraldsen met at a party held by a mutual friend in Oslo in the spring of 1959. It was not love at first sight, but there was something there as just a few days later the Crown Prince rang her up and invited her to his passing out parade at the Military Academy where he would receive his exam certificate. This was when they were captured on film for the first time, the Crown Prince and the "unknown lady". One particular journalist donned his detective's hat and managed to find out her name, but at the time nobody would have thought that she would take a place in Norwegian history. The picture taken on that summer day at the Military Academy was the only one of the two together before the bolt from the blue nine years later.

The wedding day was set for the 29th August 1968, five months after the engagement. King Olav decided that he himself would lead the bride to the altar in Oslo's cathedral as Sonja's father had died some years earlier. It was a traditional wedding with King Olav showing that he now regarded Sonja as a member of the Royal Family. Relatives from most of the European royal families were present, and, when the newly-weds came out of the cathedral to drive in an open-top car to the Palace, they were greeted by thousands along the route. There was no doubt about it, the commoner turned Crown Princess had the people on her side, even if a few still protested quietly.

King Olav's wedding gift to his son and daughter-in-law was Skaugum, the estate at Asker, where Crown Prince Harald had been born on a sunny winter's day 31 years previously. King Olav had moved to the Royal Palace in Oslo when he became King, but had kept Skaugum as his summer and weekend retreat. He now started to use the King's Manor House on the Oslo fjord, Norway's oldest royal residence, as a summer home and Skaugum became home to the young family and its children over the next thirty years.

Princess Märtha Louise was born in 1971 and was followed less than two years later by Prince Haakon Magnus (Crown Prince of Norway) who was born on the 20th July 1973.

Olav V - a focal point for his family and people

*T*he Norwegian people were to enjoy the rule of King Olav for several years yet. He was popular when he succeeded to the throne, and with time he was to become greatly loved by everyone. He was once asked the secret of his popularity, "The secret is not to think about it" he replied simply.

But the answer lies perhaps in the motto he himself adopted, and his children after him -Be yourself! This was also the first piece of advice he gave his daughter-in-law when she was to take on her many unfamiliar duties as Crown Princess. He never viewed being king as a role he had to play, and when those closest to him were asked about the differences between the King in private and public, the answer was always the same, "There is no difference".

Although he was getting older, King Olav showed no signs of slowing down at all, quite the opposite, he seemed to take on more and more duties as the years went by. He gradually became the oldest monarch in Europe, his own generation disappeared and a new generation succeeded to the throne. Each in turn came on state visits to "Uncle Olav" in Norway, and his pleasure in meeting them was quite clear to everyone. Indeed, the old King travelled about himself; he made a total of 30 state visits abroad. However, his main priority was travelling around his own country, from the largest towns to the most distant outposts. He met school outings at the Palace - he wasn't known as "the people's grandfather" for nothing. He also visited those same age as him in old people's homes. He had a particular place in his heart for old war veterans, as a former soldier he felt almost one of them. His energy and workload were to become almost

A people in mourning - when King Olav died in 1991, thousands of Norwegians went to Oslo Castle where they lit candles and foreground of this picture.

placed flowers on the snow in memory of the beloved "People's King". "Thank you" can be seen in glowing letters in the

A chain of king - flags were still at half mast on Oslo's main Karl Johan Street, when, three days after the death of King Olav, the new Royal Couple drove from Oslo Castle to the Norwegian Parliament, where the new king was to swear an oath of allegiance to the constitution.

Oath of allegiance - to swear an oath of allegiance to the constitution is the first duty for a new king. This happens in the Parliament where Members of Parliament stand to hear Harald swear to "rule over the Kingdom of Norway in accordance with its constitution and laws."

A new queen - dressed for mourning, Queen Sonja stood at her husband's side in the Parliament. She is the first Queen of Norway since King Harald's grandmother Maud died in 1938.

legendary. "They must have two kings, it's impossible for one man to do so much" said an out-of-breath Secret Service agent travelling with King Olav on one of his trips to the USA. There were many such trips, King Olav was one of the few people to have visited all the American presidents (with the exception of John F. Kennedy) from Franklin Roosevelt to George Bush.

As a young man the King, then Crown Prince, had won an Olympic Gold medal in Amsterdam for his sailing abilities. He continued to sail in the summer all his life and to ski in the winter, right up to his illness the year before his death.

The spring of 1990 was a particularly difficult time for the old king who was now approaching 87. Norway marked the 50th anniversary of German invasion and the military campaign in 1940, and King Olav was at as many of the events as he could manage. The last was the recapture of Narvik (the first town in Europe where the Germans were forced back), and King Olav was present for everything, appearing quite healthy and fit. But it later became clear that the tiring programme had left its mark. Just two days later the King was admitted to hospital with heart disease. He had suffered a brain haemorrhage and news bulletins announced that the situation was serious. But to everyone's surprise King Olav overcame this first attack of the illness, returned home to the King's Manor House at Bygdø and, as was typical of his fighting spirit, took to walking as far as he could in the park. He even invited photographers to Bygdø to prove that he was on the road to recovery.

But the evening of the 17th January 1991, the same day as the Gulf War broke out, saw the final news bulletin. First came a brief announcement that King Olav had suffered a heart attack, and then, thirty minutes later, the final announcement: King Olav was dead, Harald V was the new King of Norway.

A new king - swearing the oath of allegiance was a ceremonious occasion for King Harald, who would now take the place of his incredibly popular father.

The Church's blessing - five months after his accession King Harald V was blessed by Bishop Finn Wagle in Trondheim Cathedral. Queen Sonja was blessed directly after her husband.

Prince and Princess - Crown Prince Haakon and Princess Märtha Louise have a front row view of their parents being blessed. Märtha Louise, nearly 20 years of age, bears the order of St Olav, while the Crown Prince, not yet 18, has yet to receive either decorations or uniform, and appears wearing a morning coat for the first time in his life.

In with the new

*I*t was characteristic of the active Norwegian Royal Family that only King Harald was in Oslo when his father died. Sonja, the new Queen had taken advantage of what was to have been a quiet period to go on a language course in France. (She did of course return home, but completed the course a year later). Haakon Magnus, Crown Prince from the moment his father became King, was skiing with friends and was picked up from the mountain resort by helicopter. Princess Märtha Louise was a pupil at a riding school in Great Britain (riding had been her hobby since childhood).

Something wonderful happened in Oslo when King Olav died; Norwegians have never been ones to show their feelings, but late that evening, shortly after the death had been announced, a group of young people went to the Palace courtyard, the large open courtyard in front of the Royal Palace and placed lighted candles in the snow. Many more followed, in almost two weeks the courtyard became a sea of candles. Others came and laid flowers in the snow, playgroups and school children came with candles, drawings and salutations to the dead king. People travelled from all over the country to walk slowly past the King's bier in the Palace chapel and then to light a candle in his memory. Norway has never seen anything like this

Anyone got an umbrella? - Queen Sonja came prepared, but nobody had thought of an umbrella for the King when the heavens opened "somewhere in Norway".

ABOVE: On the road - much of the Royal Couple's time is spent visiting towns and villages around Norway. Here we see them in the unique mining town of Røros - a village so distinctive and special that it is on Unesco's list of European towns and villages most worth preserving.

LEFT: Father and son - Crown Prince Haakon has brown eyes like his mother, but from the side he looks more and more like his father.

RIGHT: Mother and daughter - Princess Märtha Louise has blue eyes, but otherwise bears a striking resemblance to Queen Sonja.

Humanitarian initiative - as Crown Princess, Queen Sonja was for a while Vice President of the Norwegian Red Cross.

demonstration of feelings which later became the subject of many sociological investigations.

King Harald did not neglect to offer his personal thanks for this national demonstration of feeling in his first New Year's speech. "The candles and all the messages in the Palace courtyard helped and comforted us through those difficult days - they gave us a strong feeling that the Norwegian people were united with us in our grief".

Despite their grieving for the dead king, the Norwegian people welcomed the new Royal Family warmly. Ten thousand people turned out to follow King Olav's final journey through the streets of Oslo and then gathered patiently in the Palace courtyard and waited for King Harald and his family to appear on the balcony for the first time as the Royal Family. They were met by modest cheers - overwhelming enthusiasm would not have been appropriate on such a day, but their sympathy was quite obvious in the spontaneous outbreak of the royal anthem and then the national anthem. Everyone knew that the new King and Queen were well prepared to take on their new royal duties. "I regard my time as Crown Prince as a pupillage" King Harald had once said some years earlier. He had been Crown Prince for 33 years when he became king and there was no doubt about the fact that he had been a good pupil.

Norway is a constitutional monarchy, but the King has closer ties with the government than is the case in most other monarchies. The King meets on a weekly basis with the government every Friday at the Palace, and chairs these meetings. The Crown Prince may sit in on a

In Lapland - on their long trip to northern Norway in the summer of 1992, King Harald and Queen Sonja naturally also visited the Lapp villages up in the northern province of Finnmark. In Kautokeino and other villages they received a warm welcome from Lapps in brightly coloured traditional dress.

Family outing - the whole Royal Family touring Norway after the blessing in Trondheim. Fortunately, security is not so tight in small villages as to stop young children making it through to the Royal Group - always a popular moment.

Caring Royals - a Royal Visit often runs to a tight schedule, but the Royal Couple always take time out to talk to older folk and war veterans, as seen here in a small coastal village in northernmost Norway.

Getting wet - the weather is not always on the Royal Family's side, but it takes more than a shower of rain to keep the Norwegians at home when the Royal Couple are visiting. These two pictures show how things can change from one moment to the next, so to speak.

meeting if there is good reason for him to do so. A new government is also announced by the King at the Palace, although it is, of course, Parliament which makes the decision.

King Harald makes a point of being present at all the cabinet meetings at the palace, sometimes even arranging foreign trips so that he is always in Oslo on a Friday. His father was the same; when he had to have an eye operation some years before his death, he made a point of being discharged from the hospital on Friday morning to be at the meeting a few hours later.

The King is also Commander-in-Chief of the Norwegian armed forces - in his younger days he was trained as an officer along with his peers, and he is also Supreme Head of the Norwegian Church. Small as the Royal Family is, the King and Queen share almost all their official duties between them. Crown Prince Haakon is in the middle of his military training and has decided to become a naval officer, and Princess Märtha Louise is back in a riding school in England for two years. There is a great deal to indicate that the Princess will undertake some sort of professional training, but it remains a secret as to just what. As long as the royal children are in education or

training, their participation in public life is limited, with the result that more falls to the King and Queen.

As Crown Prince and Crown Princess, Harald and Sonja led numerous Norwegian delegations abroad, happily combined export and culture delegations where he worked on the commercial side and she called upon her education in Art and culture, and attended to concerts. In this way they have brought Norway to the attention of the world - indeed they referred to themselves as "door-openers". It is much easier to gain contact with foreign social leaders if there is a royal name on the invitation. "It doesn't hurt to play on snob value on such occasions" said King Harald with a twinkle in his eye. Both are committed to ensuring that this small country in the north should be noticed in the big wide world which is why they are working tirelessly behind the scenes to ensure that Norway hosts the 1994 Winter Olympics in Lillehammer.

As King and Queen they are no longer allowed to "travel on business". Most of their journeys over the next few years will probably be state visits to foreign heads of state, always an important task for a new Royal Couple. In their first two years on the throne they have already managed to visit all four of their Nordic neighbours, the first being Denmark where they were received by their good friends and relatives, Queen Margrethe and Prince Henrik. Margrethe and Harald are second cousins and the two queens are very close friends who go on a week long exhausting skiing trip in the Norwegian mountains every year.

Dramatic scenery - high mountains and deep fjords are often the background to Royal visits. The Royal Yacht "Norway" anchors, the Royal Family land on the new floating jetty, the Mayor welcomes them - and the visit is under way.

State visit - King Harald and Queen Sonja made their very first state visit a family trip to their neighbours in Sweden and Denmark. Here we see a gala banquet with the Swedish Royal Couple at Stockholm Castle.

Welcome guests - Denmark's Queen Margrethe and Prince Henrik are perhaps closest to the Norwegian Royal Couple of all the European Royal Couples, and they were the first to make an official visit to Norway. The guests arrived on their own yacht to receive a warm and heartfelt welcome in Oslo.

Just as important as trips abroad are trips around Norway. In summer 1991 the entire family travelled widely around southern Norway in connection with the consecration at Trondheim. The following year they travelled on the royal yacht "Norge" for three weeks along the northern coast, visiting 62 towns in the space of three weeks. It was a marathon of a journey which required that the Royal Family and those with them were fit and healthy, not least the press corps which covered the trip from their own "press yacht" chartered especially for the trip.

Which leads us onto the relationship between the Royals and the press. Things in Norway are perhaps better than in other countries as the press is, by and large, tame in this area and does not dig too deeply into the private life of the Royal Family. But reporters are not as restrained as they were a generation ago - Crown Prince Haakon and princess Märtha Louise have long been used to being followed by the press each time they appear with a new girlfriend or boyfriend. The King and Queen have been very open with the press; they invite them to press conferences on special events and ensure a good working relationship on official occasions. In return they get a little annoyed if photographers appear when they are not wanted - it goes without saying that the Royal Family and the press have different ideas about where the border between private and public life actually lies.

Royal finances definitely fall into the private life category. For many years now it had been taken for granted that the Royal Family had a vast private fortune, and the sum of one billion Norwegian crowns was suggested after the family inherited King Olav's fortune (which also remained secret). However it was announced that this sum was quite unrealistic, although it is obvious that the family is far from financial embarrassment.

The civil list allowance has long been very low, but

Exotic visit - Crown Prince Akihito and Crown Princess Michiko, now the Japanese Emperor and Empress.

Sporting prince - the Royal Family has been heavily involved in the coming 1994 Winter Olympics which are to be held in Norway.

A princess's duty - all princesses must learn to plant trees. Märtha Louise planting one to commemorate the Royal Family's visit to the home of the author Knut Hamsun.

for many years now has been increased regularly in line with inflation. At present the King and Queen receive 21 million Norwegian crowns in total to pay their staff, to cover their travelling expenses and to maintain their private property. State property is managed and maintained on a budget of 28 million Norwegian crowns. A sum is also granted to cover rebuilding and security measures at the Royal Palace in Oslo - work which got underway immediately after the King came to the throne, and which will take several years.

It is worth noting that it is not the King and Queen who stand to benefit, the couple are more concerned that the Palace staff should have pleasant, modern working surroundings. Only once this has been achieved will money be spent on their own private apartments.

It is still not known when the King and Queen will move to the Palace in Oslo. They have always functioned well at Skaugum despite the fact that they spend their office hours at the Palace. They also fulfil all their official engagements at the Palace, from audiences with people who have received an award or some other form of distinction to huge banquets in connection with state visits. In common with all royal families, the Norwegian couple owns several properties. They have always spent summer in the countryside on the Oslo Fjord at their home inherited by the Queen from her parents. However they will spend summer 1993 in the new summer house close by and currently under construction. It is the first royal residence to have been built in Norway since Skaugum was rebuilt after the old palace burned down in 1930. Their

Princess on horseback - Märtha Louise dreamed of being a top-class showjumper, and as a child she carefully saved up her pennies for her own horse.

Along the coast - Norway has an incredibly long coastline, but with the Royal Yacht "Norway", a gift from the people of Norway to King Haakon after the war, the Royal Family can visit the remotest of islands and sail up the longest of fjords. Tradition has it that small boats sail out to meet the Royal Yacht whenever it approaches a new village.

A floating home - the Royal Yacht "Norway" was a gift from the people of Norway to King Haakon after the war, and has seen extensive service for Royal trips along the Norwegian coast. The ship was destroyed by a fire in 1985, but was quickly restored.

new home is for the family's private use and is being built from scratch as the old looked out to sea and had become a popular sight-seeing attraction for people in boats. The new house will mean more privacy during the holidays.

They inherited "The King's Chalet" from King Olav - a large log chalet in the hills above Oslo. It was built after the Norwegian national romantic style. They also inherited "The Prince's Chalet", a mountain chalet in Gudbrandsdalen where they spend every Easter and which is home to King Harald when hunting in the autumn.

The Royal Yacht "Norge" is a white-painted yacht which was a gift from the people to King Haakon after the war. It is the family's floating home and is used for travelling around Norway in the summer. When King Harald, still a keen

In the library - with bookshelves from floor to ceiling, art from Norway's Golden Age adorning the walls, and a large open fireplace, the green library at Skaugum Palace is an inviting room enjoyed by the entire family.

Master of the house - King Harald by the fireplace in the large drawing room at Skaugum. The painting on the wall is Zorn's famous portrait of Prince Carl of Sweden, King Harald's grandfather.

Celebrations - every European Royal Family was represented at Crown Prince Haakon's coming of age in the summer of 1991, and the celebrations lasted three days. Here we see the birthday boy dancing a polonaise at Oslo Castle together with his parents and his Godmother, Queen Margrethe of Denmark. The festivities at the Castle took place the day before his birthday, which is why he has no decorations to adorn his breast. He got those the next day.

Royal hug - the Norwegian Royal Couple rarely show their feelings in public, but when Sonja had christened Harald's new yacht, she was rewarded with a warm hug from her husband.

The King, Queen and Crown Prince are all keen sailors and Queen Sonja is famous for her long mountain walks in both summer and winter. She uses these walks to get to meet "normal people" in a way that would not otherwise be possible, and there is any number of villagers who have had to look twice when they suddenly meet their sportily-clad Queen on the street or in a shop.

Crown Prince Haakon enjoys sports which offer some kind of challenge - hang-gliding and white water canoeing are two of his current favourites, neither of which are without their dangerous moments. But he also has a number of cultural interests and has directed some of Ibsen's plays at school. In a television interview on his 18th birthday, he impressed the nation with his intelligent and considered replies, and announced that he thought that art and culture would come to mean more to him than sport in the future.

sailor and world champion in ocean-racing a few years ago, competes in regattas abroad, he uses "Norge" as his headquarters with his team on board as guests.

Sport and nature play an important role in royal life.

Both children have been brought up as far as pos-

A dream day - Princess Märtha Louise got on a treat with the young Norwegians on National Service when she visited a military installation. "Dream days in the Armed Forces" was one of the most original gifts the Princess received on her 18th birthday - and she got the chance to both fly in a jet aircraft and go down in a submarine.

sible like other Norwegian children; they attended state schools (there are hardly any private schools in Norway) and were allowed to choose their own friends. King Harald was brought up in the same way and has said that this, together with sport, afforded him better contact with people than would otherwise have been the case.

They maintain this contact through their large and loyal group of friends, some of whom date back to their school days. It was these friends who shielded Harald and Sonja from the world for nine years before their engagement was announced, and who never said a word about what was going on. They are still as loyal, keep a characteristically low profile and would never dream of using their royal connections to their advantage.

On the whole the Norwegian Royal Family has more freedom than other European royal families, "We are allowed to do everyday things without press releases being issued on the matter" says the King. They like to travel privately - perhaps to a European city for the weekend, where they can disappear in the crowd. Their autumn holiday in London is not to be missed, even if it is frequently combined with official engagemen.

There is every indication that they are happy with their position in Norwegian society, and that the Norwegian people are happy with them. A survey in one of the Norwegian newspapers in the New Year

Daring - Crown Prince Haakon loves sports which offer a real challenge. Paddling along rivers in a kayak, as seen here, is one of them. He also enjoys hanggliding, surfing and downhill skiing. Perhaps the Crown Prince's love of water sports is one of the reasons he chose the Navy for his military service.

showed that the Royal Family inspires more confidence than the government, parliament and other social groups. It bodes well for the future of the monarchy.

Spain

By Ismael Fuente

History

*O*n the 22nd November 1975, at the age of 37, Juan Carlos I was enthroned as the new King of Spain by the Parliament of the day. His proclamation signalled an unusual event in history. Throughout the centuries it has been most unusual for a Monarchy to fall and be restored later with greater credibility and power, as has been the case with Spain. In April 1931, after popular demand for a Republic, his grandfather Alfonso XIII suspended the Monarchy and with a heavy heart went into exile along with all the other members of the Royal Family.

Forty-four years later Juan Carlos I was made King, in accordance with the wishes of General Francisco Franco. Franco had taken over the country with the support of his Army colleagues in 1939, at the end of three years of bloody civil war, which in turn had fol-l-owed five years of mismanagement by the Republic. The civil war cost over 500 000 lives, and some estimates, which may be exaggerated, put that figure at a million. Franco held power from the end of the civil war until his death. This was the start of a regime which left in its wake death, exile, grief, hunger, isolation from the rest of the world in the long post-war period, and the political, cultural, economic and social backwardness from which to some extent the country is still suffering.

The King, Juan Carlos.

It was Franco himself who, in 1947, initiated the official return of Spain to a monarchy (which was what it had been since Don Pelayo became the first Catholic King in the 8th century). It was in 1969 that Franco appointed Juan Carlos I as his "successor with the title of King". This was despite the fact he was fully aware that the legitimate heir - Juan Carlos' father and Head of the Royal House, the 56 year old Don Juan de Borbón, who had been in

up at popular request, although it was referred to in Spain as an *experimento con gaseosa* (playing with fire).

Neither Carlos IV, Fernando VII, Isabel II, Alfonso XII, nor the Regencies of Cristina de Borbón (the queen who was regent before Isabel II came of age) and Maria Christina of Austria (acting regent for Alfonso XIII), nor even the short reigns of the "foreign" kings - José Bonaparte during the French occupation by Napoleon from 1805-1814 and Amadeo de Saboya (1871-1873) - managed to stop the slow decline of the Spanish Monarchy. This had reached its zenith with the Catholic King and Queen, Isabel I and Fernando V, who achieved the unification of the whole of Spain at the end of the 15th century. This prestige continued during the Austrian dynasty and was

King Juan Carlos I as a child.

maintained by some of the first Bourbons, such as the founder of the dynasty in Spain, Felipe V, and by Carlos III.

Nor was the young king Alfonso XIII (crowned at 16 in 1902) able to redress this self-destructive tendency. Instead, he would suffer several attempts on his life from all of which he would emerge unhurt. One took place in Madrid in

Juan Carlos de Borbón with his younger brother, Alfonso, who died at the age of 15 from an accident while they were playing with their father's revolver.

exile since 1941 - was being passed over. However, this has not detracted from Juan Carlos being the embodiment of the head of a modern State for eighteen years - a state that is fully integrated into the Western world, particularly with the surrounding countries: its European partners and Atlantic allies.

The last King, Alfonso XIII (born King in 1886 as his father Alfonso XII - married to his second wife Queen Maria Christina of Austria - had died a few months before he came into the world) had inherited all the misfortunes of the 19th century, the worst period in Spanish history. It was an unfortunate century politically and socially during which, amongst other events, there were over 110 heads of government and numerous military uprisings, with queens and generals acting as regents, some of whom were irresponsible and were gradually undermining the prestige of the multisecular institution. The country had already had experience of a republican government (February 1873-January 1874) set

1906 on the day of his wedding to Victoria Eugenia of England and another during an official visit to Paris. He was to see his government's prime ministers, José Canalejas and Eduardo Dato, assassinated in Madrid by anarchists. After many attempts at civilian government, his reign was to end with the seizure of power in 1923 by General Miguel Primo de Rivera who held it until 1930. This was the King's big mistake since, although the zealous military dictator had assured him the throne while he was in power, the cost was a fivefold increase in the political and social deterioration of the country, at the same time as isolating him from any kind of contact with the people. Although Primo de Rivera held his ground, mainly as a result of considerable improvements to the country's archaic infrastructures, he was never loved or respected and was finally removed from office in 1930. But when the King signed the appointment of Dámaso Berenguer, also a general, to succeed him as prime minister, almost everyone was aware that he was playing his last card, and that it was exactly a *naipe comodín* (wild card). All that was needed in fact were municipal elections, which were held on the 12th April 1931. The Government won but lost seats in the main cities, with the result that the people demanded a Republic and threw out the Monarchy.

However, the sacrifice of Alfonso XIII, an attractive historical figure, had been in vain. Although the Republic, which began under Niceto Alcalá Zamora and finished with Manuel Azaña as President (both great politicians in spite of everything) gave more freedom to the people, it ended in war and the subsequent division of Spain into two factions. This was never more vividly expressed than in the prophetic verses of the famous Spanish poet Antonio Machado, who died in exile at Coillioure in France within a few weeks of the end of the war.

> **"Little Spaniard who comes**
> **into the world, may God guard you.**
> **One of the two Spains**
> **must freeze your heart."**

The consequences of the War were devastating. Hundreds of thousands of Spaniards escaped death by fleeing the country (first into Europe, followed by a vast exodus to Central and South America), many others met their death, were imprisoned, suffered extreme poverty or were ostracized. For many years after the war there was little food or freedom in Spain. The country was isolated from the rest of the world as a result of the obstinacy of a visionary figure calling himself the Caudillo (Leader) of Spain and its Holy Crusade, and who considered himself responsible only to God and to History.

Nevertheless, the War gave some hope to Alfonso XIII who secretly felt that if General Franco were victorious, the Monarchy might be restored to him or his heir Juan, his fifth child and third son (heir since 1933 as a result of the written renunciations by his two elder brothers Alfonso and Jaime). He therefore sent Don Juan secretly to Spain offering to fight on Franco's side. Don Juan met with Franco's outright rejection: "Your Highness, your life is

The Bourbons

(The dynasty was established in 1700 by Philip of Anjou, grandson of Louis XIV of France, when the Austrian dynasty came to an end with the death of Charles II who left no heir. This led to a war of succession in Spain between the supporters of the French Bourbons and supporters of Archduke Charles of Austria who laid claim to the throne of Spain. The war, which lasted until 1714, resulted in the defeat of the Archduke and loss of his claim.)

Felipe V, Duke of Anjou (1700-1746)
Fernando VI (1746-1759)
Carlos III (1759-1788)
Carlos IV (1788-1808)
Fernando VII (1808 and 1814-1833) *
Isabel II (1833-1868) **
Alfonso XII (1876-1885) ***
Alfonso XIII (1886-1931)
Juan Carlos I (1975-) ****

*   After the invasion of Napoleon Bonaparte, his brother Joseph was made King (1808-1814). He left Spain when the Spanish forces won the so-called War of Independence.

**   Isabel II was three years old when she succeeded to the throne in 1833 on the death of her father. The Queen Mother, María Cristina de Borbón and the Generals Espartero and Narváez acted as Regents until 1843 when the Cortes declared that Isabel, then 13, had come of age. When she relinquished the throne in 1868 and went into exile in Paris, General Serrano acted as Regent (1868-1871). Amadeus of Aosta (1871-1873) then ascended to the throne and on his abdication the First Spanish Republic was created (February 1873-January 1874). Generals Pavía and Martínez Campos acted as Regents until Alfonso XII, son of Isabel II, returned to Spain in 1876.

***   Alfonso XIII was the posthumous son of Alfonso XII. He was born six months after the death of his father. His mother, the widowed Queen Cristina of Austria, was Regent until the Cortes declared him to have come of age in 1902.

****   The Second Spanish Republic was proclaimed in 1931. In 1936 Francisco Franco and other generals rose against the regime, signalling the start of a war which was to last until April 1939. Franco took power as a dictator until 1975 when he died in Madrid. Six years earlier (in July 1969) Franco's Parliament appointed Juan Carlos de Borbón, grandson of Alfonso XIII, as the General's "successor with the title of King". Don Juan de Borbón, Count of Barcelona, heir to Alfonso XIII, son of one king and father of another, was to be one of history's great victims and the missing link of the Bourbons.

With his parents, Don Juan de Borbón and Doña María de las Mercedes de Borbón in exile at the family home in Estoril.

too valuable to be put at risk in a war". This gave him hope which was to be quickly crushed.

The Monarch who came from exile

While in Rome in 1935, Don Juan de Borbón had married Doña María de las Mercedes de Borbón y Orleans, a royal princess of the House of the Two Sicilies, and now had a daughter, María del Pilar. In 1938, after two years of "waiting" in Rome, his second child Juan Carlos, the future King of Spain, was born. The family had just moved into a comfortable apartment in Viale di Parioli in a residential area of the Eternal City. Although adequate, it was hardly appropriate for someone who 37 years later was to become King of Spain.

Although this fair-haired rosy-cheeked child was not destined to be king by birth and only became king by chance through one of those strange quirks of history (the renunciation of his father's elder brothers mentioned earlier) there can be no doubt that he has turned out to be a gift from God to Spain. Since his father was the fifth son of King Alfonso XIII and Queen Victoria Eugenia (see the family tree at the beginning of the chapter), and therefore third in line of succession to the throne (under the Spanish Constitution the male line comes before the female), he neither expected nor aspired to become head of the House of Bourbon and the Spanish Royal Family. In fact, in 1928

when he was 15 years old Don Juan obtained permission from his father the King to attend the San Fernando Naval College in Cadiz, Spain since he hoped to reach the rank of admiral in the Spanish Navy. With the advent of the

With his father and the exiled Queen Mother, Victoria Eugenia, widow of Alfonso XIII and grandmother of Juan Carlos in Lausanne.

Republic this ambition was of course never fully achieved, although after the Royal Family left Spain, Juan de Borbón signed on in the British Royal Navy and did reach the rank of sub-lieutenant.

The heir, Alfonso, wanted to marry a Cuban citizen who was not a royal princess. A morganatic marriage such as this would have contravened a Special Royal Decree proclaimed in Spain at the end of the 18th century under which heirs to the throne were obliged to marry princesses or princes from royal houses. A few weeks before the marriage, without authorisation from King Alfonso XIII, the heir sent a document to the King voluntarily renouncing his and his descendants' claim to the throne. He was a haemophiliac, and died as a result of a traffic accident in the United States when he was 31, leaving no children. His younger brother Gonzalo had been killed in Austria four years earlier at the age of twenty, also as a result of a car accident.

This took place in 1933 and Jaime, the second son, became the new Prince of Asturias, a title which since 1344 all heirs have held until their coronation. However, Jaime was aware of his limitations and only a few days later he also wrote a similar letter to Alfonso XIII renouncing his claim and that of his sons, Alfonso and Gonzalo. The former, who died in 1989 in a foolish skiing accident in the United States, sought to take the place of Juan Carlos de Borbón during the last days of the Franco regime after marrying Franco's favourite granddaughter María del Carmen Martínez Bordíu Franco in 1972.

Unlike his brothers Alfonso and Gonzalo, Jaime had not contracted haemophilia, a rare disease where the blood is unable to coagulate properly, transmitted through the female line but which only affects males; in those days, sufferers of the disease tended to die young from haemorrhaging. Haemophilia had been brought into the Royal Family by the English Victoria Eugenia and was the source of frequent quarrels between her and Alfonso XIII, so much so that when they were in exile, although they were never officially separated, the King lived in Rome while the Queen settled in Lausanne. However, Jaime became deaf and dumb at the age of four as the result of a double mastoid operation (during which the auditory bone was forcibly broken) and was considered unfit to take on the responsibility involved. In addition, two years later he too married a commoner, Emmanuela Dampierre, whose parents, though aristocrats, were not members of a royal family, and this would in any case have made him ineligible for the throne.

This, then, is how Don Juan de Borbón, then 21, and his future children moved up to become the heir to the throne. In addition to Princess María del Pilar and Prince Juan Carlos there were to be two other children - Alfonso and Margarita. Alfonso died at the family home in Portugal in 1956 when he was almost fifteen as a result of another unfortunate accident when his brother Juan Carlos, two years older, was playing with a small revolver belonging to their father without realising that there was a bullet in the chamber.

It was in 1941 that Don Juan was to become the head of the Spanish Royal Family, when Alfonso XIII became seriously ill with a heart condition from which he had been suffering for some time, and died at the Grand Hotel in Rome at the relatively young age of 54. He had abdicated all his rights in favour of his son Juan, then 28, some six weeks earlier.

The Spanish Civil War had ended two years earlier and the Royal Family was still in a state of confusion as to the intentions of General Franco, who had appointed himself head of state and permanent head of the Spanish Government. On the one hand, *el general* (as the Bourbons referred to Franco) was sending out what were at once interpreted as smoke signals to Rome, saying that he intended to restore the Monarchy "when the time came". On the other hand however, Don Juan, and Alfonso XIII during his last months, had each begun to fear that Franco's true intentions were to invest himself with absolute dictatorial powers. In 1942 Don Juan and the Royal Family decided to move from the war-torn city of Rome to the peace of Lausanne in Switzerland, where Victoria Eugenia, the Queen Mother (who died there in 1969) was still living in exile. It was also there that Don Juan made his first public statements to the "Journal de Geneve" reminding Franco that the monarchy was the secular Spanish institution and that he was its head. These were followed by other statements, each more pointed than the last.

It was not until 1945, in a historic document known as the "Lausanne Manifesto", that Don Juan officially broke

Franco (on the right) announcing the appointment of Juan Carlos de Borbón as his successor "with the title of king" to Parliament.

off relationships with the Franco regime after denouncing the General as a dictator who had usurped power. He demanded that he should resign, recognise his failure and make way for the Monarchy as the only institution capable of reconciling the two Spains and offering a system of freedom and democracy. This system, which he spelt out in detail, was to provide basically the same freedom and democracy that the Spaniards enjoy today under Juan Carlos I.

The King presides over the ceremony of the burial of his predecessor as Head of State, General Francisco Franco.

Franco's response was to prohibit the Spanish media from publishing any reference not only to the Manifesto but also to Don Juan himself, who was then subjected to a national campaign to discredit him, carried out by various public legislative bodies and by Franco's ruling party. In addition, a Law of Succession was devised and proclaimed by the Franco Parliament in 1947 after a dubious referendum in which there were almost more "yes" votes than possible votes. This law established that his successor would hold the "title of king" but did not specify who this was to be, only that he would have to be Spanish, male, over 30, Catholic and of Royal blood.

This amounted to permanent blackmail of Don Juan de Borbón by Franco since, apart from Don Juan who historically was the only person who could legitimately be the King of Spain, this legal device of Franco's had made the way clear for other claimants. Franco had also included an article in the law to reserve the right to "disinherit" his "successor with the title of king" and appoint another person.

A democratic Trojan horse

However, a historical paradox occurred when the all-powerful Franco turned his attention to his adversary's son, Prince Juan Carlos. It was then 1948; in 1946 the Royal Family had moved from Lausanne, where they had been living quietly, to a chalet known as "Les Rocailles" in Estoril near Lisbon in Portugal, in order to follow Spanish affairs more closely and make it easier for contacts to be made with the hundreds of thousands of Monarchists in Spain. It was Franco who convinced Don Juan that his elder son should study and be educated in Spain, otherwise he would be considered a foreigner.

It is clear today that there was more than the personal regard for the Prince which the General developed over a period of time, somewhat ironically as if for the son he never had (he only had one daughter). Franco also saw in Juan Carlos an opportunity to bridge the gap between his "Monarchy of 18th July" (the date of the Army coup in 1936 and symbol of his long dictatorship) and the legitimate claim of the Bourbons to the throne, although this meant Don Juan would have to renounce his rights - rights which in any case the General totally ignored. Don Juan, a magnanimous man who had experienced the "democratic unscrupulousness" of the Dictator within the country and abroad for over three decades, quietly and regretfully made one of the great sacrifices in history by renouncing his privilege. He was a real gentleman, and after almost 40 years of censure, humiliation and insults from Franco, with the country now a democracy, the Spanish people were grateful to him for his efforts, with all that this involved in terms of his personal health. He was the son of a king and father of a king but he had never worn the Crown. It was a case similar to that of the eldest son of Louis XIV of France.

Consequently, the student prince Juan Carlos de Borbón left his first boarding school, the now-vanished Ville Saint Jean, at Freibourg. He used to spend the weekends there with his grandmother Queen Victoria Eugenia who, rather than moving to Portugal, preferred to remain with her memories in the quiet town of Lausanne in a pretty lakeside house known as "Vielle Fontaine". The present king has fond memories of this time spent with her. His secondary education took place in San Sebastian near France, decided on in the waters off this same city, during a tense interview on board Franco's yacht. His three years' military training and university education were also completed in Spain. He was thus able to make contacts with university staff and army instructors who were to play key roles on the road he was to take towards democracy as soon as he was crowned King in 1975.

On 22 July 1969 Franco proposed to "his" Parliament that Prince Juan Carlos - who at 31 was a year older than the required age - should be his successor. The response was overwhelmingly in favour. The six long years which were to pass until his coronation proved to be a true road of thorns for both Don Juan and Prince Juan Carlos. In addition to the great humiliation Don Juan suffered, many underhand attempts were made by all sources of Francoist power to set father and son against each other, though they fortunately never succeeded.

The inner insecurity Juan Carlos de Borbón suffered while he was living in the country, the absence of any kind of political activity (denied him by the regime he was to replace), the constant supervision and watchful eye of people in Franco's confidence, together with the Spanish people's lack of knowledge about his personality, his background and his duties (non-existent as he was an heir with no public engagements) had all combined to paint him as a weak character, devoid of personality and ideas for the future. Although there was no factual basis for this, as history was to demonstrate only too clearly, it was something that the opposition to the Franco regime exploited shamelessly, even going so far as to approach the "King Father" Don Juan. Instead of the democrat Don Juan was considered to be all his life, here was an "ambitious young man" intent on doing whatever was necessary to wear the crown, even if this meant going along with the whims of the Dictator against his father's wishes.

It appeared that a democratic "king" was up against a future "puppet" king. However, what few people were aware of at the time was that father and son had in fact agreed on this deception. It was an act which, while biding his time and drawing up plans for democracy, Juan Carlos concealed right up to the end. A pretence of submission to Franco, it was nothing short of a sort of legitimate "treason" against the Dictator, taking a democratic Trojan horse into the very heart of the Francoist regime in order to get the nation back into the mainstream of democracy in the old continent of Europe when the time came. All this was to put him in an unassailable position, shortly after his Coronation on the death of Franco, to surprise the world by transforming a cruel bloody dictatorship (Franco's last act, two months before his death, was to order the execution of

The present Queen of Spain, Doña Sofia, as a young girl.

five members of the terrorist organizations ETA and GRAPO) into a young, advanced democracy.

This was the reward for so much sacrifice during the dark years. In 1975/1976 political reform was promoted with great enthusiasm and the Dictator's complicated legal framework (having widely boasted that he had left everything "well tied up") was dismantled in strict compliance with the law. According to all surveys and opinion polls carried out since 1977, when free elections were held with all political parties legalised and participating, the Crown has been considered the most valuable institution by the people of Spain, although there has always been some difference of opinion as to which came second.

Queen Sofia after her engagement to the present King.

The King and Queen during their marriage ceremony in Athens, May 1962.

The King and Queen and their children (from left to right, Elena, Cristina and Felipe) before the King ascended to the throne.

King Juan Carlos I and Queen Sofia at an official engagement.

An official dinner at La Zarzuela Palace. President George Bush and ex-President Mikhail Gorbachev with King Juan Carlos I and Felipe González during the Madrid Peace Conference, October 1991.

Official

During the three years from the death of Franco on the 20th November 1975 until 28th December 1978 when Juan Carlos I sanctioned the Spanish Constitution, the King was the true driving force behind the change from a frightened humiliated people to a country free for all Spaniards, in the same way as any of its neighbours.

The King who brought democracy

This change, known in Spain as the "political transition", could probably have been carried out much faster, but it was unusual in that there were no serious upheavals in the process. This was despite the fact that the whole State machinery from the political system, administration, the repressive police, obedient legal authorities, central-ised decision-making, and the numerous sinecures enjoyed by those in various posts in the then one-party state, etc., had been planned so that all the power lay in the hands of the Dictator. His heir, permitted only a minimum of pow-er, strangely was not Juan Carlos de Borbón, as would have been logical, but his "right-hand man" throughout his life, Admiral Louis Carrero Blanco, finally appointed prime minister by the General in June 1973. However, he only

held office for six months as he was assassinated by ETA in Madrid on the 20th December that same year in one of the most spectacular attacks in the history of terrorism.

Juan Carlos I had already given some, albeit timid, indications that a new stage in the history of Spain was beginning in his first speech to the country on the day his predecessor died. He acted with such a mixture of prudence, astuteness and political courage that he broke up the Francoist apparatus without causing serious public disorder or bloodshed - apart from attacks by ETA, the extreme Ultramontane right, and GRAPO, an extraordinary terrorist organization the heads of which had been removed by the police on several occasions but which grew again like snakes.

During these six years as "successor with the title of king", Juan Carlos I had patiently and carefully worked out a plan and strategy. The only people who knew all the details of his strategy were his father, Don Juan, who finally became his principal adviser and another key figure in the transition, and Torcuatro Fernández Miranda, who was the Prince's director of studies. The King appointed him Speaker of Parliament as soon as he was crowned - a key position from which to promote the reform of the Funda-

The Barcelona Olympic Games Opening Ceremony.

The King waving to spectators at the Madrid bullring.

mental Laws (a pseudo-Constitution of the Franco regime), transforming them into a legal framework that would facilitate elections being held in as short a time as possible.

And that is exactly what happened. Others were involved alongside Fernández Miranda, but one who stood out among them was the man who actually executed the strategy prepared by the King, and was directed by the monarch at a distance. This was Adolfo Suárez, appointed prime minister a few months after the death of Franco and a man whose name will also go down in Spanish history as having won two consecutive general elections. The first was in 1977, for which his provisional government had cleared the way legally, and the second was after the new Constitu-

The King and Queen of Spain with King Baudouin and Queen Fabiola of Belgium and Princess Elena.

regime, who had despised him in his role as successor to Franco, had to take back their dire predictions for the future and the tasteless phrases they had coined (such as *Juan Carlos I El Breve*, Juan Carlos I The Brief) and other even worse epithets, as landmarks of freedom unheard of in 1975 were being achieved.

Don Juan de Borbón, who was still in exile in Estoril (Portugal), made another gesture which certainly contributed much to the general feeling. On the 14th May 1977, only a month before the election, he made over all his rights to his son at a private ceremony at La Zarzuela

tion (1978) had come into force, making him the first prime minister of a Spanish constitutional government since the time of the Republic.

During the three years from 1975 to 1978 the two Spains (the winner and the loser of the civil war) became fully reconciled. Political exiles returned and wide political amnesty was granted. The freedom of the press, freedom of speech and the right to hold meetings and demonstrations were restored. The Law of Political Reform permitting free elections to be held was devised and all political parties were legalised. But the masterpiece of political transition was, above all, the creation of the 1978 Constitution: a modern, progressive constitution with the future in mind. Moreover, it was a constitution created with the consensus of all the political parties. It was a valuable piece of legislation which signalled the reconstruction of Spanish democracy, impoverished after so many years of dictatorship.

King Juan Carlos I was firmly in control behind the scenes, moving each piece on a precariously balanced chessboard. All the opposition to the Falangist

Palace, considering him to have complied with all the requirements he had laid down for this eventuality. The many Spanish Monarchists were deeply moved; it captured the attention of the many more who were neutral, and the Republicans were put on their guard. Yet another historical anomaly had occurred: the heir to the throne had reigned for 18 months, while the head of the Royal Family remained discreetly and quietly in retirement.

Queen Sofia during a visit to Bolivia.

Juan Carlos I greets the wife of the President of Columbia on an official visit.

The King who reigns but does not govern

On that day 28th December 1978, the King, who had sanctioned the Constitution he had so ardently desired, took his rightful place as a king who reigned but did not govern, although he would continue to assist in working hard for democracy. The Charter gave him the duties which he had planned for himself during the dark years of the Franco regime, namely to be the symbol of unity and continuity of Spain, the arbitrator and moderator of the normal functioning of institutions and to represent the State, albeit with few political powers. These are limited primarily to sanctioning and proclaiming laws, summoning and dissolving Parliament, calling elections when they are proposed by the prime minister and convening referenda in accordance with the Constitution. He also has the power to propose the candidate for the office of prime minister and, if necessary, to appoint him in accordance

with election results, as well as to appoint and dismiss government ministers proposed by the prime minister, issue decrees agreed in the Council of Ministers, hold the post of Supreme Commander of the Armed Forces (Government is responsible for the defence policy), appoint ambassadors, authorise international agreements in accordance with the corresponding articles in the Charter, and declare war and sign peace treaties when so authorised by Parliament.

It is clear from this list he does indeed have very few powers. However, they are the ones necessary to enable him to arbitrate and moderate in politics from a neutral position with regard to parties and institutions, and at the same time to protect all of the people.

And this he did with great courage on the 23rd February 1981 when a large group of civil guards, led by Lieutenant-Colonel Antonio Tejero, carried out a spectacular coup taking over a full session of the Congress of Deputies, the Government and a large number of senators

The King and Queen during an official visit to Saudi Arabia.

The King congratulates a young civil guard who has just completed her training.

Joking with the Prime Minister, Felipe González after the King's skiing accident.

and holding them at gun point. They were at an extraordinary session to vote on the investiture of Leopoldo Calvo Sotelo, the second prime minister of the Constitutional Government, replacing Adolfo Suárez, who had submitted his resignation to the King after holding office for almost five years.

The true democrats who can remember the details of that sad event (which led to the imprisonment of, amongst others, the charismatic Lieutenant General Jaime Milans del Bosch and General Alfonso Armada, who for many years was one of the people in whom the King confided) spent some of the worst hours of their lives. It looked as if, with neither Government nor Parliament at the head of the nation, the six years of sacrifice to establish democracy and liberty had vanished in a few hours and the military dictatorship had returned.

However, the leaders of the coup, who had conducted

Heads of state and prime ministers of the Latin American countries at a summit meeting at the Madrid Royal Palace, July 1992.

a well-planned lightning operation, bringing out the tanks in Valencia and light artillery in Madrid, occupying (albeit somewhat amateurishly) television and radio stations and newspaper offices and generally following the recognised procedures for a coup, had forgotten to take the one key person into their calculations: King Juan Carlos. Dressed in the full uniform of Field Marshal, he confronted the rebels from his official office and, with extraordinary courage, gave orders for civil and military action. He set up a provisional government consisting of the "number twos" from each Ministry and gave his approval for orders to be sent out from the Army High Command to those Army headquarters and regiments throughout the country which were not involved in the conspiracy in order to maintain normality and force the rebels to surrender. These critical hours were concluded with a message the King managed to record and broadcast on television, which ended in the break-up of the coup and the arrest of the leaders.

After being detained for almost twenty-four hours, the first act of the leaders of the political parties, together with Adolfo Suárez - who was still the acting prime minister - was to go to La Zarzuela Palace to congratulate the King. He had saved the democracy from the most severe test it has had to undergo in the 18 years of his reign. For months and even years it was said that Juan Carlos had made more monarchists in a single day than his predecessors had in many years.

Possibly the greatest test for this young democracy was the arrival in power of the Socialist Party in 1982, with Felipe González as prime minister. This took place only

The King and Queen and their children with the Prime Minister, Felipe González and his wife.

The King and Queen receive an award at La Zarzuela Palace.

Chairing an ordinary meeting of the National Defence Committee.

The Royal Family at the opening of the Universal Exposition in Seville, April 1992.

seven years after the death of Franco, who had left everything "well tied up", but there was no upheaval amongst the civilian population in Spain who saw a change in power as being quite normal, in spite of the fact that there was no culture of democracy as there is today. Many people consider the end of the transition to be marked by the historic photograph taken on the 2nd December 1982 showing the young socialist, Felipe González, aged 40, beside the King of all Spaniards, Juan Carlos I, aged 44, as a symbol of the new, strongly emerging, democratic Spain.

The prestige of the Crown extends beyond Spain. Although foreign policy is the sole responsibility of the government, the King has made about 100 official visits abroad during his reign, spanning practically all the principal countries which share a common interest with Spain. He has been to all European countries - with the strange exception of Greece (Queen Sofia comes from the Greek Royal Family, now in exile), North, Central and South America - but not to Cuba (since neither the government nor the King support the dictator Fidel Castro), and to the leading countries of the other three continents.

Throughout his reign Juan Carlos I has been the symbol of the new Spain in the eyes of the rest of the world, a

modern progressive Spain which has rapidly been improving its relations with neighbouring countries. His influence has been such that the doors of what had up until recently been closed institutions (the Council of Europe, NATO and the European Community, etc.) have been opening up to Spain.

His heir, Felipe de Borbón, the Prince of Asturias, who at 25 is the embodiment of the values of Spanish youth, appears to be following in his footsteps with similar success. He is also one of the new instruments of foreign policy and is an important ambassador for Spain, a role he hopes to continue in the future.

Private

Although they could have taken up residence in the magnificent mid-18th century Royal Palace in Madrid, in keeping with all their predecessors from Carlos III (its first resident in 1764) to Alfonso XIII who left in 1931, the King and Queen prefer to use the small palace of La Zarzuela as their residence. La Zarzuela, where they have been living for the last 13 years, is situated in the El Pardo hills north-west of Madrid, not far from the palace of the same name which was Franco's residence until his death, and which is now used for foreign heads of state on official visits to Spain.

Living simply in a small palace

One thing the Bourbons have been quick to learn has been the history of Spain, since it might well be considered the history of their own dynasty. Juan Carlos I realised that the splendid Royal Palace was one of the reasons for the loss of the monarchy under his grandfather Alfonso XIII. Felipe V, who established the Bourbon dynasty in Spain, ordered the palace built on the ruin of the Alcázar of the Kings, which was burnt down on Christmas Eve 1734. *El rey francés* (the French king), yearning for the palace at Versailles, attempted to build a palace of a similar design, although its architectural style is not quite the same.

The Royal Palace, Madrid, used only for official events.

This was why Juan Carlos decided to carry on living at La Zarzuela, leaving the Royal Palace for the great ceremonial events. This sign of austerity, his first gesture, pleased the people. It was the same thing with the "containing wall" they erected between themselves and those who longed to form part of the Court of their dreams. The new Royal Family only intended to hold those ceremonial receptions required by protocol, with no grand celebrations, balls or other entertainments. It was their wish to remain the family they had always been - albeit a Royal Family - and live in the same small palace. Both the heir to the throne and his two elder sisters, the Infantas (princesses) Elena and Cristina, were to have their secondary education in schools rather than at the palace. They were to attend normal schools, have normal friends of their own age and generation and take part in as many normal activities as security would allow. (In November 1975 Elena was 12, Cristina 10 and Felipe 7, while the King and Queen were both 37.)

La Zarzuela Palace, the official residence of the King and Queen.

Prince Juan Carlos de Borbón married Princess Sofia of Greece in May 1962. She is a daughter of King Paul and Queen Frederica, both of whom are now dead, and the elder sister of King Constantine, who was removed from the Greek throne by the "colonels' coup" in 1967. The wedding was held with full ceremony in Athens in accordance with both Catholic and Greek Orthodox rites and followed by a honeymoon of over four months spent travelling around the world. Franco arranged for La Zarzuela to be their residential palace. Most people thought that the General would wait for six years to pass so that the Prince would comply with the final requirement if he wished to succeed to the throne, as he had to be over thirty (he was twenty-four when he married). The decision came on the 22nd July 1969 when he was over thirty-one and the three children of the marriage had been born (Elena 1963, Cristina

The spanish family together with Prince Charles and Princess Diana and their children.

1965, and Felipe 1968). It was as though Franco had been waiting for the birth of a boy, the "heir to the heir" who would ensure a "successor to the successor", part of his strange arrangement the "Monarchy of 18th July", which is in fact what happened.

La Zarzuela, like other small palaces in the neighbourhood such as La Quinta or La Casita de El Escorial (which Prince Juan Carlos had also used as an official residence) once belonged to the state. It had just been rebuilt, having been almost destroyed during the civil war. It was a simple two-floor building which has been extended over the years during the reign of the present King to fulfil his ever increasing requirements for new buildings such as offices, security and domestic services, a heliport and other facilities. A substantial area of the El Pardo hills has also been fenced in to encircle it.

A "poor" Royal family

Although more buildings have been added and security and communications systems have become more sophisticated to fulfil the needs of a modern head of the state, King Juan Carlos' official functions have increased tenfold. During the year the King receives some 25 heads of state or government together with numerous ministers and senior representatives of other countries or international or-

ganizations and institutions and, official engagements permitting, citizens or organizations and institutions who request an audience. Despite this, austerity is still one of the keynotes in the way the Crown functions. The King's state allowance for 1993 amounts to little over 900 million pesetas (approximately 8 million dollars at the present rate of exchange) on which he has not only to keep his family, associates and employees, but also to pay all the expenses of the Royal Household, apart from, of course, travelling expenses and expenses for official activities which are met by the government.

In spite of being one of the oldest in the world, the Spanish Royal Family is also one of the poorest. It should not be forgotten that King Alfonso XIII died in a hotel room in Rome; Queen Victoria Eugenia, his wife, lived for forty years in a house ("Vielle Fontaine") in Lausanne which could have made a fitting residence for a well-to-do businessman; Juan Carlos I was born in a comfortable but simple apartment in a block of flats. Prior to this, his parents had lived in an equally simple chalet at Lausanne in Switzerland, then in an ex-golf club office in Estoril in Portugal and finally, after returning from exile in the middle of the eighties, in another similarly modest property in Madrid.

In the past, during the time of Ferdinand and Isabella, and of the Austrian dynasty, the Spanish crown had been

One of the last photographs together of the King's mother and father, Don Juan de Borbón and Doña María de las Mercedes de Borbón.

The Royal Family. The King and Queen with their parents, children, sisters, brothers and sisters-in-law, nieces and nephews.

amongst the richest institutions in the world. Then, the Spanish ships and galleons were coming back from the Indies and the Antilles, laden with gold and treasures beyond price. Today the Spanish monarchy has few jewels and little property. Squandering by certain kings, invasion and looting, as in the times of Napoleon, incompetent regencies, other misfortunes and, in general, the poor administration of the property and the short-sighted view taken by some of their predecessors have resulted in the Royal Family being relatively poor compared with the households of other monarchs today.

Among the most important remaining jewels are the crown and sceptre which are kept in the Royal Palace and are both of incalculable value. The King and Queen are not known to have any estates of their own and have little private wealth. If such information were available, the Royal Family would probably not figure among the 500 richest families in the country. The Royal Palace, La Zarzuela and other palaces such as Granja de San Ildefonso, Aranjuez, El Escorial monastery, Yuste, Poblet, among others, are available for the Crown's use (although the present King and Queen have not even stayed temporarily in them), but are state-owned property, as are the many pictures, tapestries, carpets, furniture and many other extremely valuable effects in them. Not even Marivent in Majorca, the palace where they have spent each summer

The King skiing in the Spanish Pyrenees.

The King and Queen, Prince and Princesses during an official engagement.

The King in Majorca dressed for sailing.

for the last thirty years, belongs to the Royal Family (it is the property of the autonomous government of the Balearic Islands), although they have the use of it for life. All the official gifts they receive, apart from cars and other practical items, may be used temporarily by any member of the Family but are registered as general state property.

It has not been money that has supported Juan Carlos I along the path he has adopted, or if it has it has not been obvious, but the principles of democracy, modernity, progress and social justice. It is something of which at his age he feels proud (he was 55 in 1993). His father, Don Juan de Borbón, was often forced to accept donations from well-known, rich *juanistas* (his supporters) in order to maintain the dignity of the Royal House in exile and keep the monarchic cause alive Prince Juan Carlos was educated at state-owned boarding schools and institutions in Spain, and has always had to rely on the Treasury both for his and his family's expenses.

Among the few activities not frowned upon while the Prince and Princess lived in Spain were their overseas trips and visits to the spanish provinces. Not even the most bitter Franco supporters were opposed to their frequent travels; far from it, the further away they went the better, and that included the provinces. These trips not only helped Juan Carlos and Sofia to become better acquainted with the world they would be dealing with in the future, they

Princess Cristina (on the right) with her Greek cousin Alexia in Barcelona during the 1992 Olympic Games.

The King and Queen, the Prince, Princesses and government ministers cheering one of the Spanish teams during the Olympic Games.

also helped them to compare Spain's "organic" democracy (as Franco called it) with real democracy. During that period they made friends and established relationships with world leaders such as Gerald Ford, later to become President of the United States, and the President of Germany, Walter Scheel, and his French counterpart, Valery Giscard d'Estaing, amongst many others. These contacts were to prove invaluable during the first months and years of the new monarchic regime. The Prince and Princess had had to depend on financial help from pro-Royal ministries in funding their visits.

The two elder children, Princesses Elena and Cristina, having finished their studies, are now working. The heir to the throne, Prince Felipe, who is now 25 and is about to finish reading Law and Economics at university (June 1993) and three years' military training, receives an allowance from his parents of about 1.5 million pesetas (approximately 12,500 dollars) a year for his expenses. Princess Elena is teaching at a special education school in

Madrid, while continuing her studies at the university. Princess Cristina, who has a degree in Political Science, attended post-graduate courses in New York, moving on to work for UNESCO (United Nations Organization for Education and Science) in Paris. She is now living in Barcelona and still works for UNESCO.

Queen Sofia has also had first-hand experience of hardship. She was only two years old when Mussolini invaded Greece in 1940, and she was forced into exile, along with the rest of the Royal Family headed by her parents Paul and Frederica, settling in Cape Town, South Africa, until they were able to return to their country at the end of the Second World War. When she was twelve, she was sent to boarding school in Germany. Some years later, in 1967, after she had married Juan Carlos, she had the unhappiness of seeing the overthrow of her brother King Constantine.

A modest wise Royal family

From the start the Royal Family's code of conduct has emphasised the virtues of modesty, prudence and discretion, their main aim being never to put a foot wrong - an overly cautious code which, if continued, might well harm the monarchy since when they are not at official or ceremonial events they avoid the press. In fact, if one looks through newspaper and magazine, sound and film archives, there are few reports or interviews to make use of.

This behaviour probably came about because neither the Queen nor her children wanted to divert attention from the King in his important work during the first few years. The Prince and Princesses were only children in 1975, and they attended a middle class fee-paying school near La Zarzuela where over the years some of their best friendships were made, including with their Greek cousins and other members of royalty. Later, at university they again received very little publicity. In fact, to date the number of in-depth interviews given by the two Princesses amount to fewer than a dozen.

The situation was different for the heir to the throne, the youngest of the three children but first in line of succession. Even so, since his investiture as Prince of Asturias when he was eight years old, he was given very few official duties to perform, almost up to the time he began his university preparation course at Lakefield College School near Toronto in Canada, a college which was also attended by Prince Andrew of Great Britain.

As stated earlier, it is probably true that too much emphasis was placed on caution and discretion, so that the average man in the street in Spain, who knew the history of Juan Carlos I well, and to a lesser extent that of the Queen, only began to get to know the Prince and Princesses when they were already adults. There are still many facets of both Princesses which are not known at all. This is due partly to the Queen's over-protection of her daughters, and partly to a mixture of shyness and reserve about their private lives which they almost take to extremes, especially in the case of the youngest, Princess Cristina.

Until three years ago, the same thing applied to Prince Felipe, who began to take on an increasing number of official duties (visits, attending official and royal events, receptions, audiences, etc.) when he was half-way through his university course. As soon as his romance with the young Isabel Sartorius, an aristocrat and a university student, became known, he was hounded by the media. Media attention subsequently reverted to a reasonable level, bearing in mind that the Prince is almost 26, and the issue of who he marries, and who is therefore Spain's future Queen, is a matter of legitimate public interest. In particular there is a continuing debate as to whether he should marry a royal princess or not.

The fact is that Isabel Sartorius, Prince Felipe's first serious girlfriend, does not have blue blood. This has led to a lively debate in the country over whether or not the ruling on morganatic marriage (marriage out of one's own rank) should still apply, since precisely for that reason Don

Juan's elder brothers had to renounce their rights in his favour with the result, albeit indirectly, that the father of Felipe de Borbón was crowned because of a personal decision by Franco. The so-called "legitimists" are consequently arguing that Prince Felipe should comply with the Royal Sanction Decree which, since the time of Carlos III over two hundred years ago, obliges heirs to the throne to contract "equal" marriages. However, the counter-argument is actually flawless. The Spanish Constitution of 1978 lays down for the first time the conditions under which marriages of heirs may be contracted, and simply states that "a marriage may not be contracted against the will of the King and Parliament", with the result that, in the opinion of the majority of lawyers, this earlier Bourbon provision is "revoked".

Apart from that, the question has already been "settled" by the Prince himself who has stated on several occasions in recent years that he would marry "for love and anyone he wished", and that he was only prepared to comply with the Constitution. As recently as October 1992, however, he said that he was not contemplating marriage in the near future. This is another aspect which is hardly ideal, since the very essence of a dynasty is to ensure succession down the first line.

During the last eighteen years the Royal Family has clearly shown a professionalism in keeping with the times, an attitude of self-denial towards its work, a sense of responsibility in its approach towards the government (it is the government which is responsible for the king's official agenda). They have also demonstrated, albeit to a lesser extent than before, a visible presence in the daily life of the country. All the members of the royal family are keen on sport; they share a love of culture and tradition (though they have never lost sight of the importance of being in tune with the times and progress); they still remain the symbol of modern Spain and are loved and respected by the people. Opinion polls over many years have indicated that the monarchy has been and still is the institution that the people of Spain most value.

The family as individuals

Those who know the King always remark on his warm and friendly nature and his spontaneity, qualities which make whoever he happens to be speaking to feel instantly at ease, and of his ability to put himself on the same level as his interlocutor no matter who he or she might be. He has been and still is a great sportsman. He has always been keen on sailing and skiing and anything involving speed. He likes cars and engines, although a (fortunately minor) accident and his age have slowed him down a little. Most outstanding of all, however, is his professionalism - to be king does not mean being *divertido* (having fun) 365 days of the year. He has a sense of statesmanship and of his historic responsibility to maintain and to pass on to his son, at the appropriate time, the prestige, respect and affection which his people give him.

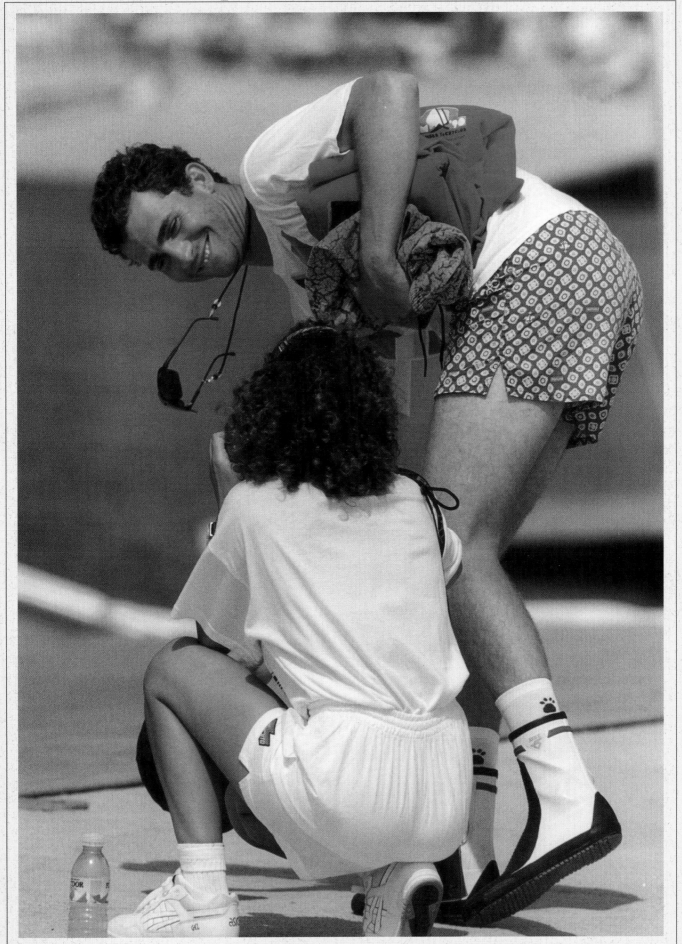

The heir to the throne was a member of the Spanish Olympic sailing team and was awarded sixth place and a certificate.

Princess Elena is an outstanding sportswoman.

has contributed much to promoting sport in Spain, and the success of Spanish competitors at the Olympic Games in Barcelona in 1992 was a great source of satisfaction to them. One of the successful competitors was the heir to the throne who was a member of one of the sailing teams that won sixth place and obtained an Olympic certificate.

Their keenness to keep abreast with what is going on in the city and in the country as a whole, means not only that they hold thousands of audiences at La Zarzuela during the year, but that they also pay surprise visits to restaurants, concerts, fashionable bars, etc., both in Madrid and in Baqueira Beret, their favourite skiing resort in the Spanish Pyrenees - although the King likes to ski in the French and Swiss Alps. This is especially true for the Prince and Princesses, who on occasion can be glimpsed at fashionable nightspots. They are particularly keen on sailing and take part in regattas in Majorca. It is there, during their annual summer holiday which lasts for about five weeks, official engagements permitting, that they feel really at ease. They have not missed a year yet, and count the weeks and even days for the summer to come so that they can go to Marivent, a beautiful site overlooking the Mediterranean.

The Heir to the Throne, Felipe de Borbón, has deliberately been left to last. He shows a mix of all of the qualities of the other members of his family, possibly with less spontaneity and less natural friendliness than his father, but for all that no less warmth. He represents the future values of the young people in Spain as we near the year 2000, while present concerns and Spain's most pressing problems are never far from his thoughts: unemployment, terrorism, the current poor economic situation and the disappearance of certain values from society today.

He also devotes time to official and ceremonial duties, both of which he carries out with great professionalism, although he also knows how to safeguard his privacy and make the most of his free time. He is known to be keen to improve himself intellectually and he is very aware of the fact that he must become the principal "asset" of the monarchy in the future. He knows that, at a time when questions are being asked about the future of the monarchy, when he will reign as Felipe VI of Spain, he will have to make every effort - as one feels sure he will - to ensure the continuity of the monarchy and democracy in Spain.

The Queen's best known quality is usually thought to be her keen intellect and sense of responsibility in her role as Queen. She is strongly enthusiastic about culture and has a passion for music, though she has other little-known hobbies such as astronomy (which her son has inherited), parapsychological phenomena and archaeology. She avoids frivolity and adheres strictly to protocol whenever she appears in public. It is possibly because of this that some people think that she is too serious, too Germanic, and above all endeavours to be too "Germanising" in her relationships with the King and the Prince, though she has made a considerable effort to become a Spaniard and eve *borbonizarse* (become Bourbon) in order to understand the complex dynasty of which her husband is the latest King. She shares some of her husband and children's enthusiasm for skiing and their love of the sea.

The Royal Family's enthusiasm for sport - apart from being good skiers, Princess Elena is an accomplished horsewoman and Princess Cristina excels at sailing - was obvious from their constant presence and support at the Olympic Games in Barcelona. It would be no exaggeration to suggest that over the last twenty years the Royal Family

Sweden

By Bobby Andström

History

King Carl XVI Gustaf is the seventh in the line of Bernadotte to succeed to the Swedish throne. He became King on the 15th September 1973 when his grandfather King Gustav VI Adolf quietly passed away at the hospital in Helsingborg. The King is married to the beautiful Queen Silvia, his chosen bride, at an unforgettable wedding in Stockholm in the summer of 1976.

After a series of royal giants such as Gustav Vasa, Gustav II Adolf, Karl XII and Gustav III, the arrival of the Bernadotte dynasty on the Swedish royal scene was the exciting and interesting result of political games and remarkable coincidences. The afternoon of the 20th October 1810 saw the arrival at Helsingborg of the tallest of

King Oscar II, King of Sweden and Norway from 1872. He renounced the Norwegian throne in 1905 and died in 1907.

Napoleon's French marshals, also the Swedish Crown Prince Carl Johan. It was a solemn and historic moment which started a new era in Swedish history. Soldiers paraded proudly, huge crowds, the bourgeoisie and farmers, adults and children, all had appeared out of curiosity to catch a glimpse of the new Crown Prince and to see him take his first steps on Swedish soil. Somewhat surprised, the welcoming committee and the general public noticed that their tall guest had arrived alone, his wife Désirée and son Oscar having been left in Paris for unknown reasons.

Helsingborg in the south of Sweden subsequently became a trade centre and was to retain its royal connections in the future. Later generations of the Bernadotte family

Per Krafft's famous painting of Carl XIV Johan's coronation in Stockholm Cathedral on 11 May 1818.

The young Prince Carl Gustaf on a celebrated procession through the streets of Stockholm together with King Gustav V and his mother Princess Sibylla.

problems and stimulate the weak economy.

After a political revolution was 62 year old Karl XIII chosen as King in June 1809 to succeed his deposed and banished nephew Gustav IV Adolf. But Karl XIII was an indolent and prematurely aged man without children. He was ill for long periods and suffered number of strokes in 1809 which left him unable to govern. However, he remained popular with his people and had done a great deal to alleviate social suffering during his active life. He was married to Queen Hedvig Elisabet Charlotta, also the King's cousin. Although a couple of her children had died whilst still very young, the Queen was a very open and happy person. She was renowned for her extreme perspicacity and regularly wrote diaries which provide a us with a picture of court life at the beginning of the 19th century.

Many had hoped that Karl August, the Danish Prince adopted by Karl XIII, would become the new King of Sweden, but he disappeared rapidly from the royal scene when, during a military parade at Kvidinge just outside Helsingborg, he fell from his horse one day in 1810 and died, probably of a heart attack.

The incident would have merited little more than a mention in Europe's royal history had the death not been hot political stuff. A number of rumours began to circulate in the royal capital to the effect that the Crown Prince had been the victim of a coup and had been poisoned.

The finger was pointed at Marshal of the Realm Axel von Fersen and the Gustavians (those thought to be closely related to the deposed King Gustav IV Adolf and his family). A hate campaign of enormous proportions really got things going. When the funeral cortege for the dead Prince reached Stockholm, Fersen was pulled from the state coach and was murdered on the street by the mob. The police and military were helpless in the midst of the bloody drama.

The same afternoon as the murder of Axel von Fersen in Stockholm, two Swedish couriers arrived in Paris to announce that the Crown Prince Karl August had died. The new Crown Prince was to be the Danish Prince Frederik

and their relatives often spent their summers in the beautiful Sofiero summer palace west of Helsingborg. It was in Helsingborg in 1973 that King Gustav VI Adolf's life came to a close and the succession decree of 1810 brought his grandson Carl XVI Gustaf to the throne.

Jean Baptiste Bernadotte's journey across the open sea from Helsingør in Denmark via Öresund to Helsingborg in Sweden was delayed 24 hours by a storm. The day before, the new Crown Prince had renounced his Catholicism and had adopted the Evangelical faith.

The fact that Jean Baptiste Bernadotte, a French Marshal and General from Napoleon's army, became Crown Prince and later Swedish King in May 1818 was the result of a long and dramatic chain of events that was not without significance. Sweden found itself in crisis and had lost Finland to Russia whilst at war. The country needed a powerful head of state to get to grips with its

the throne with Napoleon's chain in his hand. For long periods he was not needed by Napoleon, but joined his idol at the Battle of the Three Emperors at Austerlitz in 1805. Shortly afterwards in 1806 Bernadotte was made Prince of Ponte Corvo, a little enclave with just over five thousand inhabitants, near the kingdom of Naples in Italy. He also acted as General Governor in Hamburg from 1807-1809. Marshal Bernadotte had not made his name as a gifted general, but as a skilled organiser and administrator for the Emperor. He was good with his soldiers in the field and was very humane towards captured enemy troops.

There has been some speculation that Bernadotte, having got over the initial shock, welcomed the Swedish offer and decided to accept in order to secure a future position at the highest level in France.

However, the matter was not closed; the Swedish government and parliament were yet to be convinced of Bernadotte's good points. Lieutenant Mörner, who

King Gustaf VI Adolf and Queen Louise enjoying the peaceful atmosphere of Sofiero Park near Helsingborg.

Christian of Augustenborg. The couriers were Carl Otto Mörner, aged 29 and a Lieutenant in the Uppland Regiment and Senior Adjutant August Anckarsvärd. It was widely known that Mörner did not sympathise with the King in Stockholm, but instead dreamed, along with many officers and political activists, of a French war hero acceding to the Swedish throne. A Danish Prince was out of the question for Mörner who believed that Sweden would then become little more than a Danish province. Such were the beginnings of a fantastic story which was to end with the youngest son of lawyer Henri Bernadotte from the small town of Pau in southern France becoming a great Swedish leader.

Lieutenant Mörner had no power whatsoever vested in him by the Swedish state to enter into negotiations in Paris concerning the Swedish throne. Nevertheless, he contacted several of Napoleon's war heroes and asked whether they wished to become King of Sweden. However, all declined for one reason or another. But when he asked Marshal Jean Baptiste Bernadotte, the answer, after some deliberation, was yes. The marshal's career luck had changed, during the revolution he had been promoted from a private to general. When Napoleon proclaimed the Empire in the spring of 1804, he became a French Marshal and on the day of the coronation he stood beside

The young Prince and his grandfather Gustav VI Adolf.

The young Prince Carl Gustaf loved life at Haga.

helped the lawyer's son from Pau to become the successor to the Swedish throne. The 21st of August 1810 marked the official election of the French Marshal as Crown Prince by the Swedish Parliament. He was 47 years old. In November of the same year, Carl Johan (Bernadotte) was adopted by King Karl XIII and Queen Hedvig Elisabet Charlotta. He became the Crown Prince of Norway four years later.

On the 2nd November 1810, the former General in the revolution was received in Stockholm. He bided his time at Drottningholm Palace for this occasion. The crowds were out, the city was decorated to greet the new Crown Prince and the military was also present lest something unforseen should occur. However, everything went off smoothly and he delighted the people's love of pageantry. Three days later the Crown Prince gave his oath to King Karl XIII in the banqueting hall of the Stockholm Palace and received homage from all four classes of Swedish society. The oath was administered by Engeström who had worked so actively to ensure that Bernadotte was chosen at Örebro.

If the arrival of the Crown Prince had been celebrated with noise and jubilation, the arrival of Crown Princess Désirée was something of an anti-climax. She had left Paris, and her circle of friends, extremely reluctantly at the beginning of November in 1810 with her son Oscar and arrived in Helsingborg, somewhat belatedly, just before Christmas. The country which was to be her new home came as something of a shock. The climate, traditions and customs were not to her liking and when she

managed, by the skin of his teeth, to escape punishment upon his arrival home in Sweden, was placed under the next best thing to house arrest in Uppsala. This did not stop him fearlessly continuing his work to ensure Bernadotte's accession to the Swedish throne.

Sweden was in the midst of troubled times, and the parliament which dealt with issues of succession was moved from Stockholm to peaceful Örebro in the countryside to ensure that nothing could happen to disturb the peace. The King, government and committee which dealt with the matter were backing the Danish Prince Frederik Christian of Augustenborg.

Then, out of the blue, a French businessman by the name of Jean Antoine Fournier appeared on the scene as Jean Baptiste

Bernadotte's spokesman and supporter. Fournier, who had worked in Gothenburg for a time, was forceful in his proclamations that Bernadotte wished to accede to the throne. He had little to support him in his efforts other than a general letter of recommendation from the Swedish Consul in Paris and a toothpick case with a portrait of Jean Bernadotte's wife Désirée and son Oscar in the lid. Equipped with these as his only mandates and a number of liberal promises of a considerable sum of money from Bernadotte to be deposited with the Swedish Chancellor's Office, Fournier managed to dupe Prime Minister Lars von Engeström into working to promote Bernadotte's candidature. The Örebro parliament also remembered that Bernadotte had been very humane to captured Swedish officers and soldiers on the battlefield at Lübeck - all of which went in his favour and strengthened his case.

The fact that he had the support of the Prime Minister

Carl Gustaf's beloved grandfather Gustav VI died in 1973.

Carl Gustaf and the rest of the Royal Family lead the procession of mourners following the ashes of Gustav VI Adolf through the throng of grieving Stockholmers on the way to his final resting place.

finally landed in Stockholm to meet her husband Carl Johan some way out of the city, she felt that her fate was sealed. Désirée, or Desideria as she is known is Sweden, wanted from the very first to be back in Parisian court circles and drew constant attention to her poor health. At the beginning of June it was decided that the Crown Princess should spend some time in a spa town. No-one suspected when she left in her carriage that Carl Johan and their son Oscar would have to wait 12 years for her return.

In March 1811 Crown Prince Carl Johan was decreed Regent. King Karl XIII's health deteriorated and after a number of crises the Crown Prince was finally given the rule of the kingdom. The old King died on the 5th February 1818, and the Queen followed some months later. Their deaths marked the end of the Holstein-Gottorp line. It was now the turn of the Bernadottes to dictate the fate of Sweden. Carl XIV Johan was declared King on the 6th February and was crowned on the 11th May 1818.

Many held hopes that the new King would use his connections with Napoleon to take back Finland. Instead, he set about conquering Norway and joined in a coalition against Napoleon. After the battle of Leipzig where the King led the Nordic army and defeated Napoleon, he forced Denmark to relinquish Norway in the Treaty of Kiel in 1814. The Swedish Norwegian Union was founded in 1815. Over the years Carl XIV Johan became more and more conservative and devoted himself mainly to domestic politics. He died on the 8th March 1844 at the Stockholm Palace and was succeeded by his son Oscar who

reigned as King of Sweden and Norway between 1844-1859. Oscar I, who married Josefina of Leuchtenberg in 1823, worked for liberal reforms and entered into the November Treaty with the western powers during the Crimea War.

The line of Swedish kings continues with Carl XV, Oscar II and his and Queen Sofia's son Gustav V who ruled from 1907 to 1950. Gustav V, known as the tennis-loving Mr G, was married to Viktoria of Baden in 1881 and brings us into modern times. Gustav and Victoria had three sons; Gustav Adolf, Wilhelm and Erik.

During the Union crisis between Sweden and Norway Gustav was strongly in favour of keeping the Union but, when he saw that it would not last, he instead recommended that it be dissolved on the initiative of Sweden.

Swedish politics were largely shaped by the influences at the beginning of the century. One of the more notable political events was what is known as the Farmers' Rally in 1914 which was the final stage of a vicious defence debate which had been underway for several years. The Farmers' Rally had its origins in an idea conceived by a wholesaler in the university town of Uppsala. He believed that the farmers should show their loyalty to the King through their willingness to support the defence forces. On the 6th February 1914 thirty thousand farmers demonstrated at the Stockholm Palace and King Gustav V announced his own personal pro-defence ideas in what is known as the Courtyard Speech. The government had not approved the King's speech and this resulted in a con-

A moment of great ceremony at Stockholm Castle as Carl Gustaf officially becomes King of Sweden.

stitutional crisis. Prime Minister Karl Staaff tried to persuade the King to take back his speech but he refused and Staaff was forced instead to resign together with his ministers. A fifty-thousand strong procession of workers paraded past the palace two days after the Courtyard speech in support of the Staaff government. Hundreds shouted slogans and demanded a republic. But the King and his authority survived the ordeal.

This incident, together with a political decision taken in the 1950s under the government of Tage Erlander, are the only known occasions when the Swedish monarchy has really been put to the test. Tage Erlander put a stop to calls for a republic during the Social Democrats' party congresses in 1967, 1968 and 1969. Later demands for a republic were less popular and less successful.

In many ways Gustav V's long reign was happy although the Second World War and other events cast long shadows over Sweden. Pro-royalty publications told of

King Carl Gustaf is greeted by the people of Sweden. Seen here together with his sisters Christina, Birgitta, Désirée and Margaretha.

The ashes of King Gustav Adolf are carried in a cortege from Sofiero in Skåne to Stockholm Castle.

the old King and his favourite pastimes of tennis and hunt-ing. At the palace the four princesses Margaretha, Birgitta, Désirée and Christina were the objects of conti-nuous attention. The family's happiness was complete when the Royal sisters were joined by a younger brother in 1946. It started on the morning of Walpurgis Night, the 30th April. Princess Sibylla gave birth to a baby boy at 10.20, and everything went wild to quote the Stockholm dailies. The royal salute was fired 84 times on Skeppshol-men as is traditional on the birth of a Crown Prince. The whole of Stockholm congratulated itself - finally Princess Sibylla had given birth to a son after a string of daughters. The staff at the Stockholm Palace were so excited that one of the cleaners fainted. The seven pound baby boy gradu-ally grew into a young prince and the darling of the Swe-dish people.

The succession was secure for at least a couple of ge-nerations after the Heir to the Throne Gustav Adolf and his son Carl Gustaf Folke Hubertus. Few were to know that all this was to change with the death of the Heir to the Throne in a plane crash on the 26th January 1947 at Kastrup, just outside Copenhagen.

King Gustav V died in 1950 and was succeeded by his son Gustav VI Adolf who was 67 at the time. His first marriage to Margareta of Great Britain (1905-1920) pro-duced five children; Gustav Adolf, Sigvard, Ingrid, Bertil and Carl Johan. Three years after Margareta's death he married Louise, daughter of Prince Louis of Battenberg, later Mountbatten, the first Marquis of Milford Haven and Victoria, Princess of Hessen. Her death on the 7th March 1965 was grieved by the whole of Sweden.

Even as Crown Prince, Gustav Adolf was given a taste of royal duties and worked actively to preserve the monar-chy in Sweden. His sympathies with Great Britain were also popular after his parents' leanings towards Germany.

Gustav VI Adolf came to represent a completely new kind of monarchy and member of the House of Bernadot-te. His considerable interest in knowledge and learning

linked his work as Head of State with that of a scientist. Archaeology was a subject close to his heart and he devot-ed a great deal of energy to a number of burials in the Far East, Greece and Italy. He has also made impressive contributions to various scientific institutions and academies.

Swedish society has changed a great deal from a class society ruled by a King to a democracy with a constitutio-nal monarchy. In adapting himself and his role to these new demands, Gustav VI Adolf created a new type of rule characterised by democracy. In this capacity he was also a role model for his grandson Carl Gustaf who was one day to bear his responsibilities as King of Sweden.

Touring the country is one of the Royal Family's many duties.

with their roots in Sweden. Sweden also received good press reviews when American TV showed different impressions of Sweden over a whole week -everything from the structure of Swedish society, the economy, tax, the social services and art to how Swedes live and what they enjoy. King Carl Gustaf and Queen Silvia showed the "Good Morning America!" TV cameras around their beautiful Drottningholm Palace and the magnificent park.

One royal tradition which is studied with great interest, and which dates back to the Middle Ages, is that of visiting all the counties in Sweden itself. The King and his royal escorts travelled around the country getting to know local leaders and the Swedish people. It was a magnificent spectacle which always generated a great deal of interest when the King and his courtiers rode through tightly packed crowds of curious citizens.

King Carl Gustaf and Queen Silvia have kept up the tradition and have visited every county in Sweden since they came to the throne in 1973. "People are eager to show what they can produce and are proud of their work" said King Carl Gustaf on one of his trips. This was clearly the case in Blekinge, the most recent of many trips taken by the King before returning to the royal county of Greater Stockholm.

Legally, the King must perform a number of duties as the main representative of Sweden. He chairs the Information Council and the Advisory Council on Foreign Affairs. He opens Parliament and accredits foreign envoys, represents the Swedish Defence Forces and has the highest rank in the services. He also represents Sweden at the royal banquets held every year at the Stockholm Palace. Guests at the richly decorated tables also include government and parliamentary representatives, the Swedish Civil Service, the palace, business and commerce, the arts and non-governmental organisations.

Everyone listens when the King expresses himself on political issues. One such occasion was when the law was changed after considerable national debate so that the Roy-

Official

*I*t has frequently been noted in recent years that the Royal Family is a real PR asset for Sweden. The best example of this is perhaps the King and Queen's many official state visits and goodwill trips, for example the trip to the USA in April 1988. This marked the celebration of the first Swedish arrivals in America in Delaware in 1688.

The trip was widely covered by the mass media and strengthened links between Sweden and the USA - the continent with a million Swedish descendants and people

The Royal Family is granted an audience with the Pope in Rome.

Sweden's National Day is celebrated in the traditional way on the island of Skansen in Stockholm.

al Couple's first born, Princess Victoria, can become the future Queen of Sweden. It is widely recognised that the King would have liked his son, Prince Carl Philip, to be his successor. The change in the law resulted in full cognatic succession in Sweden.

As such, the royal duties will one day fall to Princess Victoria who is entitled to succeed her father and become Queen of Sweden. Even now she is in training for future duties and is attending more and more official functions. Victoria's first public engagement was when Skara celebrated its millennium; she presented the prizes for a drawing competition and signed her name in the town's guest book.

The autumn of 1973 was a dramatic time for the Swe-

The Royal Couple visit many companies each year.

Carl Gustaf and Silvia in Venice.

Meeting ambassadors at Stockholm Castle.

Kingdom meets empire - Swedish royal visit to Japan.

dish Royal Family. King Carl Gustaf's grandfather Gustav VI Adolf, fell ill on a visit to the Sofiero Palace in southern Sweden and was admitted to hospital in Helsingborg. Sweden held its breath.

It soon became clear that his illness was critical and his death on the 15th September 1973 brought with it the moment which the Crown Prince had both awaited and feared. It was now his turn to bear the historic mantle and to become the seventh member of the Bernadotte family to succeed to the throne.

When Carl Gustaf returned to Stockholm after a

It's celebration time when the Royal Couple are in town.

The Swedish Royal Couple on a state visit to Saudi Arabia, a few years before the outbreak of the fateful Gulf War.

touching visit to his grandfather's bier in Helsingborg, he was greeted by a crowd at Bromma airport. His first steps from the aircraft were extremely serious, however, when he lifted his right hand to wave it was possible to detect the traces of a smile. He had left Stockholm as Crown Price but had returned as King. The celebrations continued after his arrival at the Stockholm Palace - everywhere people sensed the feeling of history in the making and wished him well in his difficult and demanding work.

Carl Gustaf officially became King of Sweden on the 19th September 1973 in the banqueting hall of the Stockholm Palace. The crown and regalia lay alongside the silver throne which was covered in ermine. A troop of serious-looking bodyguards paraded in old-fashioned uniforms behind the King.

The King read his speech with a steady voice, "My revered and beloved grandfather became the symbol of a new

Things get jolly up in Lappland.

State visit to Queen Juliana's Holland.

The Royal Castle in the heart of Stockholm, centre of all Royal Receptions.

The Royal Couple on the way to a planning meeting at the Castle.

waved back at the sea of faces. The huge turn-out was noted in wide circles, the Swedish people are strongly attached to royalty even if the Social Democrats campaigned for its abolition.

Those close to Carl Gustaf could easily see that he quickly adapted to his new situation. Gone were the carefree days of being a Crown Prince, everything was for real now. Carl Gustaf adapted easily, few have been so well prepared when starting a new job.

Despite his favourable background, the Crown Prince's life had been rather dramatic. He was only eight months old when his father and heir to the throne, Gustav Adolf, died in an aeroplane accident at Kastrup airport outside Copenhagen in Denmark. Suddenly Crown Princess Sibylla was alone with four daughters and a son.

It was clear that the son would become King and consequently he was educated right from the start to prepare him to succeed to the throne. His grandfather King Gustav VI Adolf played an important role in this context, as did his Uncle Bertil. It was not always have been easy to curb the youngster, particularly when he was a teenager. Palace life has its drawbacks as demonstrated by Karl III who would gallop in and around the Palace. However, Carl Gustaf ne-

monarchy. I am determined to follow his good example". The coronation was a magnificent event, twenty thousand people waited outside the Palace, all wanting to see Carl Gustaf. However, he was hesitant about going out to hear the choral tributes at Lejonbacken. Courage was called for - all his life he had been brought up to be King, a role he could neither reject nor change. History had determined his fate. Carl Gustaf chose "För Sverige i tiden" [For Sweden - in our Time] as his motto.

The celebrations were unforgettable. Deeply moved he

ver emulated such activities.

The Crown Prince's mother, German-born Princess Sibylla, would in all probability have become Queen of Sweden had her husband not been killed in the air crash. She was comforted by the fact that her son was destined to become King, but did not live to see the day. She died on the 28th November 1972, the year before Carl Gustaf came to the throne.

Carl Gustaf grieved for his mother but was consoled by the fact that he had met the love of his life a few months earlier at the Olympic Games in Munich. In the youthful delirium of it all the Crown Prince suddenly saw a pair of beautiful dark eyes which had been watching him constant-

King Carl Gustaf at his desk.

The Royal Couple lend a helping hand during preparations for the Stockholm Water Festival.

Stockholm Castle is a real treasure trove of Art and Culture.

ly. His heart went "click" - a click which he later described to the international press. However, only those closest to Carl Gustaf suspected that something big was happening. The turning point came when a photographer discovered a beautiful dark haired girl in Carl Gustaf's fast-driving Porsche. It was the summer of 1973 and the Swedish romance of the century could no longer be kept a secret. I myself saw the lovely girl with her waist-length dark hair in the park at the Solliden Summer Palace on Öland. She had a beautiful smile and tried to look as if she were there purely by chance. However her name and identity soon became known, it was Silvia Sommerlath, the hostess at the Olympics and those happy days in Munich. "We are both relatively young." she said in her first interview, "It's one thing to like each other, but it will take time for that feeling to turn into love..." After that the couple were pursued constantly. Everyone felt that Carl Gustaf had chosen the future Queen of Sweden.

On the 12th March 1976 the Palace announced that Carl Gustaf and the beautiful Silvia were engaged. The official communication was as follows:

Carl XI's gallery ready for one of the year's many Royal Banquets.

"The Office of the Marshal of the Realm would like to announce that H.M. the King has on this day become engaged to Miss Silvia Renate Sommerlath, daughter of Director Walter Sommerlath and his wife Alice, née de Toledo. The announcement will be followed this evening by a family dinner at the Stockholm Palace".

The engagement resulted in genuine happiness; Sweden was to have a Queen, the King was to have a family and a new generation would pass through the palace chambers and halls. A press conference was called and the couple quite clearly beamed with happiness. The King described how his heart had gone click and Silvia was given ample opportunity to show off her talents. One of the questions put to her was, "Miss Sommerlath, do you see any particular queen as an example or role model?" "No, but I do have a king" she answered happily and smiled at her fiancé on the green sofa they were sharing.

On the 19th July of the same year their love was fulfilled with the most unforgettable wedding in the High Cathedral in Stockholm. The whole world followed the bride and groom to the altar. The improbable fairy tale of "a man of the world and a woman of the people" came true at 12.18 when King Carl Gustaf said clearly and loudly "I will" to his bride. A few seconds later Silvia became part of Swedish history by answering "I will" to the King before Archbishop Olof Sundby and a distinguished crowd of witnesses, family, nobility and special guests.

Another sensation was to be announced before the royal wedding year was out -Prince Bertil, Duke of Halland, married Mrs Lilian Craig, née Davis, on the 7th December. The wedding took place in the chapel at the Drottningholm Palace in the presence of the Royal Family and close friends and had been long awaited as Prince Bertil and Lilian Craig had unofficially lived together after a romantic

The Swedish Royal Couple Carl XVI Gustaf and Queen Silvia attend a gala.

Queen Silvia is always at the centre of the Nobel celebrations at the Stockholm Concert Hall.

Few can rival the Royal Couple as a PR asset for Sweden.

love affair during the Second World War in London. The marriage meant that Mrs Craig became the Duchess of Halland and a Swedish Princess and in this role regularly accompanies her husband in his royal duties. They can always be seen together with the Royal Couple at the annual Nobel Prize Giving Ceremony at the concert hall in Stockholm.

King Carl Gustaf has matured in his role as King of Sweden and Head of State. Royal visits and travels are combined with duties and tasks which are closer to home. Few Swedes have such a demanding workload as King Carl Gustaf. He enjoys being busy and will happily fill his diary with engagements.

The King's ability to manage his workload is attributable to his fitness. He works out and runs regularly during the summer. He also loves winter sports and regularly skis both downhill and cross-country and has completed the prestigious Vasaloppet, the world's longest skiing competition at just over 85 kilometres which attracts more than ten thousand participants each year. One of the King's favourite winter sport locations is Jämtland, Sweden's best developed winter resort which has been selected as a potential location for the Winter Olympics. The Royal Family have long owned a mountain cabin in Storlien, not far from the Jämtland pistes and ski tracks whish have been as competed on by Ingemar Stenmark and other world champions. The King often spends his winter holidays with Queen Silvia and the children, Crown Princess Victoria, Princess Madeleine and Prince Carl Philip. It was also here that he secretly brought his sweetheart Silvia Sommerlath after the sensational love story in Munich in 1972. The Crown Prince was travelling with his Adjutant Captain Bertil Daggfeldt to the seething Olympic city. He caught sight of the charming Silvia amid several pretty girls and his Adjutant made their first informal contact. The King himself has described how his heart went "click" when he met his Olympic hostess.

It would be no exaggeration to claim that the same Olympic hostess who went on to become the Queen of Sweden is widely loved. During her time in her new home-

When Queen Silvia wears the Leuchtenberg sapphires with diamonds she really deserves all the extra attention.

There's always a large crowd of well-wishers at the castle to congratulate Carl Gustaf on his birthday on the 30 April.

land she has admirably fulfilled her role as wife to King Gustaf and mother to the couple's three children. Her popularity lies largely with her charisma and also her versatility. She has moulded the role of Queen of Sweden into something new and admirable. Silvia's predecessors have also devoted themselves to various charities, but none have managed, as Silvia has, to take this charity and desire to help into a broader context. Her commitment has resulted in considerable interest in sport for the disabled at an international level and has made many people aware of this important model.

The Queen made an enormous impact when she demonstrated on television a few years ago that she could communicate using sign language. She was not happy to talk with deaf children via an interpreter, but instead diligently learnt how to talk with her hands. She wanted to have her own conversations with children and others who had lost their hearing. There was a huge reaction. Silvia received numerous letters and telegrams at the Palace. One girl wrote that her parents were deaf and communicated using sign language, but that she had always been embarrassed about using this skill when others were watching. "I'm no longer ashamed now that I've seen you using sign language," she wrote proudly. It goes without saying that the Queen was moved and delighted by this reaction.

The King and Queen of Sweden are two enthusiastic proponents of sport for the disabled. This enthusiasm dates back to their wedding in 1976 when the Swedish people donated money to the special wedding fund which was set up to offer financial support for activities for children and young people. More recently Queen Silvia travelled to the USA in 1989 on a PR trip for the book "Go for it" which was published a few years ago. The launch got underway at the highest level - during her time in the White House in Washington, First Lady Barbara Bush invited 150 influential people to lunch and Queen Silvia was given the opportunity of presenting the book on sport for the disabled. The

The Royal Couple and Princess Lilian on the way to one of the year's Royal Banquets.

Queen Silvia is one of the world's best dressed women, confident in both style and taste.

The family gathers to celebrate their father the King's birthday at Stockholm Castle.

Crown Princess Victoria is a charming young lady who will one day be Queen of Sweden.

An enthusiastic Royal Family are greeted by the people of Sweden in the outer courtyard of Stockholm Castle.

book has also been published in German and Spanish and has attracted a great deal of interest.

American television amply rewarded the Queen for having learnt sign language in its programme from the famous Gallaudet university for the deaf. Silvia was interviewed in the university's own TV studio by Marylou Novinsky in "Deaf Mosaic", a programme which has been awarded a number of prizes in the past. "It was my first ever interview in sign language", said the Queen happily when she met the press afterwards. Her only worry was that she herself had not been able to use her knowledge of sign language as the Swedish and English/American signs are so different that an interpreter is needed. However, the Queen suggested, in her creative way, that there should be an international sign language - a suggestion which met with the approval of her American hosts. She was also able to promote her cause on the peak-time "Good Morning America" when she was interviewed by the enormously popular Joan Lunden. It is thought that eight million people tuned into the programme. Interviewed for CNN by Sonya Friedman, Silvia was asked how she managed to gain the support of Barbara Bush, she replied happily, "I had met her before and knew that she is interested in issues concerning the disabled. I got in touch with her and she was kind enough to help me out."

Queen Silvia's commitment is more than skin deep; indeed she has tried out wheelchairs and other aids for the disabled and is in touch with researchers and specialists in various disabilities. She can tell you the name of the leading sportsmen and sports women, can remember their times and achievements and makes careful notes of any improvements in performance. The Queen of Sweden is al-

ways a guest of honour at the Olympics for the Disabled and other similar events. But what aroused her initial interest in young people who are disabled. "It was the King. When he went diving with blind children a few years ago, he told me that he himself felt disabled. That interested me. These days I see the real person when I talk to the disabled, I don't only see someone with a disability."

Queen Silvia also represents Sweden on a number of official occasions. Together with her husband King Carl Gustaf she undertakes a number of royal engagements which fill her working week with many meetings and public appearances. She has a great deal of correspondence and conducts several meetings in her study at the Stockholm Palace. These meetings are with all types of people, ranging from foreign dignitaries to friends from the Olympics.

The Queen must also fit in time to be a mother to the family's three children. She is helped out by skilled colleagues and loyal staff. However, her role as mother must not be neglected and is very precious to Silvia, which is why the Royal Family loves summer best of all the seasons. It is a time when they enjoy a happy and relaxed time at the Solliden summer palace on the island of Öland off the east coast of Sweden. Solliden is an oasis where the family can spend uninterrupted time with friends and relatives, swim in the sea and take day trips on the family's motorised yacht. Long happy summers recharge their batteries and give them the stamina to face royal duties awaiting their return to Stockholm. This may be school work for the children, or official duties including state visits, banquets and Nobel Prize Ceremonies for the King and Queen.

Popular relatives come to visit: Queen Margarethe and Prince Henrik of Denmark arrive in Stockholm.

Private life

King Carl Gustaf led a relatively lonely life during his younger years - at least he seemed to. His father, Prince Gustav Adolf, died before he was a year old and he was younger brother to four sisters - Margaretha, Désirée, Birgitta and Christina. He was deprived of a father figure and his mother, Princess Sibylla of Sachsen-Coburg-Gotha, was given the difficult job and responsibility of bringing up her children on her own. Of course, the help she received from the King's grandfather, Gustav VI Adolf, and her brother in law Prince Bertil should not be forgotten. The latter represented the younger generation in the family and came to mean a great deal to the Prince on account of his enthusiasm for sport. Bertil contributed a great many ideas and good practical advice to the house of Bernadotte. The Crown Prince also warmed to teachers and officers during his education. He expected to be treated as an equal, and that's just the way it was; during his training as an officer in the Swedish Navy, he had to scrub the decks just like everyone else.

He was just one of many friends as a schoolboy, from his early days at Broms school to 1966 when he took his school certificate in Sigtuna. The difference was that when his pals separated and returned to their anonymous homes, the Prince remained in the unmerciful glare of the public eye. Never before had a love affair or romance so innocent been the cause of so much sensation and first page news in the press.

Upbringing and kingly behaviour were frequently discussed in the closed circles of the Stockholm Palace. The concern was often evident from wrinkled foreheads. "The time has come for you to help me bring up the Prince", said Princess Sibylla to one of the influential men at the Palace. Perhaps it was on one of those occasions when his boisterousness had gone too far. Or when his youthful love of life did not fit in with palace and family rules.

It was therefore a happy piece of news that the Crown Prince had fallen in love with a beautiful German girl. Suddenly there was a young woman who was very close to him and who could break his isolation and dependence on older people.

Silvia was a true friend from the very beginning. She was a personality in her own right and was regularly chosen as representative hostess at the Olympic Games. She also dared to hold opinions and to stick up for them, an asset when she moved several years later to the Stockholm Palace with all its traditions and hierarchies.

She was, of course aware of the many dangers and temptations which she would encounter in her new environment. Silvia agonized over the matter more than once before she plucked up the courage to enter the world of royalty.

But, as many who followed the royal love story will recall, she did not come to Stockholm or Sweden straight away. She wished first to fulfil her obligations to the Olympic Games organisation. This was the first of Silvia's actions to leave its mark on her fiancé Carl Gustaf. It is obvious that he respects her determination and her decisions. It is well known that the King does not respect only those who bow and scrape to him.

Falling in love, getting engaged and getting married - thus Carl Gustaf metamorphosed from a happy bachelor

The beautiful Drottningholm Palace outside Stockholm is the home of the Royal Family.

with ingrained habits to a married man with a wife and family to care for. Some friends disappeared, new ones came along -not everyone could stay the course when things got serious. Here too, Silvia had a role to play in the changes brought about in Carl Gustaf. He has reached a stage of maturity which is of course linked with his personal development. Queen Silvia also remarked that it is possible to trace what has influenced his development. He is now happy and open and is extremely interested in a number of things.

Silvia also brought children into the King's life. No parent, commoner or royal can fail to be affected by their children. He clearly loves Victoria, Carl Philip and Madeleine and has played an active role in their lives and games. The family has a lively time behind the protective trees and bushes of the Solliden summer palace. The young prince and princesses rejoice in their fit father who excels at every kind of sport from wind surfing to motor cross. He loves showing them round his favourite boyhood places. The Queen looks on happily, and of course joins in the fun. This kind of close contact is absolutely necessary to her. "In the past children were kept in one compartment and their parents in another", explained the King in a radio programme broadcast from the Drottningholm Palace. "But we have managed to keep the children with us. They only need to call and we're there".

The King and Queen's first home was in the Stockholm Palace where their apartments commanded a view over the city. But it soon became apparent that the large palace in the old part of the city would not be suitable for the royal children. They were taken to the city's parks by car so that they had somewhere to play. It was also important to find

areas which were suitable from a security point of view.

Due consideration was given to all the royal palaces, it was clear in 1981 that Drottningholm would be the ideal home for the Royal Family. Drottningholm, on Lovön, is one of the highlights of Swedish architecture. This Swedish Versailles has attracted a great deal of attention since King Carl Gustaf and his family made their historic move from the Stockholm Palace to the golden Palace at Mälarstranden just before Christmas in 1981.

It would be hard to find a more suitable place for the Swedish Royal Family to live. There are traditions to maintain. In the latter part of the 16th century the State demesne was sold by Johan III's wife Katarina Jagellonika. It was a building with many towers, designed by the architect Willem Boy and commissioned by Johan III. In 1661 Hedvig Eleonora bought the property from Magnus Gabriel de la Gardie. "That year, the palace burned down" explains King Carl Gustaf. "Someone had been a bit eager when lighting the fires in one of the rooms". But the area and the environment were far too attractive to be abandoned. The following year Hedvig Eleonora had work started on a new palace with Nicodemus Tessin as the architect. However, he never saw the results of his work and, when he died in 1681, his son took over and completed the work. It is possible to see traces of the younger Tessin in a number of the interior designs, and the palace chapel was built entirely under his direction.

In 1744 Fredrik I gave Drottningholm to the young Crown Princess Lovisa Ulrika as a wedding present. She really made her mark on the palace and commissioned much-needed modernisation. In 1777 King Gustaf III allowed the government to buy the Drottningholm which was the

A Swedish family for our time (from left): Crown Princess Victoria, King Carl Gustaf, Prince Carl Philip, Princess Madeleine and Queen Silvia.

The Baroque Garden and park at Drottningholm, built at the time of Karl XII, were designed by the Tessin father and son team.

beginning of the palace's final major period of change. It is also worth noting the total restoration of the palace between 1907 and 1911 under the direction of John Böttiger and Professor Erik Lallerstedt.

This brief trip with seven league steps through the history of Drottningholm brings us to the end of 1981 and beginning of 1982. With care and cautiousness, the Ministry of Public Buildings gave the palace a well-needed technical overhaul. The King and Queen took an active part in the planning stage and could be seen on an almost daily basis picking their way through the building materials and paint pots. The aim was to create a functional home adapted to the special needs of the Royal Family.

If you stand facing the palace and look towards the facade which overlooks the park, their home is to be found on the right hand side of the palace, in the south-east wing. The family's bedrooms are situated in the tower nearest the water. There are plenty of guest rooms, a magnificent large kitchen which can cope with sizeable events, and a very private breakfast room/kitchen situated in the heart of the

family's home. It was designed to be safe for the children and easy to manage. "I love it out here." explained Queen Silvia in a conversation after the family had moved in. "Everything is so light compared with the Stockholm Palace". The Queen makes no secret of the fact that she enjoys living in the beautiful surroundings of Lake Mälaren. The King shares her views, "I think it's wonderful to have a home out here, and work to travel in to". He gestures towards Stockholm. "Everyone who lives near their work will understand what I mean. It's nice to be able to put some distance between your duties and private life, particularly if you have children".

The Palace is all the more attractive for the fact that the family has access to the beautiful walks in the palace park. During the summer the King's motorised yacht is moored outside the palace, ready to take the family on relaxing trips on Lake Mälaren or out to Stockholm's unique archipelago with more than 30,000 lakes, islands and skerries. During the holidays the King and his Adjutant take the boat to Öland and the Solliden summer palace. Queen Silvia and the children often used to prefer to make the move from Drottningholm to Öland by car - at least that's the way it used to be.

As in other countries with royal families, there has been a great deal of speculation about the future of the Swedish Royal Family. Perhaps the royal family in its present form, whereby it is required only to represent its country, is right for Sweden. The foundations of the present system were laid by Gustav VI

The Royal Wedding in June 1976 proved an unforgettable occasion.

When Archbishop Olof Sundby joined the Royal Couple in holy matrimony, Silvia Sommerlath became Carl Gustav's wife and Queen of Sweden.

with the idea of a woman on the throne. A practical example of female succession is close at hand with Denmark's Queen Margarethe who has followed in her father's footsteps in a charming and distinguished way.

State visits form a very important part of royal duties, both travelling to foreign countries and travelling to different parts of Sweden. These visits require long and detailed preparations at various levels in the palace and directly involve a number of representatives of official and cultural institutions. The Stockholm Palace is thoroughly dusted and polished, parade uniforms pressed, faithful retainers take out the cutlery and crockery from very full stocks. The state coaches are given an extra inspection in the palace stalls.

Careful thought is also given to the Royal Couple's clothes. King Carl Gustaf's uniforms and suits cause few problems - official and personal elegance are taken for granted. More time and energy is needed for Queen Silvia's wardrobe and orders are sent to couturiers and hat makers. There is also the question of which jewellery from the Bernadotte collection is to be worn on which occasions. Much of the Swedish Royal Family's jewellery dates back to Napoleonic France. The collection has grown

Adolf, and King Carl XVI Gustaf follows firmly in his grandfather's footsteps. On the first of January 1980 the law was changed, affecting one of Sweden's three constitutional laws - female succession was introduced. As a result Princess Victoria is heiress to the Swedish throne. If the idea behind the change in the law was to weaken or eliminate the Royal Family altogether, the result was quite the opposite. Crown Princess Victoria has shown great discretion in her first representative duties and public appearances. She is also a delightful young woman with clear Bernadotte features. This bodes well for Sweden and the Royal Family. It is of course impossible to know what the situation will be when she comes to succeed her father, given the way things change. The majority of Swedes are happy

and diminished over time with various inheritances and marriages.

These days the irreplaceable pieces are part of a collection which may not be depleted, and can only be added to. The piece to be worn on state visits is requested in writing and is collected from a well-guarded room in the Stockholm palace. The ornate red case is taken under high security to the room where Queen Silvia, her hairdressers and other attendants prepare for the galas in question.

Once the official invitations have been sent to the heads of state and royal families concerned, the real planning work can get underway. Dates are fixed and programmes drawn up. Consideration is given to the guests' special interests and matters that requires special attention by the Swe-

Drottningholm Palace in winter is a striking sight.

A Christmas tree is lit at Drottningholm.

dish hosts. A great deal of attention is also given to cultural events and King Carl Gustaf enjoys planning which singers and artists are to perform during state visits. One such event is the folk group which performs the entrance music when royalty and other guests arrive at the gala dinner at the palace. Other important details relating to state visits are the menus for the royal table. It is not unknown for the King to liaise with the palace chef in the kitchen and to taste the delicacies to be presented at the royal table. All in all the preparations for receiving state visits take one year from initial contact. Decisions must be made five to six months ahead of the date itself and exploratory visits are made five to six weeks before the flag is raised in Stockholm and the guests are driven in a procession to the Stockholm Palace.

Tradition dictates adherence to established protocol and a programme which is strictly followed for each state visit. Generally the guest

Winter holiday in Storlien.

head of state and security guards arrive by plane, train or, occasionally, by car. Queen Elizabeth II of Great Britain and her husband Prince Philip, Duke of Edinburgh, were guests in Sweden at the end of May in 1983 and arrived in Stockholm on the Royal Yacht Britannia. When the ship passed Fjäderholmarna in Stockholm's inner archipelago, Prince Bertil and Princess Lilian went on board to welcome the guests. Similarly, the couple usually meet other guest heads of state at Arlanda airport.

After a magnificent ride through central Stockholm to the Palace, there is an inspection of the guard of honour waiting in the inner courtyard. Official photographs, private lunch and an exchange of gifts follow. Royal guests and heads

The King and his family spend their summers on the island of Öland. There they have plenty of time to relax in the splendid Solliden Summer Palace.

Solliden Palace is the Royal Family's retreat during the summer months. It was built by Victoria, Queen of Sweden from 1907 to 1930.

of state meet the Swedish diplomats and the official programme gets underway. A gala dinner is held at the Stockholm Palace on the first evening of the visit. The second day generally begins with visits to various institutions, the Royal Armoury and Treasury at the Stockholm Palace are always enjoyable. After a busy morning it is time for the city of Stockholm to invite the guests to lunch. As a rule the guests are taken from Riddarholm to the town hall in the richly decorated barge Vasaorden, always a popular part of the programme which is followed by huge crowds on Riddarfjärden beaches.

Visits to industrial areas, musical entertainment, gala evenings at the Royal Theatre, Stockholm's opera house are also part of the programme as is a dinner where the royal guests or heads of state play host.

Many programmes also include trips to the Swedish countryside. When he was a still a Crown Prince, Japanese Akihito and his Crown Princess Michiko travelled with the King and Queen to Lapland to see for themselves the most exotic part of Sweden, the Sami culture and nature in the North.

State visits to other countries follow almost exactly the same pattern, but in reverse. The King and Queen are guests themselves and devote a great deal of time and effort to finding out about the country they are visiting, reading up about it and being briefed by diplomats and specialists from the Foreign Ministry.

The Royal Couple's outfits vary according to the time of year, climate and local customs. Suitable presents are obtained, the dinner which they are to host is discussed with the head chef and the cultural programme is fixed. Well before the Royal Couple's departure, members of the host country's press are invited to meet the couple at the Stockholm Palace to generate publicity in the host country's leading newspapers and media. Everything is in place and well prepared once the visit actually gets underway.

The King has made a total of 29 state vis-

A Royal idyll in the spacious park at Solliden.

The Royal Children love the country life.

its abroad and has been accompanied by Queen Silvia on those made after 1976. The first was to neighbouring countries Norway and Finland in 1974 where the King was hosted by King Olav and President Urho Kekkonen respectively. The following year it was the turn of Denmark, Iceland and England. In 1976 King Carl Gustaf and Queen Silvia took a notable journey on the HMS Älvsnabben to the Netherlands. In March 1977 they visited King Baudou-

Republic of Germany and Austria in 1979, Japan and France in 1980. In February 1981 the Royal Couple went on state visits to Tanzania and Saudi Arabia. In September they headed off to China to visit Peking and walk along the Great Wall of China. In January 1982 they were received by the President of Mexico, José Lopez-Portillo and in April of the same year the King travelled to Australia with his sister, Princess Christina Fru Magnuson to keep him company as Queen Silvia had been advised to stay at home on account of her condition. On the 10thof June the Royal Couple's third child was born - Princess Madeleine.

In 1983 they visited Spain and their good friends King Juan Carlos and Queen Sophia. In August it was off to Finland to visit the new President, Mauno Koivisto and his wife Tellervo. A month later the Grand Duke Jean and Grand Duchess Josephine-Charlotte invited them to a grand banquet at the palace in Luxembourg. In 1984 they visited Brazil which was particularly exciting for Queen Silvia who grew up with her three brothers in San Paolo. The following year the Swiss government invited the couple to visit Switzerland. 1986 was the turn of President Mario Soares in Portugal and President Hosni Mubarak in Egypt. In 1987 President Vigdis Finnbogadottir was host to the King and Queen in Iceland, and the following year it was the General Governor of Canada, Jeanne Sauvé. 1989 saw the couple heading off for destinations as far apart as New Zealand and Jordan. Italy was their destination in 1989. At the beginning of April President Francesco Cossiga invited the couple for a state visit. Barely a month later they visited the Vatican to see Pope John Paul II. The Royal Family visited Italy one more time that year to be present at the Birgitta celebrations in Rome. 1992 got underway with a visit to Ireland and then to Estonia, Latvia and Lithuania where they met with boundless enthusiasm after Russian-enforced isolation from the countries' Baltic neighbours.

Prince Bertil and Princess Lilian are deeply loved in Royal circles.

in and Queen Fabiola of Belgium. In 1978 President Leonid Brezhnev opened up the doors to the golden Kremlin in Moscow and took the Royal Couple on a state visit which led them to the fairy tale city of Samarkand. Then followed a whole string of state visits abroad: the Federal

The Royal Couple have also hosted a great many state visits. The first after the King's succession to the throne was that of the President of Finland Urho Kekkonen in October 1975, closely followed by King Olav of Norway in the autumn of the same year. Since then Sweden has been visited by representatives of Yugoslavia, Austria, Spain, Mexico, Rumania, Canada, Iceland, Finland, England, France, Zambia, Japan, Denmark, Algeria, the Netherlands, Germany, Israel, Portugal, Czechoslovakia, Luxembourg and Norway.

Princess Christina and her husband Tord Magnuson.

The Principality of Liechtenstein

By François Billaut

House of Liechtenstein

With a territory of 160 sq. km, the Principality of Liechtenstein, which lies between Austria and Switzerland, is one of the smallest states in Europe. In principle, there appears to be nothing in the history or geographical location to attract royalty to this Alpine country.

The origins of the princes of Liechtenstein are lost in the genealogical mists of the early Middle Ages. They probably came from the Donauwörth family of Bavarian seigneurs and seem to have lived from the 10th century in Low Austria and to have taken their name from the castle of Liechtenstein about 30 km from Vienna. The first ancestor mentioned by name is Huc of Liechtenstein who lived in the 12th century. His descendants shared in the fortunes of the Hapsburgs and acquired huge estates in the Empire. They became Princes of the Holy Roman

His Serene Highness Hans-Adam II, sovereign Prince of Liechtenstein.

Empire in 1608; Duke of Troppau in 1613 and Prince and Duke of Jaggendorf in 1623. They acquired the seigneuries of Schellenberg in 1699 and Vaduz in 1712, which after unification formed a new principality to which they gave their name. In this way, Emperor Charles IV created the three hundred and forty third state of the Germany branch of the Holy Roman Empire for them, the only one still in existence. At that time the head of the new dynasty, who was in the diplomatic service in Vienna and in the army, did not show much interest in his little country. It was not until Alois II visited Liechtenstein in 1842 that the people met one of their sovereigns. The Principality was invaded by the French in 1799 and became part of the Rhine Confederation, which gave the country full independence. In 1862 during the reign of Jean II from 1858 to 1929, one of the longest in history, the inhabitants of Liechtenstein were granted a constitution and a representative body, the Diet. François I succeeded his brother in

Princess Marie-Aglaé, née Countess Kinsky of Wchinitz and Tettau.

reduce and commute sentences and even to stop legal actions. Catholicism is the State religion.

The monarch bears the title of "His Serene Highness the Sovereign Prince (Fürst) of Liechtenstein and in Liechtenstein, Duke of Troppau and Jagerndorf, Count of Rietberg". The younger members of the family are princes and princesses of and in Liechtenstein; they all have the right to the prefix "Serene Highness". The sovereign prince has the power to ennoble and give titles to his sub-

The union of Prince François I (1853-1938) and Elisabeth von Gutman bore no children.

Prince François-Joseph II, born in 1906, succeeded his great uncle in 1938.

1929 and died in 1938. His great-nephew, Prince François-Joseph II, succeeded to the throne. He lived in Vaduz Castle, the first Prince of Liechtenstein to live in the Principality. He kept his country neutral during the Second World War and brought back to Vaduz in its entirety the dynasty's priceless art collection, which up to then had been kept in Bohemia, Moravia and Austria. Under his administration the country developed its hydro-electric potential, its industry and encouraged foreign countries to set up business in the Principality. The average income per inhabitant of Liechtenstein today is the highest of any country in Europe. Prince François-Joseph died on the 13th November 1989. His eldest son, Prince Hans-Adam II, is the present sovereign.

Apart from the Prince of Monaco, the Prince of Liechtenstein is the only European monarch to have retained real power. Under the terms of the 1921 Constitution, which has been amended several times, the person of the sovereign, the Head of the State, is inviolable and sacred. The Prince respects laws passed by the Diet but retains the power to convene, close, adjourn and even dissolve it. He appoints the prime minister and the four ministers put forward by Parliament, but has the right to dismiss them. For "the security and good of the State" he has the right of veto and the power to take the place of the legislators by promulgating laws by decree. The Prince sanctions laws, arbitrates between special interests and is protector of the national interest. The death penalty was abolished in Liechtenstein in 1987 but the sovereign has the power to

jects but normally only grants them to members of the family who have made morganatic marriages, thus losing the right to the title prince or princess.

Succession to the throne is through the male line in order of primogeniture and, by right of representation, to descendants of legitimate marriages. In the absence of a male heir, the eldest daughter succeeds to the throne and in turn is succeeded by her eldest son, with succession ensuing as previously. Before marrying, members of the House must obtain permission from the sovereign. Marriages contracted without the sovereign's consent result in the loss of the right of succession to the throne for those involved and their descendants.

Prince Hans-Adam was born on the 14th February 1945. He was educated at Vienna Schottengymnasium then at Alpinium de Zuoz College in Les Grisons. He obtained a degree in political economy at the University of Saint-Gal. Prince Hans-Adam has been ruling the country since the 26th August 1984 when his father appointed him "Lieutenant" and entrusted the future of the Principality to him.

Under the new sovereign's rule there has been an increasing tendency for the country to break away from Swiss protection. Liechtenstein has been a member of the

Perched on a rocky outcrop, the Prince's residence: Vaduz Castle.

European Free Trade Association since the 22nd June 1991. In 1992 the country rejoined the Council of Europe and became a full-time member of the United Nations Organisation. The Prince appears to wish to extend his country's independence further, without losing Swiss diplomatic representation. On the 30th July 1967 the Prince married his cousin, Countess Marie-Aglae Kinsky von Wchinitz und Tettau in Vaduz. The Princess of Liechtenstein is Chairman of the Red Cross and a number of other organisations in the country. She is particularly involved with ecological and environmental questions. A qualified graphic artist, she also very interested in seeing the promotion of Liechenstein's cultural development.

The Prince and Princess have four children. The eldest, Crown Prince Alois, born in 1968, read law at the University of Salzburg after attending the Military Academy of Sandhurst; Prince Maximilian was born in 1969, Prince Constantin in 1972 and Princess Tatiana in 1973. The Prince and Princess of Liechtenstein endeavour to avoid excess media exposure to protect the family circle.

The reigning prince has two brothers each with three children. Prince Philippe-Erasme, born in 1946, studied history and is married to Isabelle de l'Arbre de Malander. They live in Paris and have three children: Alexander, born in 1972; Wenzel, born in 1974 and Rodolphe, born

Prince François-Joseph II and Princess Regina were to die within a few months of each other in 1989.

in 1975. His second brother, Prince Nicholas, a Doctor of Law, is Liechtenstein Ambassador to Switzerland and non-resident ambassador to the Vatican. His wife was formerly Princess Marghareta of Luxemburg. They live in Berne and also have three children: Marie-Annunciata, born in 1985; Marie-Astrid, born in 1987 and Joseph-Emmanuel, born in 1989. Their sister, Princess Nora, born in 1950, lives in Spain. She is married to the Marquis de Marino; they have one child.

With nearly a hundred princes and princesses in several junior branches, the Liechtenstein family remains today one of the most extended of the Gotha line.

The sovereign couple and their children: Aloïs, Maximilian, Constantin and Tatiana.

Crown Prince Aloïs and Princess Sophie of Bavaria. Married in July 1993.

The Grand Duchy of Luxemburg

By François Billaut

The House of Nassau

*T*he Grand Duchy of Luxemburg; The House of Nassau; Luxemburg, which was founded during the second half of the 10th century, has had many ruling houses. The House of Ardennes held it until its extinction in 1336, when the country passed by inheritance to the House of Limburg, a state which provided several emperors of the Germanic Holy Roman Empire.

Luxemburg, which was founded during the second half of the 10th century, has had many ruling houses. The House of Ardennes held it until its extinction in 1336, when the country passed by inheritance to the House of Limburg, a state which provided several emperors of the Germanic Holy Roman Empire. Luxemburg, which was originally an earldom, was elevated to a duchy in 1354, sold in 1441 to Philippe the Good, Duke of Burgundy and then, after becoming a dependency of the Netherlands, passed in 1477 into the hands of the House of Hapsburg. It was a French "département" in 1797 until in 1807 the Congress of Vienna made it a grand-duchy affiliated to the Germanic Confederation, the personal property of the Orange-Nassau family, sovereigns of the new Kingdom of the Netherlands.

As it was subject to the Salic Law, under which women were excluded from the succession, when Queen Wilhelmina acceded to the throne of the Netherlands in 1890, Luxemburg passed to the eldest branch of the family, the Nassau-Weilbourgs. Grand Duke Adolphus, sovereign of the German Duchy of Nassau, who was dispossessed by William I of Prussia in 1866, was the forefather of the new national dynasty.

Descended from Dudo, Count of Laurenbourg, who lived in the 12th century, The Nassau dynasty experienced a series of sovereignties as eventful as the history of the

Their Royal Highnesses Jean and Joséphine-Charlotte, Grand Duke and Grand Duchess of Luxembourg.

two countries, the Netherlands and Luxemburg, in which it finally became established in the 19th century.

In 1905 Grand Duke Adolphus of Luxemburg was succeeded by his son, William IV. The male line of the

Adolphe (1817-1905) Duke of Nassau until 1866, Grand Duke of Luxembourg in 1890.

1897, Grand Duke Adolphe surrounded by the princes in his family.

Marie-Anne of Portugal, wife of William IV.

Grand Duke William IV (1905-1912).

Grand Duchess Marie-Adélaïde reigned from 1912 to 1919.

House of Nassau finally became extinct on his death on the 25th February 1912. The Grand Duke and his wife, the former Princess Marie-Anne of Portugal, had six daughters. Under a family statute, promulgated in 1907 and ratified by the Chamber of Deputies some months later, the Law of Succession was amended so that women could at last accede to the throne. Thus in 1912, the eldest daughter, Marie-Adelaide, became the reigning Grand Duchess.

After she was accused, probably unfairly, of being pro-German during the First World War, the young sov-

Grand Duchess Charlotte came to the throne in 1919 and restored the prestige of the dynasty.

ereign was forced to abdicate in 1919 in the face of hostility from some of her people and the Allied Armies. She entered a convent taking the name "Sister Marie of the Poor" and died in 1924 at Hohenburg Castle. Her youngest sister, Charlotte, took the constitutional oath on the 15th January 1919.

During this troubled period the Luxemburg monarchy owed its salvation entirely to the remarkable personality of the young sovereign. She immediately called a referendum and, after receiving over 80% of favourable votes, was able to begin her reign on a sound footing. During the German invasion in

Grand Duchess Charlotte and her children: Jean, Elisabeth, Marie-Adélaïde, Charles and Alix.

In 1944 the current sovereign fought for the liberation of his country under the pseudonym "Lieutenant Luxembourg".

On 9 April 1953 Jean, then Grand Duke apparent, married Princess Joséphine-Charlotte of Belgium.

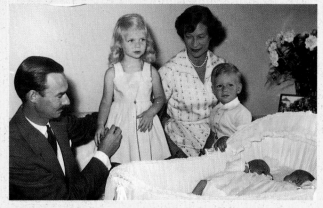

The Grand Dukes apparent and their first born: Marie-Astrid, Henri and twins Jean and Margaretha.

1940 the Grand Duchess and her government in exile were a symbol of the country's independence. The German authorities requested Charlotte, who had fled first to Portugal then to Great Britain, to return to Luxemburg. Her proud reply was "My heart says yes, but my reason says no!". The Germans occupied the country and oppressed its people but were unable to suppress the spirit of the nation. In the eyes of the Allies, the Grand Duchess had saved the moral integrity of her country.

In 1919 Charlotte had married Prince Felix of Bourbon-Parma, brother of Empress Zita of Austria,

The current Grand Duke apparent Henri of Luxembourg, Crown Prince of Nassau, born in 1955.

Grand Duchess apparent of Luxembourg, née Marie-Thérésa Mestre.

Queen of Hungary, both children of Robert I (1848-1907), the last sovereign of the Duchy of Parma. Six children were born of the marriage. Grand Duchess Charlotte reigned happily until 1964, when she abdicated in favour of her son and heir, Grand Duke Jean. She died peacefully 21 years later, surrounded by the love and respect of her people and her family.

Grand Duke Jean of Luxemburg is also Prince of Bourbon-Parma through his father. The Prince of Parma branch originated from the second son of Elisabeth Farnese and Phillip V, first Bourbon king of Spain, a grandson of King Louis XIV of France. The present Sovereign is therefore a member of the Capetian House, the only family in the world which can trace its ancestry back to 852, to Robert the Strong, Count of Angers, great grandfather of Hugues Capet, founder of the French dynasty and the Grand Duke's ancestor to thirty-one generations.

As he inherited the Crown through his mother's family, on the 28th July 1987 the Grand Duke renounced the family name Bourbon on behalf of himself and his whole family. The dynasty therefore now bears the name of Nassau only, while the title of Prince of Bourbon-Parma no longer exists.

The full title of the Grand Duke is "By the grace of God, Grand Duke of Luxemburg, Duke of Nassau (Prince of Bourbon-Parma), Count Palatine of the Rhine, Count of Saygn, Königstein, Katzenellenbogen and Diez, Burgrave

of Hammerstein, Seigneur of Mahlberg, Wiesbaden, Idstein, Merenberg, Limburg and Eppstein". The present Grand Duke and his children still use the form of address "Royal Highness", which comes from the House of Bourbon-Parma. However, Luxemburg had previously employed the specific forms of address "Their Grand-Ducal Highnesses". The eldest son and heir has the title Heir to the Grand Duchy of Luxemburg, Crown Prince of Nassau (Prince of Bourbon-Parma). The other members of the family are princes and princesses of Luxemburg and Nassau (princes and princesses of Bourbon-Parma).

The rules of succession to the grand ducal crown were laid down by a House of Nassau family agreement in 1783, the family statute of 1907 and the Grand Duchy Constitution. Within the Nassau family the crown is hereditary and is passed down the male line in order of primogeniture. If there are no direct or collateral male descendants of the House, the crown is passed in order of primogeniture through the female line of the ruling dynasty. Princes of the grand ducal house may not marry without the sovereign's consent, otherwise they and their issue lose their right of succession, titles and forms of address. The heir apparent has full right to the crown as soon as the throne is vacant, either as a result of the death or the abdication of the holder.

Under the terms of the country's constitution, the su-

Jean, Grand Duke of Luxembourg. Lieutenant General of the Kingdom in 1961, he acceded to the throne in 1964.

Joséphine-Charlotte, Grand Duchess of Luxembourg. Daughter of King Léopold III of Belgium and the unforgettable Astrid of Sweden.

preme authority is vested in the nation. The Grand Duke only exercises executive power. He sanctions and promulgates laws and makes his decision known within three months of a vote in the Chamber of Deputies. A sanction is an act under which the Grand Duke gives his consent to a provision passed by the Chamber of Deputies, thus giving the provision the nature of a law. Promulgation is the act by which the Grand Duke orders the publication and application of a law. If, within a period of three months after approval by the Chamber of Deputies, the Grand Duke has not sanctioned a law, the provision passed by the Chamber becomes null and void. The Grand Duke concludes treaties, which must be approved by law and published as laid down. He is Commander-In-Chief of the Armed Forces. He makes appointments to civil and military posts, apart from where the law dictates otherwise. He presides over the Council of State when he sees fit. He may be represented by a prince of royal blood, who then takes the title of Lieutenant for the Grand Duke. The representative must reside in the Grand Duchy and take an oath to the effect that he will observe the Constitution. All sessions of the Chamber are opened or closed by the Grand Duke or a proxy appointed for the purpose. The Grand Duke may convene the Chamber for extraordinary meetings at the request of one third of the deputies. He may adjourn the Chamber or dissolve it.

Justice is administered by the courts and tribunals in the name of the Sovereign, who has the right to remit or reduce sentences passed by judges.

The Grand Duke enjoys active and passive legation rights : he may send diplomatic envoys to foreign Monarchs and Heads of State, and may receive their envoys. He may sign credentials and appoint ambassadors.

He has retained the rights and privileges of royalty, namely the right to pardon, to mint money, to confer titles and award civilian and military honours.

Grand Duke Jean was born on the 5th January 1921 at the Chateau Colmar-Berg. He received his primary and secondary education in the Grand Duchy and later went to Ampleforth College in England as a boarder before reading law and political science in Canada at the University of Quebec. He enlisted with the Allied Forces in the Second World War and in June 1944 took part in the liberation of his country under the name of Lieutenant Luxemburg. He has been a Member of the Luxemburg Council of State since 1951 and in 1961 was appointed Lieutenant-Representative by Grand Duchess Charlotte, thus receiving authority to exercise the sovereign's power on behalf of his mother. On the 12th November 1964 the Grand Duchess abdicated in favour of her son. Grand Duke Jean has continued to achieve the two principal ambitions of his predecessor's reign: to improve the welfare of his people and to give his country a leading part in the construction of Europe.

Grand Duke apparent Henri of Luxembourg at a military review.

February 1981 and already have five children: William born in 1981, Felix born in 1984, Louis born in 1986, Alexandra born in 1991 and Sebastian in 1992. The Princess is actively involved in charity, especially in assisting the handicapped. The royal couple's simplicity and kindness has earned them great popularity and the love of the people of their country. Prince Jean and Princess Margaretha, the third and fourth children, are twins and were born in 1957. Prince Jean lives in Paris where he married Helene Vestur; they have four children: Marie-Gabrielle born in 1986, Constantin born in 1988, Wenceslas born in 1990 and Carl-Johann born in 1992. The Prince has renounced his right of succession to the throne. Princess Margaretha is married to Prince Nicholas of Liechtenstein. The youngest child of the Grand Duke and Grand Duchess, a son Prince William, was born in 1963 and is not yet married.

Finally, the Luxemburg family includes another four sisters of the Grand Duke: Princess Elisabeth, Duchess of Hohenberg born in 1922; Princess Marie-Adelaide, Countess Hencke of Donnersmarck, born in 1924; Princess Marie-Gabrielle, Countess of Holstein-Ledreborg, born in 1925 and Princess Alix, Princess of Ligne, born in 1929. Their brother, Prince Charles, who was born in 1927 and died in 1977, had two children - Prince Robert of Luxemburg born in 1968 and Princess Charlotte born in 1967.

On the 9th April 1953 he married Princess Josephine-Charlotte of Belgium, eldest daughter of King Leopold III and sister of the present King of the Belgians. The Grand Duchess is particularly concerned with social problems in the country. She is President of the Luxemburg Red Cross. The Royal couple, who are keen on maintaining the traditions of a Christian family, lead simple modest lives and avoid excess media coverage of the Royal Family.

Jean and Josephine of Luxemburg have five children. Princess Marie-Astrid, born in 1954, is married to Archduke Carl-Christian of Austria. Prince Henri, the heir to the Grand Duchy was born in 1955, studied in the Duchy and in France, then went to Sandhurst in England for his military training. He read economics and political science at the University of Geneva, where he met his wife-to-be, Maria-Teresa Mestre, the daughter of a middle-class Cuban refugee living in Switzerland. They were married in

The Principality of Monaco

By Vincent Meylan

House of Grimaldi

he Principality of Monaco; House of Grimaldi; Monaco, one of the world's smallest states with its territory of 1.5 hectares and population of 23,000, is a product of historical accident. Documents dating back to the 5th century B.C. refer to a Ligurian settlement on the rock. Its Roman fortifications made the wild isolated site an ideal haunt of pirate bands throughout the early Middle Ages.

Monaco, one of the world's smallest states with its territory of 1.5 hectares and population of 23,000, is a product of historical accident. Documents dating back to the 5th century B.C. refer to a Ligurian settlement on the rock. Its Roman fortifications made the wild isolated site an ideal haunt of pirate bands throughout the early Middle Ages. It was towards the end of the 12th Century that the rocky Mediterranean outcrop first came to the attention of the powers that be. The Counts of Provence, Vassals of the Holy Roman Empire, realising its strategic significance and doubtless keen to get rid of the pirates, acquired the title of "Seigneury of Monaco".

Their suzerainty was short-lived. In 1162 and 1191 the Emperor granted the newly created seigneury to the city of Genoa. At this time, most of Italy was torn by internal strife between the Ghibellines, supporters of Imperial supremacy, and the Guelphs, holders of Papal power. Monaco's future independence was to be one of the minor repercussions of this political struggle.

In 1297 the Ghibellines took power in Genoa and the great Guelph families, erstwhile masters of the city, began

Monaco past and future: Prince Rainier with his grandchildren.

their long exile. Among those driven from his home was Francesco Grimaldi, who resolved to use force of arms to establish a fief for himself and his descendants. Was his choice of the Monaco headland an arbitrary decision? Or had Francesco's ancestors, as some historians claim, al-

Louise-Hippolyte Grimaldi, Princess of Monaco at the beginning of the 18th century.

Princess Caroline (1793-1879).

Prince Albert I (1848-1922) and his wife, Lady Mary Douglas-Hamilton (1850-1922).

Prince Charles III (1818-1889).

Princess Charlotte (1898-1977).

Prince Albert 1ᵉʳ.

Prince Louis II (1870-1949), grandfather of Prince Rainier.

ready governed Monaco on behalf of the Counts of Genoa a century earlier? There is no proof either way.

What we do know is that, on Christmas Eve 1306, Francesco and his brother Rainier disguised themselves as monks and had the gates of the town opened for their troops to enter. This famous episode has left its trace on the Principality's Coat of Arms, which depicts the Grimaldi shield "with silver and gules fusil" held by "two friars each brandishing a sword". Genoa would pursue its claims to the territory throughout two centuries of siege and battle, and it was not until 1482 that Louis XI consented to take the fief under his protection on the understanding that it lay "outside the boundaries of the Realm". This recognition of independence was reiterated in 1489 and 1512 by Charles VIII and Louis XII, and also by the Dukes of Savoy, whose power extended to both sides of the Alps. In 1524, a political realignment brought Monaco the protection of Charles the Fifth and and with it recognition for the little State's independence from the Holy Roman Empire and Spain.

The title Prince of Monaco first appears in an official act in 1612, and was formally recognised by France in 1641 under Louis XIII. In the meantime, the Princes of Monaco conquered the neighbouring fiefs of Menthon and Roquebrune. These two towns, previously enfeoffed to Savoy, were included in the independent Principality of Monaco. Around the same period,

Louis XIII conferred on Prince Hercule de Monaco the French titles of Duke of Valentinois, Marquis des Baux and Count of Carlades.

The Grimaldi line died out for the first time in 1731. As Antoine I had no sons, the throne went to his eldest daughter, Louise-Hyppolyte, wife of Jacques of Goyon de Matignon. The latter, youngest son of a family of Norman origin, agreed to carry on the Grimaldi name and arms.

1793 saw the end, albeit temporary, of the fine structure erected by the seigneurs and princes of Monaco. In February of that year, the little State's citizens proclaimed the downfall of their princes and transferred their allegiance to the French Republic. In fact, for decades the princes had danced attendance at the Court of Versailles, spending only brief periods on their Mediterranean lands. Honoré III and his eldest son were imprisoned. Joseph, the youngest son went abroad, while his wife remained in Paris to die on the scaffold. For twenty one years, Monaco was without its independence.

In 1815 the Grimaldis returned to power. The territory inherited by Honoré had been bled dry, destroyed by the years of anarchy. Nevertheless, his subjects were not unduly impressed by his authoritarian rule. His brother and successor, Florestan I, was no more successful in his own vain attempts to restore the Principality's economy, despite the support of his wife, Caroline Gilbert. Notwithstanding his populist initiatives and his liberalism - reduced taxes and excise duties, free schools and shelters - by 1848 a fair number of his subjects seemed ready for armed insurrection. Menthon and Roquebrune rebelled, demanding assimilation into the kingdom of Piedmont Sardinia. Following a referendum by the French and Italian governments in 1861, they were definitively integrated into France. It was just two years later that the wizard who would restore the Monegasque Rock to its former splendour appeared on the scene.

The seaside resort company entrusted with exploiting the territory's tourist potential was set up in 1856, but did not really take off until 1863 when Charles III appointed Louis Blanc as its director. Gambling, which was banned in neighbouring states, was to transform Monaco into a luxury resort and divert an inexhaustible stream of gold into the princely coffers. In 1866 the Principality, which had been reduced to the single town of Monaco with the integration of Menthon and Roquebrune into France, underwent a fictitious enlargement. At Louis Blanc's request, Charles III signed the decree for the creation of Monte-Carlo, a new city dedicated to gambling, pleasure and tourism. Its success soon exceeded every expectation and has never waned, although gambling today represents only a minute proportion of the Principality's resources.

Just after the Great War, the resolution of a further minor difficulty over civil status enabled the Grimaldi line to be perpetuated for a second time. In 1918, the French

131. MONTE-CARLO *Les enfants de S.A. le Prince de Monaco*

Two little children in Monaco: Prince Rainier and his sister, Princess Antoinette.

government became concerned about the continued bachelorhood of Louis, the 48 year old heir to the Principality. They were afraid that, in the event of his death, the throne might pass to German princes, the Dukes of Urach, descendants of Princess Florestine of Monaco. The powerful Third Republic enforced a Treaty of Alliance on Albert I,

Miss Grace KELLY

Grace and Rainier, Hollywood star meets Prince Charming.

Constitution

Would it be correct to describe the Principality of Monaco as Europe's sole surviving absolute monarchy? There is no doubt that the powers granted to the Prince under the Constitution of the 17th December 1962 are virtually unlimited.

Article 3 states : "Executive power shall be vested in the Prince". Article 4 adds : "Executive power shall be exercised by the Prince and the National Council". This Council comprises 18 members elected on the list system by direct universal suffrage for a five year term. Under Article 66 of the Constitution, the role of the National Council is to "debate and pass laws". However, paragraph 2 of the same article states: "the power to initiate laws lies with the Prince". In other words, the National Council can veto laws proposed by the Sovereign but has no legislative power of its own.

The financial provisions afford another particularly striking example of the Prince's omnipotence. The State budget is passed annually, as in all European countries. It

Prince Rainier divides his leisure time between sport and his family.

the Sovereign Prince, involving considerable restrictions on the Principality's foreign and economic policy. If the dynasty were to die out, Monaco would become French territory.

To avoid this eventuality, the heir, with his father's agreement, adopted the love child who had been born in Algeria in 1898 of his liaison with Mademoiselle Juliette Louvet. Consequently, in 1919 Charlotte Louvet became Her Serene Highness Princess Charlotte of Monaco, Duchess of Valentinois. In 1922, she married Count Pierre de Polignac, descendant of an ancient line of French feudal nobility. Like Jacques of Goyon de Matignon, his wife's distant ancestor, Count Pierre de Polignac agreed to renounce his name, arms and title and adopt those of his father-in-law. He became his Serene Highness Prince Pierre of Monaco. Two children were born of this union : Princess Antoinette in 1920, created Baroness of Massy in 1951, and Prince Rainier, the present Sovereign, in 1923.

In 1944 Princess Charlotte renounced her right to the throne in favour of her son. On the death of Louis II in 1949, Rainier became Rainier III, Sovereign Prince of Monaco. Three children were born of his marriage in 1956 to Grace Patricia Kelly : the heir Prince Albert, Marquis des Baux, and the Princesses Caroline and Stephanie.

The future of the Principality: Albert, Caroline and her children.

covers all public revenue and expenditure and sets guidelines for the Principality's economic and financial policy. It includes expenditure attributed to the Royal Household, in other words, to the Prince and his family. Under Article 40 of the Constitution, the Civil List levy has priority over all expenditure out of general budget revenues. The not in-considerable financial security his Serene Highness thus en-joys is far from the least of the royal prerogatives. Even in a serious economic crisis, his al-lowance would be at the top of the Principality's spending pri-orities.

Finally, under Article 88, "Judicial power shall be vested in the Prince, who delegates the exercise of that power to the courts and tribunals". The principle of the separation of powers, a democratic safe-guard dear to Voltaire and Rousseau, is thus a trifle com-promised in the Principality.

The Crown Prince is a great winter sports fan.

In reality, Prince Rainier enjoys powers which might be the envy of many a head of state. Yet to his credit, there is no sign of his ever having given his fellow citizens any cause for complaint.

Within his own family too, the Sovereign's authority is absolute. The law of succession (Articles 10 to 16 of the Constitution) states : "The crown of Monaco is hereditary within the legitimate succession of the Prince in order of primogeniture, with priority to males in the same order. In the absence of legitimate descendants, succession may pass to the Sovereign's child by adoption and to the des-cendants of the latter". The formula is vague enough to offer the Sovereign Prince considerable latitude. Indeed, it will be remembered that the principle had already been put to the test in 1918, when Prince Albert I permitted his heir Louis II to adopt his natural daughter Charlotte Lou-vet. This child became Her Serene Highness Princess Charlotte of Monaco, and her son Prince Rainier now oc-cupies the throne.

This constitutional arrangement, unique among Euro-pean monarchies, is of particular significance in the case of Princess Stephanie and her descendants. Her son, Louis Ducruet, was born out of wedlock and is at present barred from from his grandfather's or uncle's succession. How-ever, if Prince Albert's line were to die out and Princess Caroline's children refuse to accede to the throne, Prince Rainier, or his son Albert, the present heir, would have the right to adopt Louis Ducruet and make him Prince Louis III of Monaco.

It is not beyond the bounds of possibility that Prince Rainier might one day bestow a title on one of his daugh-ters. In 1951, he awarded the title of Baroness of Massy to his sister, Princess Antoinette. Her three children, Elisa-beth, Christian and Christine, all bear the title Baron or Baroness of Massy after their first names.

The whole question of titles as it affects the Prince's family is somewhat complex. All those who bear the Gri-maldi name, whether by birth, marriage or adoption, have the title prince or princess of Monaco. They all have the right to be addressed as Serene Highness. The eldest son and heir carries the title of Crown Prince.

In this sphere too, as is usual, the wide powers the Constitution grants the Prince include complete control over the titles of his relations. Article 16 lays down the principle : "Orders, titles and other distinctions are in the gift of the Prince". It was under this ordinance that Prince Rainier's sister was created Baroness of Massy some forty years ago. The Crown Prince is the Marquis of Baux. The Prince not only has the power to grant titles to his children and members of his family, but also to withdraw them at will.

It is traditionally said that the Prince of Monaco is Europe's - perhaps even the world's -most titled monarch. However, the plethora of titles to which the Grimaldis lay claim needs to be seen in context.

Over the centuries, as a result of some brilliant marital alliances with the upper echelons of the French nobility, the Princes of Monaco acquired a number of titles which - with the agreement of the King of France - became part of their heritage. Duke of Valentinois, of Estouteville, of Ma-zarin, of Mayenne ; Prince of Château-Porcien, Marquis of Baux and of Chilly, Count of Carladès, Thorigny, Ferette, Belfort, Longjumeau, Than and Rosemont ; Baron of Buis, Altkirch and Saint Lô, Lord of Saint-Rémy, Matignon and Isenheim : these are all titles held under French law.

However, to this day they remain subject to French law which is particularly strict in this field. Since no French title can be handed down through the female line - except with the agreement of the Head of State - they are thus technically considered extinct, and they do not feature in any dictionary of the nobility. And indeed, it is hard to understand how Prince Rainier's mother, Princess Char-lotte, who was born not only female but out of wedlock, could have inherited these titles, let alone passed them down to her son. In the eyes of French law, the Prince of Monaco possesses just one title - apart from those which are purely Monegasque - that of his father, Count of Po-lignac.

Nevertheless, the Prince's family continues to use some of these titles. When Princess Charlotte gave up her right to the throne, she was made Duchess of Valentinois. Purists of French nobility law generally take the view that these titles are Monegasque creations with no validity beyond the Principality's borders. All the same, the country and its government have never voiced any objection.

The Royal Family

The birth of a son to Princess Stephanie marked a new chapter in the tale of the Princes of Monaco. In fact, the history of the Grimaldis does read rather like a romance. Even in the 17th and 18th centuries, the family was conspicuous for its troubled amours. One princess was the mistress of Louis XIV. Another gave up husband, palace and Principality to throw in her lot with a prince of Condé, in the end becoming his wife. In more recent times, the eventful and fluctuating family chronicle has provided material in plenty for the media. On 9 April 1956, the report of Prince Rainier's wedding to Grace Kelly, one of American cinema's most famous stars, was borne into homes throughout the world by newspapers, radio and even television. That day marked the beginning of the Grimaldis' love affair with the press, with the emergence of an utopian picture of Monaco as a fairy tale land ruled by its dashing prince. It was an image that the births of Princess Caroline in 1957, Crown Prince Albert in 1958 and Princess Stephanie in 1965, did nothing to dispel. It was only with the story of Princess Caroline that the first discordant note was introduced.

From the age of 16, her undeniable beauty, her spontaneity and high spirits made Caroline a favourite quarry for the whole world's paparazzi, and with her somewhat mercurial behaviour she presented an easy target for criticism. After a protected childhood, she began a degree in political science in Paris, switching to psychology. Although she was a promising student, she dropped out of university in 1978, when she discovered love in the person of Philippe Junot, a charming bachelor 17 years her senior.

Stéphanie, Princess of Scandals.

Despite her parents' opposition, Caroline persisted. And on the 29th June of the same year, in the presence of a mass of photographers and actors and a sprinkling of royal highnesses, Her Serene Highness Princess Caroline of Monaco became Mrs. Philippe Junot.

The honeymoon was short and far from sweet. Caroline was young and immature, keen to escape from the stuffiness of the family circle. Without pause for thought, she had succumbed to the charms of a man who himself was none too sure of his choice. Their divorce after two years of marriage was undoubtedly one of the hardest ordeals Princess Grace ever had to face. Her deep religious convictions, her faith and sense of duty, all were affronted by her eldest daughter's marital breakdown. Nevertheless, her maternal feelings were stronger still, and Caroline found refuge and comfort with her parents.

Her second marriage, to Stephano Casiraghi, ended even more tragically. The Italian born businessman was killed in a powerboat accident in September 1989. Three children were born of their six year marriage, Andréa in 1984, Charlotte in 1986 and Pierre in 1987. The children have no titles and do not appear in the line of succession to the throne. Nevertheless, if the Crown Prince were to remain a bachelor, it is not inconceivable that his elder sister, and her children after her, might one day occupy the ancestral throne. There is nothing in the Constitution to prevent it.

A year before Caroline's marriage, an earlier tragedy had thrown the Grimaldi family and the whole Principality into mourning. It was the end of summer 1982 when Princess Grace was killed at the wheel of her car as she drove down the Grande Corniche. It is ironic that it was on the same road, almost thirty years before, when starring with Cary Grant in one of Alfred Hitchcock's most celebrated films, "To Catch a Thief", that she had her first introduction to the little State which was to become her second homeland.

When Princess Grace died, some of Monaco's luck seemed to die with her. Since that sad event, the specialist magazines have published regular exclusives on Prince Rainier's fleeting romances with princesses or mysterious strangers. It would appear, however, that His Serene Highness has no plans to make a new life for himself. The Prince devotes most of his time to his country and his family. Under his reign, Monaco has come to function like an industrial enterprise. As a businessman, graduate of some of the finest French, Swiss and English schools, Rainier III has been single-minded throughout his reign in his efforts to transform his country into a modern state. He began with the tourist industry, with the creation of a marina and new beaches, improvement of the hotel infrastructure and, in particular, the installation of an exceptional security system.

In the early sixties, the Prince turned his attention to the processing industries, like flour-milling, ceramics, textiles and printing. His dynamism has not gone unrewarded, and today the Principality's economy remains extremely healthy.

Prince Rainier's life has been no bed of roses. The archives of the Principality record a troubled childhood torn between two parents whose marriage of convenience had turned out far from happy. At an early age, the heir to the throne left for England to be educated at the well-known schools of Summerfield and Stowe. He returned to France shortly before the Second World War after spending part of his adolescence at the famous Rosey College in Switzerland. He studied at the universities of Montpellier and Paris. In 1939 he enlisted in the French army, and in 1947 was awarded the Cross of the Légion d'Honneur for his services.

Much harder to define is the personality of the Prince, who, though a man of action, is also a very private man. Very little is known of his personal tastes and his pastimes.

In his youth he enjoyed boxing and he remains a keen sportsman. Despite his very heavy schedule, he is usually to be seen in the audience at the Monte-Carlo Formula 1 Grand Prix and the Tennis Open. Like all the Grimaldis, he is a sailor.

Since the death of her second husband Princess Caroline has led a quiet life.

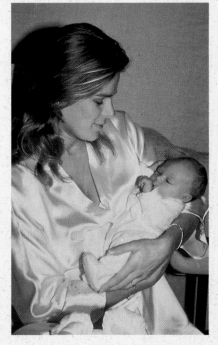

Louis Ducruet and his mother.

He owns a yacht on which he frequently cruises in the Mediterranean. He is also closely involved with the oceanographical museum founded by his great grandfather. He makes regular visits to his property at Marchais in the Aisne. This estate, inherited from his mother Princess Charlotte, is all that remains of the considerable French lands accumulated by the Grimaldis over the centuries. It consists of a 17th century chateau and a beautiful hunting domain where he can indulge his love of shooting.

Credit for the revival of the arts in the Principality is often attributed to Princess Grace and her eldest daughter, but it would be unjust not to recognise Prince Rainier's important role in this sphere. The literary award he endowed some years ago, the Prince Rainier III prize, was perhaps a reminder of the poems he himself wrote as a young man. The Prince was also actively behind the transformation of the National Opera, and the creation of the Television and Circus Festivals.

In the same spirit of cultural enrichment for the Principality, Rainier III nurtures two private projects, both of which now fall within the public domain : his private zoo in the Palace gardens and his collection of vintage cars. The zoo is already open to visitors, and in the future the Prince would also like to see his cherished car collection transformed into a public museum. Finally, there is one sphere in which Prince Rainier is particularly active - the preparation of Albert, the Crown Prince, for his future role.

It has been said of this young man that he is "good in every respect", every mother's dream son. Certainly, in comparison with his somewhat flamboyant sisters, he comes across as totally serene. Unlike Princesses Caroline and Stephanie, his school and university education has been conventional in every way. After going to school in Monaco, in 1976 he followed family tradition by joining the French Navy as a cadet. After a tour of several months aboard the "La Jeanne", he entered the American University

Grace and Rainier received great names from all over the world in Monaco: Prince Philip Duke of Edinburgh.

of Amherst in Massachusetts to read political science, German and art history. He graduated in 1981 in the presence of his mother, Princess Grace, and his two sisters. Finally, he spent a few months as a trainee in an American bank in New York, learning the fundamentals of banking and real estate. All in all, therefore, his upbringing was faultlessly conventional.

For some years the Crown Prince has devoted most of his time to the affairs of the Principality, assuming responsibilities delegated to him by his father. Since his mother's death, he has also been President of the Monaco Red Cross. The only question mark over the Prince's future is his marriage. For a long time it was said that Princess Grace wished her son to marry a princess of royal or at least princely blood. Just as his elder sister was seen as a likely match for the Prince of Wales, it was suggested that Prince Albert intended marriage to Lady Helen Windsor, or perhaps one of the Spanish princesses. So far, the young Prince has shown more interest in American born models or actresses, so press speculation may well be proved wrong. Perhaps we will one day see blazoned across the world's media a repeat of Grace and Rainier's sensational romance. But for the moment, Prince Albert himself is doubtless as much in the dark as we.

If Albert was the obedient son and Caroline the beauteous Princess of fable, Her Serene Highness Princess Stephanie of Monaco has without question been cast in the role of the ugly duckling. The commentators have found plenty to criticise in the baby of the family. Until she was 18, her lack of discipline, scholastic shortcomings and failure to dress according to the conventional expectations of

a princess, met with public and media indulgence, and sometimes even amusement. Since then, Prince Rainier and Princess Grace's last-born has shown few signs of improving her image.

In career terms, her path has been far from smooth. Not remotely interested in formal university education, the young Princess left school with the ambition - shared by many a young girl - to enter the fashion world. But in her case, it was an ambition that her mother's friends were well placed to help her fulfil. Marc Bohan, a longtime Director of Christian Dior, was an old friend of the Royal Family. He naturally offered to take Stephanie into his team and give her some hands-on experience in the world's top fashion house, and for several months she clocked on at the famous House of Dior in Avenue Montaigne. At that time work colleagues and employers alike were unanimous in their praise for her as a professional, a workmate and a designer. At the end of this period of training, Stephanie went into business for herself with a swimwear collection designed in collaboration with her friend Alix de la Comble. This first collection, entitled - like their company - "Pool position", met with great success.

To promote her collection, Stephanie even accepted an offer from France's most famous fashion magazine "Elle" to work as a model for her own designs. Rumour has it that this move was not altogether to Prince Rainier's taste.

Following this first venture, Stephanie decided to become more directly involved in the art world. Her first record "Ouragan" went rapidly to the top of the charts and the Top 50, and was the tune on everyone's lips throughout Europe for a whole summer. The next discs were less successful. Stephanie moved to the United States, hoping to improve her professional skills with singing and dancing lessons. Unfortunately, this is as far as her musical career was to go.

In the meantime, reporters and photographers had been keeping the world a breast of the Princess's various love affairs. Her first love was Paul Belmondo, son of the famous French film actor. He was a calm, well brought up young man who undoubtedly helped restore her psychological and emotional balance, which had been seriously undermined by her mother's death. However, the romance was not to last long, as Stephanie preferred adventure to the entice- ments of enduring love. Her second lover was also closely connected with the world of French cinema. Anthony was the son of an- other famous actor, Alain Delon. Discreet walks in the gardens of the Prince's palace and intimate meals in small restaurants in the ca- pital, soon gave way to fren- etic evenings in clubs and night spots. Again, the ro- mance only lasted a few months. The next affair, with yet another cinema personality, the American actor Rob Lowe, was short- er still.

For the last ten years Prince Rainier has had to shoulder the responsibilities of power alone.

Towards the end of the Eighties a new escort appear- ed in the fickle princess's entourage. As a prospective son-in-law, Mario Jutard fell far short of the ideal. His troubled private life and vague professional background were hardly in tune with the princely image of the Grimal- di family. However, he and Stephanie lived together for several months in the United States. The Princess was very much in love and even had her fiancé's features re- corded for posterity in one of her video clips. It was not long, however, before Mario Jutard was replaced by an American record producer, Ron Bloom. It is not known whether or not Prince Rainier considered him for a time a possible future husband for his daughter, but unlike Stephanie's other suitors, he was seen several times at Monaco in the company of the Royal Family, and was even invited to the Annual Circus Festival and other exhi- bitions in the Principality.

Worse was yet to come. In 1989 Princess Stephanie announced her engagement to Jean-Yves Le Fur. A re- ception attended by certain members of the Grimaldi fam-

ily was held one evening in a fashionable Paris restaurant. Official photographs were taken. Stephanie, proudly sporting her engagement ring, was shown tenderly ent- wined around her beloved. The affair was again a short one. Jean-Yves Le Fur quietly faded from the Monegas- que scene and from the Princess's life.

Stephanie went to live with with one of her former bodyguards, Daniel Ducru- et, and last December gave birth to a son, Louis. For the moment, her career as an artist seems to be in sus- pension.

For years psychologists and journalists have been hypothesising about the causes of Stephanie's rebel- liousness and non- con- formity. The trauma of witnessing her mother's tra- gic death is most commonly cited. Does this explain the instability of the black sheep of the Grimaldi fa- mily? Time alone may tell.

Prince Rainier seems unsure of his own stance. The media were quick to point out his absence from the clinic when his younger daughter gave birth to his fourth grandchild.

By contrast, his only sis- ter, Princess Antoinette, took the trouble to congra- tulate her niece in person. Opinions about this mem- ber of the Royal Family vary widely. Princess An- toinette is undoubtedly very popular in the Principality. Until Princess Grace's arrival on the scene, she undoubtedly performed the difficult role of First lady brilliantly. After presiding at cultural events, dances and official openings at her brother's side, it was said that she found it very hard give way to her sister- in-law. Her private life gives considerable insight into her strength of character and personality. Her first marriage in 1951 was to a Monegasque lawyer and top tennis player, Alexandre Noguès. They had three children, Elisabeth, Christian, and Christine who died in 1989. After three years of marriage, Princess Antoinette divorced. In 1961 she remarried, this time to Charles Rey. There were no children from this marriage which also ended in divorce in 1973. Finally, in 1983 Princess Antoinette was married for the third time - to a man ten years her junior - the dancer, John Gilpin. This marriage was even briefer than the previous one, as John Gilpin succumbed to a heart attack a few weeks after the wedding. The entire Royal Family rallied round the widow in her grief with one exception, her own son, Baron Christian de Massy.

Father and son in perfect harmony.

A number of years earlier, the Baron had broken off all contact with Monaco and the family. In "Palace", a book published in the early Eighties, he revealed the other side of family and political life in Monaco. His comments, which were not always complimentary to his mother and uncle, certainly explain the estrangement which followed. The only person who found favour in his eyes was his aunt, Princess Grace. Of her he wrote: "She was the only one in the family with any humanity".

Albert: Monaco's future in the 21st century.

Heads of non-reigning Royal Houses

By François Billaut

In order of antiquity :

The French Royal House

Capetian dynasty, reigning from 888 with Eudes, King of the Francs and King of France from 987.
A branch of the Bourbon-Orléans dynasty.
Henri, Count of Paris; Head of the French Royal House.
Title by right: Henri VI, King of France and Navarre.

The Count of Paris was born on the 5th July 1908 at the Chateau du Nouvion-en-Thiérache in the Aisne. He married Princess Isabelle of Orléans and Braganza in Palermo on the 8th April 1931. The couple had eleven children. He became Head of the French Royal House on the death of his father, Jean of Orléans, Duke of Guise on the 24th August 1940.

His Royal Highness the Count of Paris in front of a portrait of his direct ancestor, King Louis XIII.

The Austrian-Hungarian Royal House

Hapsburg-Lorraine dynasty. 1276 for Austria (Hapsburg), 1439 for Hungary (Hapsburg) ; a hereditary imperial house in 1804 (Hapsburg-Lorraine).
Otto, Archduke of Austria; Head of the Imperial House of Austria and Royal House of Hungary.
Title by right: Otto I, Emperor of Austria, King of Hungary, Bohemia, etc.

His Imperial and Royal Majesty Archduke Otto of Austria.

Archduke Otto was born in Reichenau, Austria, on the 20th November 1912. He is the son of the last Austrian sovereigns, Emperor and King Charles and Empress and Queen Zita. He became Head of the Imperial and Royal House on the death of his father on the 1st April 1922. He married Princess Régina of Saxe-Meiningen on the 10th May 1951 at Nancy; they have seven children.

The Portuguese Royal House

Capetian dynasty. Founded by Alphonso I in 1112.
Burgundy branch which became Braganza.
Duarte, Duke of Braganza; Head of the Portuguese Royal House.
Title by right: Duarte III, King of Portugal and the Algarve.

The Duke of Braganza, who was born in Berne, Switzerland, on the 15th May 1945, became Head of the Portuguese Royal House on the death of his father, Duarte of Braganza, Duke of Braganza, on the 24th December 1976. The Portuguese Royal House is a branch of the Capetian house founded by King Robert II of France.

His Royal Highness Dom Duarte of Portugal.

The Russian Imperial House

Romanov (Oldenburg-Holstein-Gottorp) dynasty. Tsar in 1613. Maria Wladimirovna, Grand Duchess of Russia; Head of the Russian Imperial House.
Title by right: Maria I, Empress and Supreme Ruler of all the Russias.

Grand Duchess Maria Wladimirovna was born in Madrid on the 23rd December 1953. On the 22nd September 1976 in Madrid she married Prince Franz-Wilhem of Prussia, who became a member of the Russian Orthodox Church and took the title of Grand Duke Michel Pavlovitch of Russia. They have one son, Grand Duke George Mikhailovitch of Russia. Grand Duchess Maria Vladimirovna became Head of the Imperial House on the 21st April 1992 on the death of her father Grand Duke Vladimir Kirilovitch. Grand Duchess Maria's claim to be "Head of House" contested by several cousins.

Their Imperial Highnesses Grand Duchess Maria of Russia and her son.

The Prussian Imperial House

Hohenzollern dynasty. King in Prussia 1701, King of Prussia in 1742, German Emperor 1871.
Louis Ferdinand, Prince of Prussia; Head of the Imperial German House and Prussian Royal House.
Title by right: Louis Ferdinand I, German Emperor, King of Prussia.
Prince Louis Ferdinand was born in

Prince Louis-Ferdinand of Prussia, his daughter-in-law Princess Donata and Crown Prince Georges-Frédéric.

Germany on the 9th November 1907 at Marmor Palace, while his grandfather Kaiser William II was on the throne. On the 2nd May 1938 he married Grand Duchess Kyra Kyrilovna of Russia, who disappeared in 1967. There were seven children from the marriage. He became Head of the Imperial and Royal House on the 20th July 1951 on the death of his father Crown Prince William.

The Royal House of the Two Sicilies

Capetian dynasty. Charles of Bourbon, King in 1735. Two Sicilies branch of the Bourbons.
Ferdinand, Duke of Castro; Head of the Two Sicilies Royal House.
Title by right: Ferdinand IV, King of the Two Sicilies.
The Duke of Castro was born on the 28th May 1926 at Podzamczé Castle in Poland. On the 25th July 1949 he married Chantal de Chevron-Villette at Giez in Savoie; there were three children from the marriage. He became Head of the Two Sicilies Royal House on the death of his father Rénier of Bourbon-Sicily, Duke of Castro, on the 16th January 1973.

His Royal Highness Prince Ferdinand of Bourbon of the Two Sicilies, Duke of Castro.

The Italian Royal House

Savoy dynasty. King of Piedmont and Sardinia in 1713, King of Italy in 1861.
Victor Emmanuel, Prince of Naples; Head of the Italian Royal House.
Title by right: Victor Emmanuel IV, King of Italy.
The Prince of Naples, son of King Umberto II and Queen Marie-José of Italy, was born in Naples on the 12th February 1937. On the 7th October 1971 he married Marina Doria in Teheran. The Prince and Princess of Naples have one son, Emmanuel Filiberto, Prince of Venice, born on the 22nd June 1972. The Prince of Naples became Head of the Royal House on the death of his father on the 18th March 1983.

Their Royal Highnesses the Prince of Naples, the Princess and their son the Prince of Venice.

The French Imperial House

Napoleon-Bonaparte Dynasty. Napoleon I, Emperor in 1804.
Louis, Prince Napoleon ; Head of the French Imperial House.
Title by right: Napoleon VII, Emperor of the French.
Prince Napoleon was born on the 23rd January 1914 in Brussels. He became Head of the French Imperial House on the 3rd May 1926 on the death of his father, Prince Victor Napoleon. He married Alix de Foresta on the 16th April 1949 ; they have four children. Prince Napoleon is also a descendant of the kings of France through his mother, formerly Princess Clementine of Belgium, great granddaughter of Louis Philippe I, King of France.

His Imperial Highness Prince Napoléon.

Royal House of Bavaria

Wittelsbach dynasty. Elector, king in 1805.
Albrecht, Duke of Bavaria; Head of the Bavarian Royal House.
Title by right: Albrecht I, King of Bavaria.

The Duke of Bavaria was born in Munich on the 3rd May 1905 during the reign of his grandfather King Louis III. There were four children from his marriage with Countess Marie Draskovich of Trakostjan, deceased in 1969. Duke Albrecht became Head of the Bavarian Royal House on the 2nd August 1955 on the death of his father, the Crown Prince Rupprecht.

The Royal House of Wurtemberg

Wurtemberg dynasty. Duke, then Elector of Wurtemberg, king in 1805.
Carl, Duke of Wurtemberg; Head of the Royal House of Wurtemberg.
Title by right: Carl II, king of Wurtemberg.

The Duke of Wurtemberg was born on the 1st August 1936 at Friedrichshafen Castle. On the 21st July 1960 he married Princess Diane of France at Althausen Castle; there are six children of the marriage. He became Head of the House of Wurtemberg on the death of his father, Duke Philippe, on the 15th April 1975.

The Saxony Royal House

Saxony dynasty. Elector of Saxony, king in 1806.
Marie Emmanuel, Margrave of Meissen; Head of the Saxony Royal House.
Title by right: Marie Emmanuel I, King of Saxony, Margrave of Meissen.

The Margrave of Meissen was born at Prufening Castle on the 31st January 1926. On the 23rd June 1962 he married Princess Anastasia-Louise of Anhalt. There are no children from the marriage and the other princes of the Royal House have lost their dynastic rights as a result of marriage with commoners.

The Royal House of Hanover

Brunswick-Luneburg dynasty. Duke of Brunswick and Luneburg, King of Hanover in 1815.
Ernst August, Prince of Hanover, Duke of Brunswick and Luneburg; Head of the Hanover Royal House.
Title by right: Ernst August V, King of Hanover, Duke of Brunswick and Luneburg.

The Prince of Hanover was born in Hanover on the 26th February 1954. On the 28th August 1981 he married Chantal Hochuli in a marriage which was recognised as valid by the Head of the House. There are two children from the marriage. He became Head of the Hanover Royal House on the death of his father, Ernst August IV, on the 9th December 1987.

The Yugoslavian Royal House

Karageorgevitch dynasty. Sovereign Prince of Serbia 1842, King 1903, King of Yugoslavia in 1929.
Alexander, Prince of Yugoslavia; Head of the Royal House of Yugoslavia.
Title by right: Alexander II, King of Yugoslavia.
Prince Alexander of Yugoslavia was born in London on the 17th July 1945, the only son of King Peter II of Yugoslavia. He became Head of the Royal House on the death of his father on the 3rd November 1970. He had three children from his first marriage to Princess Maria da Gloria d'Orleans and Braganza on the 1st July 1972; the marriage ended in divorce and annulment by the church in 1985. The Prince married again on the 21st September 1985, this time to Katherine Batis.

His Royal Highness Prince Alexander.

The Greek Royal House

Schleswig-Holstein-Sonderburg-Glücksburg dynasty (The Danish Royal House). King of the Hellenes in 1863.
Constantine II, King of the Hellenes, Prince of Denmark.
   King Constantine was born in Athens on the 2nd of June 1940. He is the son of King Paul I (1901-64) and his Queen, born Frederika of Hannover (1917-81). After the death of his father he ascended the throne and married, on the 18th of September 1964, his cousin, Princess Anne-Marie of Denmark. In December 1967 his attempt to overthrow the military junta failed and he and his family had to leave the country. In 1973 Greece was proclaimed a republic and the King is now living in exile in London. There are three sons and two daughters from the marriage.

Their Majesties King Constantine and Queen Anne-Marie of the Hellenes.

The Rumanian Royal House

Hohenzollern-(Sigmaringen) dynasty. Carl I, Sovereign Prince in 1866, king in 1881.

Michael I, King of Rumania, Prince of Hohenzollern.

King Michael of Rumania was born on the 25th October 1921 at Foischor Castle in Rumania. He reigned from the 20th July 1927 to the 8th June 1930 and from the 6th September 1940 to the 29th December 1947 when he was forced to abdicate by the Communist government.

On the 10th June 1948 he married Princess Anne of Bourbon Parma at the Royal Palace in Athens; there are five daughters of the marriage.

Their Majesties King Michael and Queen Anne of Rumania.

The Montenegro Royal House

Petrovitch-Niegosh dynasty. Sovereign Prince 1860, King in 1910.

Nicolas, Prince of Montenegro, Head of the Montenegro Royal House.

Title by right: Nicolas II, King of Montenegro

Prince Nicolas of Montenegro was born in Saint-Nicolas-de-Pelem in the Côtes-du-Nord on the 24th July 1944. He is the great grandson of King Nicolas I (1841-1921).

The Prince became Head of the Royal House on the death of his father, Prince Michael of Montenegro, on the 24th March 1986. He married France Navarro on the 27th November 1976; there are two children from the marriage.

His Royal Highness Prince Nicholas of Montenegro.

Royal House of Bulgaria

Saxe-Coburg Gotha dynasty. Sovereign 1887, King in 1908.

Simeon II, king of the Bulgarians, Duke in Saxony.

King Simeon, son of King Boris III, was born in Sofia on the 16th June 1937. He was proclaimed king on the death of his father on the 28th August 1943. When the country

was proclaimed a Republic on the 9th September 1946 after a referendum held by the Communist government, the young king left his country. The King married Señorita Margarita Gomez-Acebo y Cejuela on the 21st January 1962 in Vevey in Switzerland; there are five children of the marriage.

His Majesty King Simeon of the Bulgarians.

The Royal House of Albania

Zogou dynasty. King in 1928

Leka I, King of the Albanians.

King Leka was born on the 5th April 1939 at Tirana. He was the only son of King Zog I (1895-1961) and his Queen, formerly Countess Geraldine Apponyi de Nagy-Appony.

On the 15th May 1961, shortly after the death of his father, an Albanian national assembly in exile proclaimed him king. He was recognised by General Franco as head of a government in exile. On the 10th October 1975 he married Susan Cullen-Ward at Toledo; there is one son from the marriage

His Majesty King Leka of Albania.